© 2003 by Melanie Arnold

About the Author

ED RUGGERO is the author of *Duty First: A Year in the Life of West Point and the Making of American Leaders*, in addition to five novels about the military. He is an experienced keynote speaker on leadership and leader development, and was an infantry officer in the United States Army for eleven years.

COMBAT JUMP

THE YOUNG MEN WHO LED THE

ASSAULT INTO FORTRESS EUROPE,

JULY 1943

ED RUGGERO

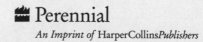
Perennial

An Imprint of HarperCollins*Publishers*

HarperCollins books may be purchased for educational, business, or sales promotional use. For information please write: Special Markets Department, HarperCollins Publishers Inc., 10 East 53rd Street, New York, NY 10022.

First Perennial edition published 2004.

Designed by Joseph Rutt

The Library of Congress has catalogued the hardcover edition as follows:
Ruggero, Ed.
    Combat jump: the young men who led the assault into Fortress Europe, July 1943 / Ed Ruggero.—1st ed.
        p.   cm.
    Includes index.
    ISBN 0-06-008875-3
    1. World War, 1939–1945—Campaigns—Italy—Sicily.   2. United States. Army. Airborne Division, 82nd—History.   3. United States. Army—Parachute troops—History—20th century.   4. World War, 1939–1945—Aerial operations, American.   5. World War, 1939–1945—Regimental histories—United States. 6. Airborne operations (Military science)—History—20th century.   I. Title.

D763.I82S448   2003
940.54'2158—dc21

                                                          2003047819

                        ISBN 0-06-008876-1 (pbk.)

        04 05 06 07 08   ❖/RRD   10 9 8 7 6 5 4 3 2 1

To Jack Norton,
who inspired me to tell this story

CONTENTS

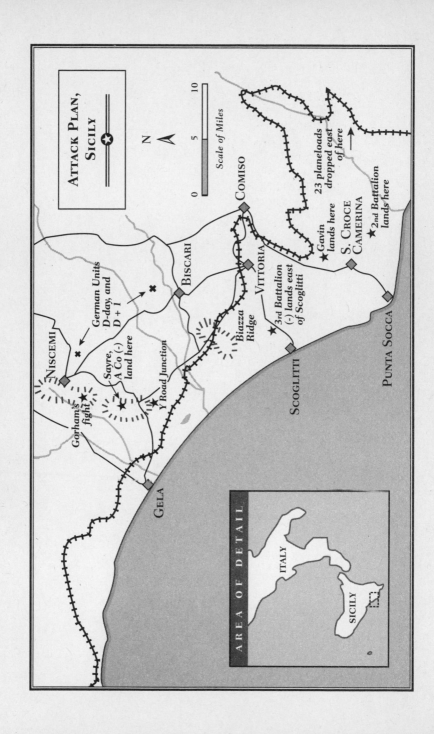

ATTACK PLAN, SICILY

N

Scale of Miles

0   5   10

NISCEMI

Gorham's fight

Sayre, A Co (-) land here

German Units D-day, and D + 1

Y Road Junction

GELA

BISCARI

Biazza Ridge

3rd Battalion (-) lands east of Scoglitti

SCOGLITTI

VITTORIA

COMISO

Gavin lands here

23 planeloads dropped east of here

S. CROCE CAMERINA

2nd Battalion lands here

PUNTA SOCCA

AREA OF DETAIL

ITALY

SICILY

PROLOGUE

Jim Gavin struggles against the hundred-plus pounds of gear strapped to his body, scrambling to gain footing on the deck of the bucking aircraft. A few of the seventeen other men sitting hunched in the darkness look up. Others are sleeping or lost in their own thoughts. Gavin checks his watch yet again and looks out the starboard windows of the C-47 Skytrain, hoping to see the dark mass of Sicily rising out of the Mediterranean, but there is nothing except the occasional flash of moonlight on water. No amount of wishing can make the enemy-held island appear, so Gavin is on his own to fight the rising feelings of panic.

At thirty-six, Colonel James M. Gavin has been a soldier for his entire adult life; his whole career has been in preparation for this night. In his first combat action, Gavin is leading a force of just over thirty-four hundred men,[1] who will be the first American soldiers to set foot on what Adolf Hitler has called *Festung Europa*, or "Fortress Europe." In the skies behind Gavin are another 225 aircraft, all heading for the same action, all filled with men who are counting on him to lead them to victory, and Jim Gavin cannot entirely dismiss the notion that he is lost.

He climbs past the outstretched legs of his troopers to the cramped cockpit of the aircraft, where he and the pilots search for the landmarks that would tell them they are on the right course. But there is nothing below the plane except a dark sea.

As midnight approaches, the men in the aircraft spot the dark hulls of the invasion fleet, steaming for the beaches. Most of the troopers find this sight comforting, but it is one they aren't meant to see. The frustrated Gavin knows the pilots are supposed to fly a course over the open water between the American and British convoys, which are on widely separated, parallel tracks for the southern coast of Sicily. Looking down on the blacked-out armada, Gavin can't tell if he is looking at the British or the American force. Either way, it seems plain that the Navy is probably not in the wrong place, which means he must be. And now he wonders if the ships' nervous antiaircraft gunners will fire on them.

Besides all the predictable worries of a commander going into battle for the first time—who will perform well? who poorly? have I prepared my men for every contingency?—Gavin carries an additional burden. He is doing what no American commander has ever done before: taking a large body of men into combat by parachute drop, to spearhead a massive seaborne invasion. It is a gamble at best, and an invitation to disaster at worst. If the paratroopers fail in their mission to block the German counterattacks that are certain to hit the beaches come daylight, the enemy might push the invading force back into the sea. This would leave the airborne units cut off behind enemy lines with a choice between capture or destruction. Besides the slaughter sure to ensue, such a debacle would throw off, for a year or more, the entire Allied effort against Hitler. Gavin would go down in history as the man whose failure doomed the newly formed U.S. airborne.

Another worry: Gavin's men have made only two night jumps since arriving in North Africa in April. The first resulted in so many broken legs, arms, and backs that the second had to be stage-managed: only a token number of troopers made the jump; the rest began their training already on the ground. But here they were, about to make a difficult night jump, and this time mistakes would be measured not in lost training, but in lost lives.

Gavin knew, all during the planning phase, that their first big challenge was simply getting from the departure airfields in North Africa to the right drop zones in Sicily. There wasn't time for all the pilots to get in enough night training. The flight path, which began at twelve different departure airfields in Tunis, took the planes over 185 miles of featureless, open sea between Africa and Malta. Without sophisticated navigational aids, the inexperienced pilots had to rely on dead reckoning, calculating airspeed and compass direction to get a rough idea of when and where they should make landfall. But the strong cross winds played havoc with their plans. Just before takeoff, a young airman from the weather station had come running up to Gavin's plane.

"Colonel Gavin? Is Colonel Gavin here?"

"Here I am," Gavin answered.

"I was told to tell you the wind is going to be thirty-five miles an hour, west to east." Then, perhaps realizing what this news meant for the paratroopers, the man added, "They thought you'd want to know."[2]

Gavin had canceled training jumps when the wind exceeded fifteen miles an hour: there was too much risk of the paratroopers being blown far from their drop zones, or of being dragged to their deaths across rugged ground by their chutes. This wasn't a training jump, of course, and there was no calling it off. Gavin was left to imagine the cost, in broken limbs and broken bodies, for these men he had trained.

Now, in the air above the Mediterranean, Gavin can see that the wind is pushing the air armada off course. The bumpy ride is also making some of the troopers violently airsick. Weighted down with up to 120 pounds of equipment, the men are all but trapped in their seats. The ones who get sick throw up in their own laps, and in the cramped interior of the planes, the tangy smell of vomit is mixed with the engine exhaust fumes.

The pilots of Gavin's plane completely missed both landmarks on the flight from North Africa: the small island of Linosa and, incredibly, the 300-square-mile island of Malta. This Allied-held island was supposed to be lit up as a navigational beacon to help guide the air armada, but neither Gavin nor his pilots see it. Instead, the young colonel sees the tiny wingtip lights marking the aircraft, but even these are not reassuring. The inexperienced pilots, fearful of midair collisions, allow their planes to drift apart; the farther apart the planes, the more widely scattered the troopers will be on the ground.

The pilots check the time. It is past the point when they should have seen the big island, where they were supposed to turn left to a northerly heading. It doesn't take an experienced navigator to figure out that the strong northwesterly winds have blown them off course. They cannot simply keep on this heading, so the plane begins its turn. Gavin and the pilots hope to run into the 190-mile-long coast of Sicily.

Sitting in the dark aluminum tube of the C-47, Gavin has plenty of time to consider that perhaps the critics have been right. Even Eisenhower, the theater commander, had his doubts about an airborne spearhead. Maybe the idea of parachuting troops onto the battlefield *is* ludicrous.

But the time for questioning is past. Gavin is riding the crest of a huge wave of men, aircraft, ships, and landing craft. Once set in motion, there is no calling it back. Every passing minute brings those ships closer to shore, and the men down there are counting on the paratroopers. He and the thirty-four hundred men under his command, all of them hurtling forward somewhere out in the moonlit night, *must* get to the battlefield.

Then, finally, Gavin can see land . . . but it is on the *wrong side of the aircraft*. Where have the pilots taken him? Is this Sicily? Or have they been blown so far off course by the strong northwesterly winds that they are looking down on the Italian mainland? Have they completely missed the nearly two-hundred-mile-long southern coast and instead made landfall on the east side of the island? Is the entire air armada about to be dropped in the wrong place?

Walking with the peculiar waddle of a man strapped into a tight parachute harness, and loaded with the accoutrements of war—helmet, main and reserve parachutes, rifle, ammunition, trench knife, hand grenades, rations, canteen, entrenching tool, gas mask, flashlight, first aid kit, map case—Gavin makes his way to the door, hooks his hands on the inside of the fuselage, and leans out into the hundred-mile-an-hour slipstream to look for landmarks.

Sicily or not, he and his men are going. He gave specific orders that every man would jump; the only people staying on the aircraft will be the pilots. Squinting into the wind, Gavin can see searchlights and the strangely beautiful arcs of tracers reaching up. They have, at least, made it to some part of the war.

Gavin turns to the man behind him, a twenty-three-year-old sergeant named Nick Kastrantas, who is a skilled mapmaker and translator.

"Scared," Gavin says over the roar.

Kastrantas, thinking it was a question, nods and yells back, "Yes!" Then the young sergeant realizes that Gavin is probably talking about his own feelings. The old man is giving him permission to be frightened.

The red light by the door comes on, indicating that the pilot thinks they are close to the right drop zone.

"Stand up!" Gavin shouts over the roar of the engines.

The troopers are happy to oblige. No one wants to be crammed inside the plane, helpless and immobile, when the antiaircraft starts tearing at the thin aluminum skin of the C-47.

"Hook up!"

The seventeen men—each planeload is called a stick—behind
Gavin hook their static lines to the overhead cable running the length
of the plane. The static line, thus attached to the aircraft, will pull
each man's parachute from its pack before separating. The troopers
struggle to keep their balance as the plane bucks in the strong wind. It
will be very difficult for the heavily laden men to pull themselves upright should they fall.

"Check equipment!"

Each man does his own check—helmet, chinstrap, web lines,
weapon—and then checks the parachute of the man in front of him.

"Sound off for equipment check!"

Now the men can hear the firing from below, although it is not yet
close. There is no panic. They have practiced these same maneuvers
hundreds of times, have made dozens of training jumps together back
in the States. There is comfort in the repetition of something so familiar. Besides, everyone wants out of the aircraft.

Starting with the last man in the stick, they begin counting, each
slapping the man in front of him.

"Seventeen, okay!"

"Sixteen, okay!"

"Fifteen, okay!"

When the count reaches Gavin in the doorway, he turns his face
into the wind, the darkness, and the war that waits below.

- 1 -

IN THEORY

The United States Military Academy at West Point was a backwater assignment in the winter of 1941. While the cadets studied the Napoleonic Wars and waited out the endless gray days in upstate New York, the Army was in an uproar. America's first peacetime draft had been signed into law during the hot summer of 1940, though the term of enlistment for draftees and federalized National Guard troops was optimistically limited to one year. Although large segments of the public still hoped the war raging in Europe and Asia would pass America by, a million men were about to be inducted into the armed forces. Whatever happened in the diplomatic world, the nation was girding for war. For professional soldiers like Captain James M. Gavin, the only prudent thing to do was to prepare.

Gavin was thirty-three years old that winter, tall and slender—his nickname was Slim Jim—with movie-star looks and a passion for athletics. He was also one of the most junior officers assigned to the Academy's Tactical Department. He didn't draw one of the plum assignments for a "Tac," overseeing the military development of a company of cadets, but his duties did include supervising the seniors who ran the cadet corps. Like other members of the Tactical Department, he spent time enforcing the mind-numbing minutiae of regulations:

inspecting how cadets folded their clothes, polished their shoes, cleaned their weapons and their rooms. Officers in the Tactical Department also taught classes about the organization of the Army and the role of the junior officer. Major Johnny Waters even instructed cadets on the proper table etiquette an officer and a gentleman needed to know. Waters was aided in this by his wife, Bee, who was herself the daughter of a not-yet-famous West Pointer named George Patton.

Though classes on the Army supply system were necessary, they were hardly inspiring, for instructors or cadets. Fortunately, the department was also responsible for teaching tactics: how small elements actually battled the enemy, the artistry of fire and maneuver, the use of artillery and machine guns and tanks to overwhelm an enemy position or defend a hilltop, all the things the cadets, as future combat leaders, had to master. Jim Gavin shone as a teacher, and the cadets could see the fire in the young infantry officer as he coached them on the technical side of their new profession. Like all good teachers, Gavin wasn't satisfied with simply covering the curriculum; he expanded his students' horizons to an in-depth study of modern war. He wanted the cadets to see the bigger picture.

In his classes, often conducted in the high-ceiling rooms above the mess hall, where the cadets learned to draw engineering diagrams of bridges, roads, and machinery, Gavin took the cadets on a world tour of modern military organizations. Together they dissected the German Wehrmacht—at that point the world's most formidable and successful army—studying how it was built and how it fought. The young captain and his younger charges discussed how the Germans blended tanks and low-flying attack aircraft with their maneuver formations, how they coordinated all the arms—artillery, air power, armor, and infantry—to bring the greatest amount of force to bear on the critical spot on the battlefield. The cadets began to understand that war, particularly since the introduction of the internal combustion engine and all that did for speed, required a complex set of skills. It was more than a matter of training individual soldiers and pointing them toward an enemy (which had proved so disastrous in the trenches of World War I). The modern commander had to choreograph air and sea power, had to communicate over vast distances to put his units at the exact right place at the exact right time, with the right arms and the will to use them. He had to master new techniques: faster artillery, motorized formations, more lethal weapons. He had to understand his enemy, and that understanding had to go beyond organization, tactics, and weapons. It had to include the social system that put enemy soldiers on the battlefield, all the cultural and political factors that made men fight.

Gavin was soft-spoken for a soldier, but he made the war headlines come alive, and in his teaching there was always an undercurrent, that this was knowledge the West Point class of 1941 would soon put to use. The lessons on how small units fought were often conducted over sand tables, large flat boxes filled with dirt the instructor used to shape hills and valleys, like museum dioramas. (Although the organizations varied depending on the mission, the basic element in the infantry was a squad of ten or eleven men, led by a sergeant. Three to four squads made up a platoon, led by a lieutenant, and three or four platoons made up a company, commanded by a first lieutenant or captain. West Point cadets who went into the infantry could expect to become platoon leaders.)

Gavin would brief the cadets on situations they might face as platoon leaders. While these lessons were designed to help cadets see and understand how to employ soldiers, they had another use as well. Gavin and other instructors added elements to drive home the point that warfare, especially the up-close kind of fighting they would see as junior officers, was often a confusing mix of incomplete information, rapidly shifting priorities, and the highest stakes imaginable.

Most important, Gavin wanted his cadets to think—not just spit back programmed responses to questions about military history or tac-

tics. Although he didn't invent it, the technique he used would become the norm in all the forces Gavin would command: he pushed de-
cision-making down to the level where decisions would actually be
made, to the junior leaders on the ground.

The cadets gathered around the table, and the slim captain gave
them the bare essentials.

> You are here. Your view is blocked by this hill, though you can
> hear firing on the other side. The unit on your right has inex-
> plicably disappeared—they may be in front of you or behind
> you—either way your flank is exposed. If you get too far ahead
> of the rest of the body, you may be cut off. If you fall too far
> behind, your comrades may be cut off. Your commander wants
> you to push ahead; he thinks you can get behind the enemy
> position on the next ridge. But the ground in front of you is
> open, so your men will be exposed to enemy fire and will be
> visible to any artillery spotters on this hill.

The cadets analyzed the problem, trying to recall all they had
learned in their summer training, in their poring over tactics manuals,
in their earlier discussions with officers. Then came the question that
would become a hallmark of what Gavin (and later, his airborne commanders) asked a generation of junior leaders: "What do you do now?"[1]

The cadets responded: This is what I would do if I were the squad
leader. This is what I would do as platoon leader, as company commander. For Gavin, it was critical that the cadets think through the
tactical problems, and that they do so quickly. He was not interested
in whether they could memorize what this or that historical figure had
done. He wanted them to understand, and be able to explain, the ra-
tionale for their decisions. His class was tough, and cadets who dared
go in unprepared regretted it. But his incisive mind and dedication to
his profession drew the young men to him.

On Sunday afternoons, the young captain and his wife, Peggy, held open house, and cadets trudged up the steep hill behind the barracks to spend some of their free time in his circle. The discussion ranged over events in Europe and Asia, how the German army had managed to defeat the French and push the British off the continent, how they had reduced the Low Countries and conquered Norway.

One subject that particularly fascinated Gavin in 1941 was something entirely new in the annals of warfare: the use of parachute troops.

After the September 1, 1939, invasion of Poland that marked the beginning of fighting in Europe, the whole world became familiar with a new term, *Blitzkrieg*, German for "lightning war." The key element of the blitz was the coordination of the combat arms—the tanks, the close air support, the artillery, and the infantry—to strike at the enemy's command structure, supply system, transportation network, and front-line troops all at once. By the spring of 1940, the Germans added another element to this lethal mix when they used parachutists to spearhead their invasion of Belgium, the Netherlands, and Luxembourg. Small units of paratroopers jumped into the Low Countries ahead of the advancing ground troops to seize key brides over the Maas and Waal Rivers. They achieved almost complete surprise, suddenly appearing where they weren't expected—and where the defenders were not ready to fight them. The German paratroopers quickly overran the bridge defenses and held them until the tanks and infantry arrived. Even more impressive was the attack on Fort Eben Emael, a key strongpoint in Belgium that was supposedly impregnable to land attack. The fort fell quickly to the highly trained infantry who jumped directly on top of its defenders.

Later in 1940, after France had fallen and it looked as if Hitler would invade England, the British expected that German parachutists would spearhead the invasion. They diverted tremendous resources to defend against troops who could quite suddenly appear almost anywhere. Thus even the threat of an airborne attack could force the enemy to spread himself thin.

Of course, reports on exactly how the Germans employed their airborne forces were unavailable to the American Army, so much of what Gavin could learn was pieced together from the sketchy dispatches—most from defenders—that did get out of occupied Europe. As he thought about how the U.S. Army might use such troops, Gavin also relied on the work done by military theorists between the world wars, who had considered the parachute as a way of delivering combat troops behind enemy lines. The technical challenges were daunting.

During World War I, some pilots had been outfitted with parachutes to enable them to escape disabled planes. A pilot had to get clear of the aircraft—sometimes by climbing out on the wing—jump, and pull a cord releasing a small "pilot" chute that then tugged the main chute from its pack. This was a lot to accomplish on a plane that was going down, maybe even spinning out of control or flipping upside down. It was nearly impossible if the pilot was wounded.

In 1923 the U.S. Army Air Corps parachuted a machine gun and crew, but the experimentation ended there; the tight Army budget left little room for research and development. The Soviets, who also studied the possibilities, thought parachutists should be lightly armed and fight as guerrillas, harassing the enemy's rear echelons, disrupting supply lines, ambushing messengers. Soviet reasoning was practical: airplanes of the time were small and in limited supply, so there was no way to deliver large bodies of troops who could fight as a conventional unit. As cargo planes got bigger and more reliable, the Soviets experimented with mounting larger-scale assaults led by parachute troops. A common training scenario called for the parachutists to seize an enemy airfield and wait for more heavily armed reinforcements whose planes would land on the captured strip. There was no question that soldiers could parachute into battle; the question was whether they could be delivered at once, in a tight formation, with enough combat power to significantly affect the course of a fight.

While a small coterie of professional soldiers theorized about tactics, the U.S. Army tinkered with smaller adjustments that had bigger potential rewards. Early enthusiasts liked the idea of a parachute that opened quickly and automatically as the troopers left the aircraft. Thus the U.S. Army adopted the static line, a strap that attached to a fore-and-aft cable running the length of the troop compartment. When the jumper left the plane, the static line played out very quickly. The line ended in a cloth tape tied to the top of the packed chute. When the trooper reached the end of the static line, the force of his fall pulled the chute free, then broke the tape.

The adjustment had several effects. Frightened jumpers might forget to pull a release cord; static line jumping was safer. Since the chute deployed quickly, paratroopers could jump at low altitudes, limiting the amount of time they spent in the air as targets for enemy ground troops. Finally, jumpers could leave the aircraft in a tight line, one right after the other, as fast as they could follow the man in front. This meant less dispersion on the ground. A few seconds between jumpers translated to hundreds of yards between men when they landed, and the object, on the drop zone, was to form a unit and concentrate firepower rapidly.

Jim Gavin was one of several bright young officers who worked out these challenges in a series of articles in the *Infantry Journal*. At some point Gavin stopped seeing this as merely a mental exercise and began recognizing his work for what it was: the groundwork for an American airborne force.

The challenges were formidable. In the United States, which was just gearing up for large-scale production of war materials, cargo planes were in short supply and low on the list of priorities. The principal military cargo plane then in use was the sixty-three-foot-long

Douglas C-47, called the Skytrain. Its name was somewhat misleading, as it could carry only eighteen to twenty fully loaded paratroopers. The twin-engine workhorse had a top speed of 230 miles per hour and a range of 3,600 miles. Scribbling away in his office in the cadet barracks, Gavin could easily determine that dropping a single battalion of infantry required more than 50 planes. A regiment filled about 150 aircraft. Large-scale airborne operations, if they were ever going to come about, promised to be very expensive. Besides finding all the aircraft, the crews had to be trained to fly in giant formations that would deliver the paratroopers to the right places. This meant long-range formation flying, probably at night, with radio silence and blacked-out aircraft, over unfamiliar territory; and that was all before the antiaircraft fire started.

Even though Congress had reluctantly agreed to large infusions of cash for the military, there was a deafening clamor for those funds as each service raced to get itself on a war footing. (When Germany invaded Poland in September 1939, the U.S. Army ranked seventeenth in the world, with less than 190,00 men in uniform.)[2] Many of the million men who would be drafted as a result of the new legislation would not even have modern rifles, so it was very difficult for the chief proponent of airborne forces in the U.S. Army, Colonel William C. Lee, to get any funds at all.

Nevertheless, in June 1940, Lee had been able to convince the War Department that the United States Army should at least experiment with the notion of using parachute troops. Thus was born a platoon of fifty volunteers, called the Test Platoon, commanded by William T. Ryder. This tiny group began conducting tests from a dirt strip along the banks of the Chattahoochee River in Fort Benning, Georgia, the home of the U.S. Army Infantry School.

Throughout his year at West Point, Gavin read everything he could find about the Test Platoon, about the German advances in airborne operations, and the battles involving paratroopers. Even though the total number of qualified parachutists in the United States Army was smaller than West Point's Corps of Cadets, Gavin was thinking on a bigger scale: about massed formations of paratroopers that could have a significant impact in modern battle. This tendency—to think far ahead of the status quo—was one of Gavin's lifelong traits.

James Maurice Gavin was born to Irish immigrant parents in Brooklyn, New York, on March 22, 1907. His parents died before he was two years old, leaving him stranded in a Catholic orphanage. He was soon placed with another Irish immigrant family, Martin and Mary Gavin of Mount Carmel, Pennsylvania. The Gavins were poor, and their adopted son and an adopted daughter, Mary, were expected to work to help support the family. A childhood photo shows the children, one standing on each side of Martin. They are on a dirt path that leads to crooked wooden steps, but they look scrubbed and well fed. Their clothes are clean and their smiles genuine.

Early on, Jim Gavin showed signs of both his ambition and his leadership abilities. By the age of eleven he managed two newspaper delivery routes, and was the local agent for three out-of-town newspapers. By thirteen, he had added two Sunday routes and had two other boys working for him. He had always been an avid reader, and over the years he worked his way through the entire Mount Carmel public library.

For Gavin's parents, as for many immigrant families, education was a luxury they couldn't afford. When Jim finished the eighth grade, his parents decided that he'd had enough schooling, and Gavin went to work full-time, first as a store clerk and then as a filling station manager. Although his schooling was interrupted, he managed to stay out of the mines, where so many of his schoolmates went to work. Yet Gavin knew that he needed an education to get anywhere in the world, and he had his sights set on a much wider world than Mount

Carmel. His parents couldn't help him, so he would have to do it on his own.

On the day he turned seventeen, Gavin left for New York City, armed with a sharp mind, a keen ambition, and little else. His goal: find a way to educate himself. A little more than a week later, on April 1, 1924, he signed papers at an Army recruiting office, passing himself off as an eighteen-year-old. His first duty station after basic training was the Panama Canal Zone, and while there he took the entrance exams for West Point, which were open to enlisted soldiers. Even though he had only an eighth-grade education, he passed the exams and was admitted the following summer. He graduated with the Class of 1929, ranking 135 out of 290.[3]

The Army suffered with the rest of the country during the Great Depression, with Congress frequently cutting both its strength and its pay. There was little in the way of advancement, and even World War I veterans were often reduced several grades as cutbacks rolled through the ranks. Yet Gavin had found a home. The Army served him as it did so many young men from modest—or in Gavin's case, less than modest—means. It gave him an education, it gave him respectability, and it gave him opportunity, if not for promotion, then at least for travel and the chance to work with talented leaders. Gavin continued to read widely, especially in military history, and he worked on his writing skills as well. By 1940 he had published several articles in professional journals; he was making a name for himself as a thinker and innovator.

By the time of his assignment to West Point, he had found a focus for his considerable talents: Gavin believed that the United States could and should field an airborne force, but that it should be unlike anything else ever tried. The Americans should take it a step further than the Germans had, putting together an entire combined arms team of airborne infantry, artillery, engineer, signal, and medical units that could strike the enemy where he was weakest—in the rear eche-lons. In traditional linear warfare, this was an arena populated by supply troops, communications centers, and field hospitals, all important—and vulnerable—assets. As part of an amphibious invasion, airborne forces could land between the beaches and inland enemy forces, holding off counterattacks as the assault force struggled to get men and equipment from ships to shore. Paratroopers could seize airfields, which would then be available as bases for U.S. attack aircraft supporting the invasion.

In 1940 and '41, there weren't enough planes, there weren't enough trained parachutists, and there was no doctrine telling how such forces should fight or be resupplied by air. But there was a coterie of officers, scattered around the Army, who believed it was possible. Jim Gavin was one of those men.

In the spring of 1941, West Point's senior class, numbering a bit over four hundred, gathered to hear a visitor from the War Department. For most of their cadet careers, the war in Europe had seemed a distant thing. In fact, after the fall of France in 1940, it looked to cadets that perhaps Hitler would be satisfied with his conquests. Even though he hadn't succeeded in conquering Great Britain, that island was isolated and outgunned. The Germans and the Soviets were still allies, which gave Hitler access to vast sources of raw materials.

Most of the young men gathering for the lecture were thinking about graduation, about the new freedoms that life after West Point would bring. Some held on to hope that the war might pass them by; others were afraid that they might miss the chance to serve in combat. Lieutenant Colonel Mark Clark had come from the War Department to clear up those questions for the class of 1941.

"The United States is going to be in a big war," he said. "Your class is going to lead the way with the small units. Your leadership is going to be the key to our victory."[4]

Clark's plainspoken announcement did not exactly electrify the class. They were young men with bright futures. Besides, they were used to officers herding them into stuffy rooms and making pronouncements designed to shake them up. Like young people everywhere, their first tendency was to ignore the things that middle-aged men told them were true.

Clark's talk did resonate with one of the cadets in the room, however. Jack Norton was the First Captain, the senior chosen to command the entire Corps of Cadets. Like many of his classmates, Norton was looking forward to a long and well-deserved leave after graduation, but Clark's message made sense to Norton because it fit with what he'd been told by his mentor, Jim Gavin.

Gavin was responsible for overseeing the cadet staff, which included Norton and his roommate George Brown.[5] Gavin took a personal interest in the cadets under his charge, and Norton looked up to the soft-spoken captain with the quick mind.

By the spring before his graduation, Norton had become such a regular visitor at the Gavins' Sunday open houses that, on occasion, the Gavins even asked him to baby-sit their daughter, Barbara, while they attended mandatory social functions at the Academy.

As 1940 turned to 1941, as the cadets counted down the days until graduation, as they daydreamed about new posts and travels, Norton had his sights set on more than becoming a good infantry lieutenant. He wanted to marry Leslie Cameron Smith, a Vassar coed who had turned up at the window of his ground-floor streetside room one day in 1938, tapping lightly on the glass. When Norton and his two roommates went to the window, they found a beautiful young woman with a pretty smile, dressed in a pleated skirt and argyle sweater, who said she was looking for a cadet named Marshall Carney. The quick-thinking cadets all answered, "I'm Marshall Carney!" Her laugh, they agreed later, was a thing of beauty, and just what was needed to brighten their Spartan all-male world.

Two years went by before Norton, with a little more free time available to him, asked her on a date. The young couple hit it off right away, and Norton became a regular visitor at the Smiths' home in Bronxville, New York. By the autumn of 1940, Norton was thinking about marriage, but Leslie had other plans.

Leslie was an excellent student at Vassar, and if Norton had any doubt that she was dedicated to science, she dispelled it one day as the two of them sat in "the Boodler's," a soda fountain where the cadets took their dates. Somehow, the conversation turned to children and then—much to Norton's discomfiture—to reproduction. Leslie, who was already preparing to be a doctor, used a napkin to diagram for Norton the human reproductive system. This was simply not a topic of conversation between young men and young women in 1941. Norton was embarrassed, in part by his own ignorance, but he also admired Leslie's unorthodox attitude.

If Norton was an optimist about the world beyond West Point's gates, Leslie was a realist. She planned on going to medical school—an unusual step for a woman in 1941—and that wouldn't be possible if she was traipsing around from one dusty Army post to another behind an underpaid husband. Besides, there were dark things on the horizon, and their conversations about the future had a troubling undercurrent. War was coming, and Jack Norton, who had trained for years to be a soldier, would wind up as close to the action as he could get. He could read Leslie's concern, and even he had to admit there was a chance he would not come home. Why would she want to start her adult life as a widow?

Norton's roommates, perhaps trying to make the inevitable easier to take, reminded him that the last thing he could afford was a wife. Still, he held out hope as the winter of 1940–41 turned to spring. He had not formally proposed, so, his thinking went, she had not really turned him down. Not yet, anyway.

In May 1941, just a month before Norton was to graduate, the Germans shocked the world again by staging history's largest airborne invasion. A force of nearly twenty-five thousand men came out of the sky over the British-held island of Crete. The attacking force included parachutists, glider-borne troops, and elements of two mountain infantry divisions that landed once the paratroopers secured runways for them.

Because the Allies had already broken some high-level German codes, the island's defenders—a collection of British, Australian, New Zealand, Palestinian, and Greek troops—had advance warning of the invasion. The German paratroopers suffered huge losses: nearly 44 percent of the attacking force became casualties, including more than three thousand men killed outright, with another eight thousand wounded. The attackers also lost some 170 out of the 530 aircraft involved.[6]

Nevertheless, the Germans overwhelmed the Allied forces, pushing them off the island in a smaller version of the humiliating evacuation at Dunkirk. Some fifteen thousand British troops got away, but they also left behind some twenty-seven thousand killed, wounded, captured, and missing. To the Allies, particularly to the Americans, the attack on Crete looked like another example of German prowess. The enemy had appeared out of the sky and routed a much larger defending force. The fact that the British had been given warning—thanks to the immensely talented code-breakers working outside London—was not widely known, even among the highest levels of the military.

More important, no one on the Allied side knew how badly the Germans had been mauled. From the U.S. side of the Atlantic, it looked as if everything had gone well. In the eyes of American army officers, particularly those of General George Marshall, the Chief of Staff, Crete proved that the airborne invasions could work.

Unknown to the Allies, Hitler had decided exactly the opposite. Up until May 1941, Hitler's forces had never suffered such appalling losses (that would all change within a few months when the Germans launched *Barbarossa,* the invasion of the Soviet Union). Hitler declared the invasion a disaster and told his general staff that "the days of the paratrooper are over."[7] The Germans would not launch a large-scale airborne assault for the rest of the war. That would fall to the Allies.

The Germans' apparent success on Crete electrified many in the U.S. Army, and Jim Gavin was one of those. In April 1941, he had put in for a transfer to the new Parachutist School at Fort Benning, but West Point's Superintendent turned him down, both because Gavin had been at the Academy for less than a year, and, as he noted, Gavin, "so far as I know . . . is not particularly fitted for this type of duty."[8]

But Gavin was undeterred, and he contacted Colonel William C. Lee, the "father" of the airborne movement, who had the ear of General Marshall. Gavin's orders came through.

West Point's graduation was preceded by a week of dances, parades, and outdoor receptions for the cadets and their families. Many parents worried about the war in Europe and Asia, but during "June Week," in the warm sunshine and new green of spring, it was possible to forget— for a while at least—what might lie ahead. The Academy looked its best, from the neatly trimmed grass of the parade ground to the smartly turned out cadets, and droves of visitors and family members turned out to watch the ceremonies.

Norton was proud to have Leslie on his arm for the receptions. The trim girl with the curly hair looked more resplendent each time he saw her, from the garden parties to formal dance. The one blot on the week was that Norton's father, Augustus Norton, could not get up to

West Point to see his son graduate. The elder Norton, who had worked in shipping after his Army career, had been recalled to active service to oversee the vast expansion of port operations in New York, where much of the $7 billion in aid authorized under the Lend-Lease Act was beginning to flow to the war zone.[9]

Jack Norton spent most of his graduation leave at the Smith family camp in Maine, staying until the last possible moment and dragging out what he feared might be his last leave for some time. He stayed so long that he had to drive straight through—Maine to Georgia—to arrive at Fort Benning on time. There was more traffic than there had been through the years of the Great Depression. The country was slowly awakening, the "Hooverville" settlements of jobless men were disappearing, and work was easier to come by. Along roadsides up and down the coast, men in uniform were hitchhiking, looking for rides to the Army camps springing up in the vast undeveloped stretches of backwoods America. Norton drove south, bumping along on paved and unpaved roads, toward an uncertain, exciting future.

Behind him lay Leslie and her books, the camp in Maine, and the comfortable routines of civilian life. Ahead of him was Fort Benning, the home of the Infantry School, where the United States Army was stamping out new soldiers, noncoms and officers for a fighting force that some said might number in the millions. Jack Norton was on his way to take his place on the great stage set.

When Jim Gavin arrived at Fort Benning on August 1, 1941, the post was sweltering in the dog days of late Georgia summer. In the mornings, a thick blanket of moist air covered the riverside post like wet wool. Even the simplest physical labor became difficult, and crisp uniforms were sweat-soaked within minutes. Anyone with a choice avoided exertion during the blistering daytime hours, especially out of doors. Gavin drew his overalls and reported for the intense physical training that the Army demanded of its aspiring paratroopers. Gavin had developed a reputation as one of the Army's most intelligent officers; at airborne school he proved that he was as physically tough as he was mentally agile.

Jack Norton, now a brand-new second lieutenant, looked up his mentor when he arrived at Benning. Although Gavin was superbly fit for his age, the airborne school was designed to challenge the mostly twenty-something soldiers who came through. The troopers were doing hundreds of push-ups in the course of a day, and Gavin told Norton about the difficulty of climbing, hand over hand, the thick rope that stretched to an overhead pole some fifteen feet up. Some of the classes were washing out half the number who started.

The airborne was creating its own image as an elite outfit. Recruiters who visited other posts to seek volunteers pitched the new branch as the "best of the best." For starters, they looked it. Thanks to the rigors of airborne school, the men were physically fit and looked like soldiers. Beginning in 1941, the parachutists began to change their uniforms to create a distinct style. Some of these changes were practical, some were in recognition of their special status, and others were—at least in the eyes of soldiers who weren't airborne qualified—just showmanship.

First came the airborne wings, the metal badge worn on the uniform shirt. The design that came from the Army's department of heraldry in Washington was uninspiring, so Major William "Bud" Miley, commanding the 501st Parachute Battalion at Fort Benning, assigned an officer to come up with something better. A few days later, Lieutenant William Yarborough presented several options to his boss, including a sort of fourragère, a braided cord to be worn over the left shoulder. His favorite was an open chute with powerful wings extending from the base. After getting the necessary approvals in Washington, Yarborough took the design to an old-line Philadelphia jeweler, Bailey, Banks and Biddle. The lieutenant left Philadelphia with 350 of the badges, cast in silver. On the night before the first badges were awarded, Yarborough and his wife sat up cutting out small cloth ovals, in the unit colors of red and blue, that the soldiers pinned between the wings and the uniform blouse.

The paratroopers didn't stop there. They developed a round cloth patch, with embroidered wings, to be worn on the side of the overseas cap. They created their own field uniform, with extra oversized pockets (the troopers had started out wearing mechanics overalls, but the pockets were all sealed shut by the parachute harness). They even wore cloth name tapes, which old-timers thought smacked of too much individualism, putting "me" before "we." But perhaps the most distinctive uniform item was the jump boot.

Originally, the troops had been issued a boot developed for artillerymen. It had high sides, to help prevent twisted ankles, but it also had a strap and buckle that crossed the instep. Since a jumper's feet sometimes wound up above his head in an airplane's slipstream, there was a danger that the buckle could become entangled in the parachute shrouds. Fouled shrouds would keep the parachute from opening, and the tangled jumper would fall fast, trailing an unopened chute the troopers called a "streamer."

Yarborough cut away the boot's strap and buckle, and added a bubble-shaped metal toe cap, covered in leather. He also cut the forward edge of the heel to a forty-five-degree angle, as there had been instances of jumpers tripping on the deck rings of aircraft as they shuffled toward the door.[10]

The troopers kept their boots highly polished, and, to better show them off, they began to tuck the bottoms of their trousers into the boot tops, a practice they called "blousing." They even bloused their dress uniforms, and began referring to any man who wasn't a paratrooper as a "straight leg" soldier (because their trousers hung straight to their shoes), or, more derisively, just a "leg." Sometimes, a fashion-conscious general officer who was not a paratrooper showed up at Fort Benning wearing the smart-looking footwear, and there wasn't much the troopers could do. But enlisted men around Fort Benning who were not paratroopers knew not to be caught wearing the boots. Sometimes the paratroopers just made the straight-leg soldier hand them over—meaning he had to find his way back to his unit is his stocking feet. Sometimes the boots were forcibly removed.

The regalia was eye-catching, and for a lot of young men putting on a uniform for the first time, the attraction was no small thing.

Then there was the issue of hazardous duty pay, or simply "jump pay." Trainees brought in by the new draft received twenty-one dollars a month, and could expect small raises if, for instance, they qualified as expert with their weapons. Enlisted paratroopers got an extra fifty dollars a month, a 130 percent raise. Officers got one hundred dollars a month in jump pay.

But when it came to recruiting volunteers—and all paratroopers were volunteers—the best selling point was the airborne's reputation as one of the hardest assignments in the Army, a reputation the leadership deliberately cultivated. As the sharply dressed recruiters scoured the basic training posts and visited the new divisions, they spread a clear message: only the toughest men would make it through the training and earn the right to wear the silver wings. Only the fearless would even try.

This recruiting approach served two purposes. First, it attracted exactly the kind of risk-takers the airborne needed—after all, its mission was to jump from an aircraft in flight,[11] behind enemy lines, most likely at night. If the unarmed plane wasn't brought down by enemy fire, and if a man's chute opened properly, and if he didn't break his legs or back landing on a building or a wall, and if he didn't get dragged across the ground by a billowing chute, and if he didn't get shot in those first minutes of vulnerability as he struggled to get out of his harness and remove his weapon from its carrier, and if he could find his buddies and his leaders, then all he had to do was survive combat.

Second, the danger and tough training contributed to an invaluable sense of esprit among those who made it through jump school and eventually to an airborne unit.

The men even poked fun at the danger they faced, adding verse after verse to the gory song they called "Blood on the Risers," a long tale of a rookie trooper who dies when his chute fails to open. When they'd been drinking they sang it, loudly and badly, to the tune of "The Battle Hymn of the Republic."

The risers swung around his neck, connectors cracked his dome
Suspension lines were tied in knots around his skinny bones
The canopy became his shroud; he hurtled to the ground
AND HE AIN'T GONNA JUMP NO MORE!

Gory, gory what a helluva way to die,
Gory, gory what a helluva way to die,
Gory, gory what a helluva way to die
AND HE AIN'T GONNA JUMP NO MORE!

He hit the ground, the sound was "splat," his blood went spurting high
His comrades then were heard to say, "A HELLUVA WAY TO DIE!"
He lay there rolling round in the welter of his gore
AND HE AIN'T GONNA JUMP NO MORE!

There was blood upon the risers, there were brains upon the chute
Intestines were a'dangling from his paratrooper suit

He was a mess, they picked him up, and poured him from his
   boots
AND HE AIN'T GONNA JUMP NO MORE!

The new culture being built around the airborne wasn't the only change apparent at Fort Benning; it wasn't even the most noticeable. The entire sprawling post seemed turned on its head with change. Civilian contractors swarmed over the piney hills, clapping together wooden barracks by the hundreds, along with orderly rooms and medical clinics and mess halls and headquarters buildings. Firing ranges were scratched out of virgin woods, roads cut, and vehicle maintenance areas created.

Great drafts of men arrived nearly every day: they had to be housed and fed and trained, issued weapons and uniforms and hundreds of items of individual equipment, from shoe polish and toothbrushes to steel helmets and GI socks. The citizen soldiers had to learn Army discipline and customs—everything from how to wear a uniform and render a salute, to how to negotiate the chow line. The Army had to find doctors and dentists and truck drivers and railroad men; it had to train surveyors and military police, photographers and mechanics, cryptographers and radio operators. And it had to create the legions of infantry that would form the backbone of the Army if America went to war.

All of this tremendous change was being foisted on an organization that had, between the wars, been neglected to the point of suffocation. The interwar Army developed a rigid caste system rivaling anything the British army had ever created. With little money for training and less chance for promotion, the officer class, in particular, became more and more enamored of ritual and tradition.[12] There were more than a few people concerned that the sudden tremendous growth of the Army would so dilute the customs and mores that it would not really be the United States Army any longer. Some of the niceties of the peacetime Army, which had existed at a much slower pace, simply fell by the wayside.

South Carolinian Ed Thomas, one of the young men who suddenly found himself in uniform, didn't think he'd joined the "old" Army he'd heard about in the Reserve Officers Training Corps (ROTC) program at Georgia Tech. His friend and fellow lieutenant, Joe Gibbons, had read up on the customs and courtesies of the service and wasn't ready to abandon the old ways. When the unit to which the men were assigned, C Company of the 503rd Parachute Infantry Regiment, got a new commanding officer, Gibbons hauled out his summer white dress uniform and persuaded Thomas to borrow a similar outfit so the two could call on their new commander at his quarters one evening, as had been the custom between the wars. The only other officer Thomas could find who even owned the fancy uniform was a fellow nicknamed "Big Swede." Predictably, Thomas swam in Big Swede's uniform. But the two brand-new lieutenants were eager to fit into the culture, and they made their way to the corner of the post where married officers lived, Thomas self-conscious in his ill-fitting formal uniform.

Captain James Gavin answered the door in sweaty field overalls. Instead of inviting them in for cocktails, chitchat, and an exchange of engraved calling cards, he and his subordinates exchanged a few words. Then the exhausted Gavin went back inside to rest for the next day's training.

As he walked back toward the bachelor officers quarters, feeling even more ridiculous in someone else's dress whites, it occurred to Ed Thomas that Company C was going to be part of an Army that put training first. He took the lesson to heart.

Gavin was soon pulled from C Company to airborne headquarters by Colonel Bill Lee, who put the talented young officer to work writing one of the first doctrinal manuals for this new form of warfare, *The Employment of Airborne Forces.* The officers in the Provisional Parachute Group put in long hours, working out the details of how such an organization should be equipped and how it should fight.[13]

Gavin was happy to be among men who were as excited as he was by the prospect of creating a new arm of the service, one whose potential to be decisive on the battlefield was all out of proportion to its size. But as much as he liked the intellectual challenge of creating a brand-new doctrine, Gavin never lost sight of his main goal: he wanted to command troops.

FROM EVERY
CORNER
OF THE LAND

While Jim Gavin was working through his first autumn with West Point's Tactical Department, watching cadet parades and Saturday football games, a twenty-five-year-old sergeant in the Texas National Guard named Edwin Sayre became part of the massive call-up of troops swelling the Army.

Sayre was a genial man with an easy smile, dark hair, and a round face. When he found that the training day at Texas National Guard Camp didn't start until 5:00 A.M., he felt as if he'd been given a vacation. The workday back on his father's dairy farm near Breckenridge, Texas, started at 3:00 A.M. By the time the bugler blew reveille, turning the soldiers out for morning formation, Sayre's parents and siblings had already been at work for two hours. Not only that, but he now had Sundays off. Running the Sayre Dairy, where more than one hundred cows needed milking every day, was a 365-day-a-year operation.

For most of the year, weekly drill consisted of two hours of marching, handling the Springfield '03 rifle, and learning the rudiments of Army life. He got to spend time with boys he'd known all his life, and for every drill period, Sayre received the grand sum of one dollar.

Like a lot of people in Texas, Sayre didn't have to look far on his family tree to find military people. His great-grandfather, a Georgia native, had been a surgeon in the Confederate Army. When Sherman's army laid waste to a wide swath of the south in its March to the Sea, most of the family property was destroyed. Moving west after the war was easier than starting over again in ravaged Georgia.

Sayre's father, Arthur, leased a ranch on the Navajo reservation in New Mexico. It was in the ranch house that young Ed Sayre was delivered, with his mother's sister acting as midwife, on December 19, 1915. By the mid-1920s, the family had moved to Breckenridge, Texas, about a hundred miles west of Fort Worth. Men there were making the tremendous sum of $150 a month in the oil fields. It was good money for hard work, and it allowed the family to save enough to buy a dairy farm. Running the farm was also hard work, but not as dangerous as working on the oil rigs.

After high school, when Sayre went north for a semester of college in Nebraska, the country was in the grip of the Great Depression, and Texas suffered through a long drought that turned the middle of the country into a vast dust bowl. There was no money for school, and Sayre had to return to Breckenridge and the family farm. The Texas National Guard, besides giving him a chance to spend time with friends instead of with cows, offered a way to earn a little money at a time when every dollar was important.

Even so, Arthur Sayre didn't think joining the guard was a good idea. When his son announced that he wanted to enlist, he said, "I really wish you wouldn't."

In those lean years between the wars, when America tried to forget about armies and foreign entanglements, many Americans thought that being a soldier was just a step or two above being a convict, or an indentured servant. But young Sayre was persistent, and his father sent him off with the admonition, "Go ahead, then, be a bum!"

As it turned out, the guard offered more than pocket money and a chance to get away from the dairy farm for two weeks every year. In 1935, with the nation in the grip of the Depression, with few opportu-

nities available for young men, the guard offered advancement to a
man with ambition. Sayre rose to the rank of sergeant by the time he
turned twenty-one, in 1936. And even though platoon sergeants in the
guard only wore the three stripes of a buck sergeant—the lowest grade
of noncommissioned officer—Sayre was proud of the work he was
doing.

He studied correspondence courses to further his military education. A man could work his way through basics such as map reading
and military history, on up through more sophisticated subjects, like
the organization of the Army supply system, even on to military justice.
There were levels of difficulty to correspond to higher ranks; not that
there were any real promotions to be had. But the courses at least
opened the possibility that a man could be promoted.

Sayre, who was always looking for a challenge, took the courses,
studying at the kitchen table in his parents' home, extending his already long days by an hour or more each evening. There were times
when he was puzzling through some problem in logistics or tactics or
regulations that his buddies would drop by. Sometimes he went with
them; sometimes he put up with the ribbing and kept studying. One
weekend a month, he'd report to the converted garage that served as
the armory in Breckenridge to enjoy the company of the other soldiers.

Sayre's regiment was called to active duty when the Thirty-sixth Division, Texas National Guard, was put in federal service in October
1940. Many of the men packing their uniforms and equipment were
questioning their decision to join the guard, which had seemed like a
nice, safe way to put in a year of service to the country—none of it
very far from home—while avoiding the draft and the regular Army.
Even with the mobilization, many of the men were still happy with
their choice. These optimists said that since the call-up was only for
one year—it said so right on their orders—chances were that the

Thirty-sixth Division would spend the whole time at some stateside post.

In fact, twelve months was barely enough time to get a collection of units, dragged together from the corners of the largest state, to operate as a single, lethal war machine. There was just too much to do. By the time the sergeants taught them fire and maneuver and weapons maintenance and employment, by the time the officers learned how to plan and call for artillery fire, by the time they drew all the right equipment and learned how to take care of it—from radios to trucks to the newfangled jeeps—the year would be over. If war broke out after that, quite a few of these men figured, they'd be safe at home with their discharge papers.

A lack of training wasn't the only thing standing between the Thirty-sixth and full combat readiness. Like many National Guard units, the Texas division was rife with politics. Since the men in any particular unit were often from the same hometown, many jobs were handed out based on political connections rather than ability. Some of the battalion commanders were in their fifties, which was about three decades too old for the rigors of leading ground troops in combat.

But once the division came under the control of the War Department, things began to change. George Marshall, the Army's Chief of Staff, had already decided that the war was going to be fought by young men. He sent regular Army officers, men he knew and trusted, out to the National Guard divisions with orders to shape them up. There was a lot of housecleaning to do, with older and unfit men being identified and moved out, and younger ones trained and promoted to fill the critical leadership positions.

The Thirty-sixth Division moved to Camp Bowie, Texas, about seventy miles due south of Breckenridge, close enough for Ed Sayre to make it home on a weekend pass. There, the units expanded their training. At their home bases, they'd been limited to conducting squad and platoon maneuvers, since the armory could only field a small number of men. At Bowie, the exercises got bigger, with battalions of 400 to 500 men maneuvering through the sage and gullies.

Sayre taught his men how to move at night, how to attack an enemy position, how to shoot and operate like a team. A good bit of what he knew was book knowledge, but he saw every day as a chance to try things out on the ground, to see what worked and what didn't.

Even though Europe had been ablaze for a year and Japan had been at war in China for more than four, a vast number of Americans still believed that it was possible that the United States could stay out of what they saw as a foreign war. Sayre wasn't so optimistic, and he approached his combat training seriously, believing he would use it soon.

In the same month that the Thirty-sixth Division was called to active service, the Luftwaffe pressed its bombing raids on British cities, including London and the industrial midlands of England. American newspapers were hardly neutral; headlines and stories talked about the bravery of the British populace in the face of German air raids on the industrial cities. When President Roosevelt called up some naval reservists, the Republican opposition and some vocal isolationists accused the president of moving America closer to war.

On December 6, 1941, Sayre had a weekend pass, so he made arrangements to take a high school friend, Deana Slaughter, on a Sunday-afternoon date. The couple planned to see a movie at the theater in town, then have an early dinner afterward. Sayre would then drop her off at her home outside of town before hitting the two-lane road leading south from Breckenridge toward Camp Bowie. The bumpy Texas roads always made the trip an adventure, and a flat tire could throw off his timing just enough so that he'd be late if he wasn't careful. Deana was not a serious girlfriend; the two had met in grade school and had gone out a few times; also, Sayre believed that it wasn't the right time to make long-range plans.

Sayre didn't like the movie much, but Deana did, and Ed enjoyed spending time in the company of a young woman, instead of with hundreds of men. When the two emerged blinking in the sunlight after the dark of the theater, they could tell something had changed. There were more people on the street, talking in excited tones, speaking with strangers in small groups.

"The Japs bombed Pearl Harbor," Sayre heard a man say.

"Where's Pearl Harbor?" Deana asked.

"Hawaii," Sayre said.

Ed took Deana by the hand and walked toward a store whose owner had placed a big radio set in the open doorway. The news bulletins were sketchy on details, but the big picture was clear. On a sunny Sunday morning, the U.S. fleet had been attacked while at anchor in Pearl Harbor, Hawaii.

"All military personnel are to report immediately to their duty stations," the radio announcer said solemnly.

As 1941 came to a close, Berge Avadanian, a twenty-three-year-old Massachusetts native, landed a great job that allowed him to travel and even afford a car. After more than a decade of the Depression, the economy was finally picking up in earnest. There would be time and money for him to return to college later. For now, he was enjoying himself.

In early December, Avadanian was working in northern New Jersey, training managers for newly opened Howard Johnson restaurants. The job required some traveling, but Avadanian was young and unmarried, and he didn't mind being on the road. His territory included the New York area, and he took full advantage of a city night life that had been jolted awake. For the first time in his adult life, people had money to spend, not only on essentials like food and clothing, but even on things that were purely fun.

A musician friend of Avadanian's, Danny Kenyon, was touring with Louis Prima's band, and Avadanian arranged his schedule so that he could make it to the club. This was almost too good to be true: he'd get to hear one of the hottest bands on the club circuit, maybe even meet Louis himself. And of course, the club would be filled with young people who'd come out for a night of dancing.

The morning papers would be filled with the predictable mix of news about the war and the big debate in the United States: Would FDR's policies drag the United States into the war? But those concerns were for the morning, when Avadanian could sit down with the newspaper and coffee. On a Saturday night filled with lively music, it was easy for a young man to think about more pleasant things.

Everything changed on Sunday.

At 2:22 P.M., Roosevelt's press secretary released a brief statement saying that the Japanese had attacked Pearl Harbor, Hawaii. The first radio news broadcasts began reaching East Coast audiences almost immediately. Avadanian was at work in the restaurant when the reports started coming in. Customers and staff alike stopped moving, shocked into stillness. They stared at the radio in disbelief, numbed and unable to comprehend what they were hearing. The Japanese had attacked America? They had somehow made it all the way across the vast Pacific Ocean without being detected, and had managed to launch an enormous attack that was a complete surprise? How could such a thing happen? What was the Navy doing? How had they been caught off guard?

It was all anyone could talk about. Strangers spoke to one another in public places, in trains and restaurants and bars. They scoured the newspapers for details, listened to radio reports that offered maddeningly little that could help them make sense of how their world had changed. Ships were sunk, men were dead, and the debate about America's slow slide into war was suddenly over. The war had come to America.

Monday, December 8, was another workday, so Berge Avadanian dressed in his white coat and went to the new restaurant he was opening. The staff couldn't concentrate on the mundane tasks at hand: stocking pantries, keeping inventory and accounts. They were too angry that the United States had been played for a sucker, that the Japanese had launched a sneak attack, that the fleet had been asleep and unprepared, and they were angry that, until recently, Japan had been one of America's principal trading partners, that tons of scrap iron had been shipped from the West Coast to Japanese factories, and had obviously been returned in the shape of bombs and torpedoes.

A little after noon, the employees all gathered around a radio to hear the president's address, scheduled for 12:30. As Avadanian listened to Roosevelt's characterization of December 7 as "a date that will live in infamy," he had a moment of clarity. Roosevelt's speech lasted just a few minutes, but it was long enough for Berge Avadanian's world to change.

He stood up, took off his white Howard Johnson coat, went outside to his car, and pointed it toward New York City, stopping when he reached the first recruiting station in lower Manhattan. There was already a line reaching out the door, and Avadanian had to wait. The other young men were in the same mood he was in: they all wanted to do something, and they all wanted to do it right away. Judging from the conversations he heard around him, most of the men wanted to fight the Japanese, but Avadanian's mind was on another potential enemy. Germany had not yet declared war on the United States (that would come on December 11), but Avadanian believed that Hitler posed the bigger threat: his war would be in Europe, fighting the Germans.

Avadanian approached a Navy recruiter first. He had some notion that he wanted to sink the U-boats that were strangling Britain's lifeline. But the Navy recruiter told him he couldn't make any promises about where Avadanian would wind up. Just a few steps away, though, was an Army recruiter who didn't want the eager volunteer to walk out the door.

"We've got something here that might interest you," the recruiter said. "Something new."

That was how Berge Avadanian learned of the airborne. Not only did it offer a chance to serve with the Army's best-trained troops, but there was also an incredible bonus of fifty extra dollars a month. Since he was about to go from twenty-eight dollars a week to twenty-one dollars a month, the jump pay was not a small consideration. Besides, Avadanian figured, he had some experience that would pay off, maybe give him an advantage when it came to training. As a kid he used to jump from the second-story loft of the family barn with a big umbrella, landing in piles of hay stacked below. And at the 1939 World's Fair in Flushing, New York, he had paid seventy-five cents for one of the more popular thrill rides: visitors were strapped into a harness beneath an open parachute, then hoisted nearly two hundred feet into the air, where a latch released the chute and the "parachutist" drifted to a soft landing in plowed-up earth. (The Army adapted a similar design for its jump towers at Fort Benning.)

Avadanian's family was worried, but they were also proud of his impetuous decision. Eventually, his mother would hang a flag with three blue stars in the window of the family home, meaning that she had three sons in the nation's service.[1] Avadanian was not alone. The same mood was sweeping the country, and tens of thousands of young men did exactly the same thing Avadanian did: they set aside their lives and stepped forward to volunteer. It was an emotional decision, certainly, but without the flag-waving and patriotic rhetoric the previous generation had heard as they lined up at recruiting and induction centers during the Great War. The men who gathered before countless recruiting sergeants in the aftermath of Pearl Harbor had about them more of a quiet determination. They would need it to get through what lay ahead.

When it came time for Berge Avadanian to report to the recruiting station, he hocked the only civilian suit he owned at a pawn shop right across the street from the depot, pocketing the eight dollars and figuring it would be a long time before he needed a civilian suit again.

The year that saw the formation of the 505th Parachute Infantry Regiment, 1942, was a dire one for the Allies. In the Pacific, the Japanese handed stunning defeats to a massive U.S. force in the Philippines, and captured the British stronghold of Singapore. The first ray of hope reached America in April, when the public learned of Colonel Jimmy Doolittle's air raid over Tokyo. Although the raid did little damage and did not affect the outcome of the war, it did boost American morale during a bleak time. (It also confused the Japanese, who could not figure out how land-based heavy bombers had reached the home islands.)

Hitler had broken his treaty with the Soviet Union and launched a massive surprise attack in June 1941. By 1942, across a front that stretched over a thousand miles from the Baltic to the Black Sea, huge German and Soviet armies were locked in a death struggle, with the Wehrmacht still advancing in spite of suffering more than a million casualties. Joseph Stalin had pleaded with his British and American allies to get into the fight. The view from Moscow was straightforward: Hitler was at war with three major powers in Europe, but only one of those nations, the Soviet Union, was doing any substantial fighting. Stalin wanted his allies to open a second front that would draw off some of the German resources clawing at the heart of the Soviet Union. If the USSR collapsed, which seemed highly likely in 1941 and into 1942, not only would Hitler control vast new resources for his war machine, but his millions of combat veterans would be available to crush the British and keep American troops out of Europe.

As German land forces fought deeper into the Soviet Union, the German navy was winning the battle for the Atlantic. In early 1942 Admiral Karl Donitz, commander of Germany's U-boat fleet, allowed his aggressive commanders to push all the way to the U.S. coast. America might well be the arsenal of democracy, but every tank, rifle, bullet, and soldier that would fight Hitler first had to cross the Atlantic; Donitz saw this shipping bottleneck as a strategic opportunity. If they couldn't reach Europe, it didn't matter how many tanks or infantrymen the United States produced.

The submarine commanders were thrilled by what they saw when they surfaced near the U.S. coast. With the wartime economy booming, with tourists and servicemen spending money freely, coastal cities like New York, Atlantic City, and Miami refused to enforce blackouts. Their bright lights silhouetted merchant ships in what became a shooting gallery for Donitz's skippers. In January 1942, a single U-boat patrolling off New York Harbor sank eight ships, including three oil tankers in one twelve-hour stretch. On February 28 a U-boat torpedoed and sank the USS *Jacob Jones,* within sight of the New Jersey coast; only 11 of the 136 sailors on board survived. On April 10, a U-boat surfaced off Jacksonville Beach, Florida, and used its deck cannon to sink the tanker SS *Gulfamerica.* The U-boat captain watched through binoculars as thousands of tourists gathered on the beach to see the tanker burn.

Commander Reinhard Hardegen wrote in his log: "All the vacationers had seen an impressive special performance at Roosevelt's expense. A burning tanker, artillery fire, the silhouette of a U-boat—how often had all of that been seen in America?" On June 15, in broad daylight, a German U-boat torpedoed two American freighters within full view of thousands of Virginia Beach bathers.

And these incidents were just the most spectacular. U-boats patrolling the Atlantic were sinking Allied ships faster than they could be replaced. By June 1942, German U-boats had sent to the bottom more than 4.7 million tons of ships and cargo, including one-fifth of the fleet carrying Jamaican aluminum ore (for aircraft production) to the United States. Oil-carrying capacity was shrinking by 3.5 percent every month. In June 1942, Army Chief of Staff George Marshall concluded: "The losses by submarines off our Atlantic seaboard and in the Caribbean now threaten our entire war effort." Another month or two of this slaughter, he figured, and the United States would be unable to deliver the men and equipment necessary to fight in Europe.[2]

A German spring offensive in 1942 rocked the Soviets again, and when Soviet Foreign Minister Vyacheslav Molotov arrived in London in May, word was waiting for him that the Germans had overrun the Crimean Peninsula. The gallows humor in the British capital was that Molotov spoke only four words of English: "yes," "no," and "second front."[3] While Molotov fumed, Churchill talked endlessly about the British struggle in North Africa, where, as Molotov surely knew, the British faced only a fraction of the German might the Soviets were battling.

Molotov next traveled to Washington, where FDR's staff worked with him on a joint communiqué about the absolute necessity of opening a second front in Europe in 1942. But Churchill was soon on his way to Washington to dissuade his American allies from a premature assault on Europe. Churchill had watched Britain commit a large force to fighting on the continent in World War I, only to see much of a generation slaughtered in the trenches. In a single day's fighting along the Somme River front in July 1916, the British suffered twenty thousand killed. It was not a lesson easily forgotten, and it was a mistake Churchill was determined would not be repeated in this war. Instead, Britain adopted a peripheral strategy: isolate the enemy through blockade, attack his war-making plants with bombers, keep open the supply routes to America and the oil fields of the Middle East, contain Axis expansion, and launch small-scale attacks on Fortress Europe.

The chief problem with this strategy was that it presumed that the Soviet Union could survive. And in 1942, that was not clear.

In April 1942, President Franklin Roosevelt sent General George Marshall, the Chief of Staff of the United States Army, to London to discuss this second front with Prime Minister Winston Churchill. Roosevelt cabled Churchill: "Your people and mine demand the establishment of a front to draw off pressure on the Russians, and these peoples are wise enough to see that the Russians are killing more Germans and destroying more equipment than you and I put together."[4]

The taciturn George Marshall, who richly deserved the title history would award him as the architect of American victory, knew that the British were reluctant to commit to a cross-channel invasion in 1943, which was the soonest the Allies could hope to build up sufficient force in England to hurl at the Continent. Marshall worried that the Soviets might collapse, that all those hundreds of German divisions would then be available to Hitler in the west.

Dwight Eisenhower, commander of U.S. forces in Europe, shared the view that opening a second front was critical to Allied success. This was not purely altruistic, but a cold assessment of what would happen if the Soviet Union collapsed. Ike noted, in July 1942, "We should not forget that the prize we seek is to keep eight million Russians in the war."[5]

American strategists, especially Marshall, pushed for an attack on Europe. Churchill's mission was to get them to put off such an assault at least until 1944. If he had to commit to smaller invasions sooner than that, he was willing to compromise.

For his part, FDR believed he had to get the American war machine in action somewhere. Facing congressional elections in November 1942, Roosevelt wanted to show voters that the United States was committed to the war against Hitler.

As the winter of 1941–42 gave way to the spring, the pace of change at Fort Benning accelerated. The post was awash in infantry trainees: newly commissioned officers, recruits, and draftees from all corners of the country. The fort itself grew, swallowing up huge tracts of pine woods south of the old post and alongside the Chattahoochee River. Tiny backwoods communities were displaced, houses razed, family cemetery plots fenced off. The names of these vanished hamlets came to be associated, instead, with road intersections and training areas in the trackless woods. The air crackled with reports from scores of rifle ranges. Farther away from the main post, mortar rounds *carrumphed* on cleared impact areas. Spotters adjusted fire, and sweating crews practiced putting rounds where the infantry wanted them.

On weekends, the khaki crowds were so thick in the tiny downtown of Columbus, Georgia, that pedestrians spilled from the impassable sidewalks and onto the streets. Clubs, speakeasies, and brothels attracted crowds of soldiers, particularly on the weekends following paydays. War had already changed the face of Europe; it was changing this corner of southern Georgia, too.

Jim Gavin, whom West Point's Superintendent had noted was "not particularly suited" for the airborne, had been promoted twice and was now a lieutenant colonel, about to take command of the newest regiment forming at Fort Benning. The 505th Parachute Infantry, activated on July 6, 1942, was a skeleton unit. In the earliest days, the men spent a good bit of time simply waiting for the unit rosters to fill up as new men finished training and became available.

When Cloid Wigle, a farmer from Oregon, was assigned to H Company, there were only eight other men in an outfit that would be home for more than a hundred. Although only a private, Wigle frequently encountered Gavin, the regimental commander, simply because there were so few men in the unit. When the troopers played football in the company street, Gavin sometimes joined them. In one contest, Wigle knocked the much bigger Gavin to the ground. The colonel bounced on the hard-packed dirt, and Wigle had a passing thought that he'd made a mistake.

"How can a little guy like you hit a man so hard?" Gavin asked. He stuck out his hand and shook Wigle's. Wigle figured the paratroopers were really going to be a rough-and-tumble lot, just as he'd been promised. And it started with the boss.

Gavin looked for the same attitude in the subordinate commanders he chose for the new regiment. He found what he was looking for in Arthur Gorham, commander of the First Battalion.

Gorham, who turned twenty-seven in January 1942, was a 1938 graduate of West Point who had played some football at the Academy. Six feet tall, lean and muscular, with dark hair, a long face, and bright eyes, he often joined the pick-up games of baseball or football the troops played in their off-duty hours. As with Gavin, the soldiers considered it a good sign that the young officer was willing to take a few shots.

Gorham's first assignment as a paratrooper was with the 503rd Parachute Infantry. Like many of the commanders who would come to dominate the airborne, Gorham demanded a great deal from his troops, especially when it came to physical fitness and the technical details of their work. He was a stickler for clean weapons, clear communications, and deep foxholes, which he knew would keep men alive in combat. He was also an unconventional thinker, a good trait in a paratrooper and one he encouraged among his men.

In one training exercise, Gorham's unit was to take part in a large-scale assault on MacDill Army Air Base, near Tampa, Florida. The plan was for the paratroopers to fly from Fort Benning, jump onto drop zones about a mile from the field, then quickly assemble for an assault.

The objective was to capture the airfield and the base operations building. The "enemy" would be straight-leg infantry troops from Camp Blanding, Florida.

One of Gorham's new lieutenants, Ed Thomas (who had visited Gavin wearing Big Swede's dress whites), made an outlandish suggestion. Thomas told Gorham that a young woman he'd met while in college lived in St. Petersburg, Florida. He didn't know her very well, but he knew that St. Petersburg was not too far from Tampa, and he had a plan. Gorham approved and the young woman agreed to be a part of it.

The drop zone was centered on a major intersection, and Thomas asked his friend, Helen, to park her car at that intersection with a bedsheet on the top of it as a signal to the pilots. The sheet proved unnecessary; on this daytime drop, the aircrews put the troopers right on the DZ.

After shedding his parachute, Thomas took three men from his platoon and ran to the car, where they loaded up, with the lieutenant behind the wheel and an excited Helen in the back with another soldier. Thomas drove the car right up to the main gate at McDill. He stopped, as required, and when the gate guard approached, one of the troopers jumped out, stuck the muzzle of his weapon in the guard's stomach, relieved him of his sidearm, and jumped backed into the car before the guard could react.

Thomas and his cohorts followed the directional signs to the operations building. It was unguarded, but the door was locked. The lieutenant used the butt of his pistol to break a glass pane on the door, then let himself in. A startled exercise judge in the operations center ruled that the paratroopers had been captured, although the enemy forces had no one inside the building who could actually do such a thing. Thomas figured that the umpire was unwilling to let the exercise stop so early.

A photographer who happened to be on hand for the exercise took a photo of Helen and her paratroopers, and in the accompanying story called Helen "the Mata Hari of MacDill Field."

THE OH-FIVE

Within weeks of the attack on Pearl Harbor, Ed Sayre and the rest of the 36th Division were on the move to Camp Blanding, Florida. Like many of the posts growing all across the country, Blanding was a sprawling hive of activity when the Texans arrived. Facing an acute shortage of officers, the division allowed four hundred noncommissioned officers to take a written test, an examination for a direct commission as a lieutenant. When Ed Sayre sat down and looked at the questions, he smiled to himself: the material was drawn directly from the correspondence courses he'd studied at his parents' kitchen table back in Breckenridge. Sayre finished in the top 10 percent, and soon wore the brand-new gold bars of a second lieutenant.

While he was training at Camp Blanding, Sayre heard about the new corps of parachute troops being formed. Like a lot of the men who wound up at airborne school, Sayre was at least partly attracted by the substantial bonus pay. At the time, a second lieutenant's pay was $125 a month; the bonus pay for airborne officers was an additional $100.

Unfortunately for Sayre, the Thirty-sixth Division didn't want to let him go. His performance as a junior officer had been solid, even though he had not received any formal training at the Infantry School.

When he requested reassignment to airborne school, the commanding general of the Thirty-sixth Division disapproved it.

His immediate boss summed it up for him. "We've been spending a lot of time training you and getting you ready. We're not going to invest all that and then hand you off to some other unit."

Sayre contented himself with preparing his men for what lay ahead, but he didn't lose interest in the airborne. One day he got a call from a friend who worked for the adjutant general, the office that handled all administrative paperwork in the division.

"The division commander is on leave for a while," Sayre's friend told him. "If you carry your request up here yourself, I'll see that it gets out of division headquarters with an approval."

Sayre filled out the paperwork again and hurried to headquarters. His friend was as good as his word, and as soon as the orders were typed, Sayre packed his bag and headed out of the division area before someone could change them back.

Sayre had his orders, but he had to make his own way to Fort Benning. The Thirty-sixth Division wasn't about to fund his travel, and the parachute school didn't have the budget. Sayre found himself hitchhiking through northern Florida, a heavy canvas duffel bag on the ground by his feet. Fortunately, the sight was common, and it wasn't hard for a serviceman in uniform to catch a ride.[1]

In the late spring of 1942, many of the men who would form the core of the Army's first airborne forces were going through jump school, and Sayre joined them in May. (There were plans for two airborne divisions of eighty-four hundred men each.) Because his class had a large contingent of junior officers, Sayre was assigned to a training platoon made up of lieutenants and captains (all ranks went through the same training). They signed in, dropped their canvas bags on a bunk, and began swapping stories they'd heard about the training ahead.

Some of the stories were alarming: tales of physically fit men who couldn't handle the running and the push-ups, and who dropped out even before they started hurling their bodies from airplanes.

Airborne school was four weeks long. "A" week was mostly physical training to harden the men, not so much for the rigors of jumping, but for landing. Jumping was a test of nerve; landing safely was a test of physical toughness.

They lined up to jump from small platforms—three, four, five feet high—into sawdust pits where they practiced the tumbling roll called the "parachute landing fall." The idea was to control what happened. The ideal stance, just before impact, feet together, knees bent, arms stretched overhead. Once a man made contact with the ground, he rolled onto his side, protecting his head and using the fleshy part of the torso to soften the impact. The trainees practiced this countless times, from increasing height, until it became second nature.

There was a particular emphasis on building upper body strength. Parachutes in use in 1942 had no steering mechanism, so the only way a rapidly descending soldier could guide his chute was to pull down hard on the risers, the thick straps above each shoulder that ran from the body harness to the thinner lines (called shrouds), which were in turn connected to the bottom rim of the parachute. This tugging collapsed the parachute just enough to change the aerodynamics. Pull down on the risers over the right shoulder, and the jumper slips, or drifts, to the right. This kind of maneuvering became important close to the ground, as jumpers tried to avoid landing on top of buildings, fences, and trees.

Since upper body strength was so important, the trainees at jump school were always doing push-ups—any minor infraction or hesitancy in training would get a man dropped for twenty, thirty, or more. The men had to climb hand-over-hand up thick ropes, without using their feet to clamp the rope.

And they ran. Everywhere.

Running was the sine qua non of airborne school, just as long marches with full field equipment were a staple of infantry training. Men who showed up at Benning with a few extra pounds soon shed the weight and began to take on the look of lean fighters.

The physical training wasn't a problem for Sayre, who was as compact and lean as a piece of beef jerky. He got through A week and B week without too much difficulty. During the second week, the men learned about maneuvering their parachutes by yanking on the risers. They learned how to strap on the harness: the trick was to always to make the harness tight enough so that the jumper was ready for the opening shock. A loose harness, while more comfortable on the ground and in the aircraft, meant a lot of play, and the opening shock would break a man's legs or arms, or crush his testicles. A too tight harness cut off circulation during the hours they spent trussed and waiting to board an aircraft or flying to the drop zone.

By the third week, the trainees were ready for the packing sheds. These buildings were ovens in Georgia's early summer, but this was not a place to get drowsy or fail to pay attention. For it was here the men learned to lay out the chute on the long tables, to remove tangles and check the static lines and carefully pack the parachute so that it would deploy instantly. The men were closely supervised during this phase, for obvious reasons. Any deviations or flaws in this work and the trainee had to start over again.

The jump school training area was dominated by the 200-foot towers, like huge construction cranes, that were visible from much of the sprawling post. On training days, even from a distance one could see tiny paratroopers being hauled up beneath fully opened parachutes that were hooked to a large hoop. Once at the top, the man had to indicate that he could hear the sergeant on the ground (who then knew the man wasn't paralyzed with fear and could follow commands). Then the big ring went up another half foot, tripping a release mechanism, and the trooper floated to the ground. The towers had four arms, so that no matter which way the wind was blowing, at least two down-wind arms could be used without a trooper being blown into the superstructure.

For Sayre, the most daunting prospect was not the 200-foot towers or, during the last phase, the "real" jumps from the boxy C-47 aircraft. Instead, he was surprised to find that his nemesis was the 34-foot tower, mock aircraft fuselages set atop thick poles. Trainees climbed a long staircase, wearing just the harness portion of a parachute rig. Once inside the fuselage, a noncom hooked the harness to an overhead trolley, which in turn rolled on a cable running to the ground. Thus prepared, the trainee resembled some kind of human ski gondola.

In the mock fuselage, the men practiced everything that took place right before and right after a man exited an aircraft. The jumpers were tucked in tightly, in a single file, as the eighteen men that made up a "stick" would be in an actual jump. They shuffled to the door, each keeping close to the man in front of him. When the jumpmaster, positioned beside the door, yelled "GO!" the jumper leaped into space, tucking himself into a tight, almost fetal body position, and readied himself for the shock of the parachute opening. On the tower, this was just a sudden sharp upward tug as the man's weight fell a few feet. Then the harness—with the jumper dangling below it—slid along the downward-sloping guide wires. At the bottom, the jumper practiced his parachute landing fall.

For some reason, thirty-four feet was just the right height to frighten many of the men. Anything lower didn't seem dangerous, and most things higher felt more like an amusement ride—almost surreal, too high to worry about. But thirty-four feet was just high enough to bring out the fear, and Ed Sayre was one of those who worried about that tower.

Anticipating this fear, the trainers at airborne school spent countless hours conditioning the men to react to commands. Paratrooper trainees practiced "shuffling toward the door" and jumping out of mock aircraft on the ground. More important, they learned to respond instantly to the jumpmaster's "GO!" There was no time for hesitating in the doorway, no time to think, just a constant relentless pressure, both real and mental, to clear the aircraft.

Just to ensure that no frightened jumper blocked the doorway for others, the men were taught never to put their hands on the inside of the aircraft door; the hands always went on the outside. That way, a man who hesitated had nothing to grab on to and could easily be pushed out the door by the guy behind him, or by the sheer weight of an eighteen-man stick of troopers hurrying for the door. The effect, depending on one's point of view, was either heroic—a group of men in a tightly knit team, defying their own fears—or pathetic. They looked a bit like lemmings, hurling themselves into the void on command, simply following the man in front.

Eventually, Sayre overcame his fears. The training helped, as did the fact that the enlisted men watched the officers carefully to see how they would react. The officers were supposed to be leaders, especially when it came to doing something dangerous or unpleasant. Sayre was determined to do his duty.

In June 1942, Sayre and the other men who'd stuck it out were called into ranks to hear a senior officer read the orders that made them all Army parachutists. Sayre was proud of his accomplishment: he'd made it through one of the toughest schools the Army had. He could now wear the silver wings of a parachutist, and he would see a significant pay raise at the end of the month. At the order "stand at ease," Sayre put his hands in the small of his back and let his eyes fall on a tall, slender lieutenant colonel he'd never seen before. The colonel did not have a strong speaking voice; even so, there was an air of confidence about him. He was, Sayre figured, a commander.

"We're putting together a new unit," Jim Gavin told the assembled junior officers. "The 505th Parachute Infantry Regiment."

Then Gavin produced a sheaf of papers and held them in front of him.

"I've reviewed the records of the men in this class, and I believe some of you are good enough for the five-oh-five. If I call your name, take a step forward."

Gavin read about twenty names, Lieutenant Edwin Sayre's among them. As instructed, Sayre picked up the duffel bag containing all of his uniforms and got on the truck waiting in the company area. It was an easy leap onto the tailgate step and only a short ride over to the 505th area. It was also a journey that would have a tremendous impact on Ed Sayre's life.[2]

The truck took Sayre and the other junior officers just a few miles from main post to an area of Fort Benning called "the Frying Pan," a low bowl of sand and pine trees along the Chattahoochee River, which separates Georgia from Alabama. The Frying Pan was one of the few flat areas on post, a natural choice for a runway. From here, Air Corps planes could take off with their loads of paratroopers. Sayre's experience in the National Guard paid off. Arthur Gorham, commander of the First Battalion of the 505th, recognized Sayre's skills and made him executive officer of B Company.

Sayre hadn't come across any West Point graduates in the Texas National Guard, and had met only a few since volunteering for airborne school. So far, his impressions had been positive. That continued with Gorham, who, at twenty-seven, was only a few years older than Sayre. Gorham didn't want to become buddies with his men, but he treated them well and fairly, and respected their opinions. Gorham also knew the technical details of his job, from Army administration to how to maneuver rifle companies. He shared with his boss, Jim Gavin, a way of welcoming officers to the unit.

"So you're an officer, huh?" the senior leaders greeted new arrivals.

"Around here that means the first one out the aircraft door and the last one through the chow line."

Like Gavin, Gorham also spoke quietly. In spite of his youth, he had an almost fatherly demeanor. He shared the hardships and he treated the men with respect, from privates on up through his battalion executive officer, Major Walter Winton. Winton could see, in the way Gorham talked to the troops, that he had a genuine concern for their welfare.

This didn't mean the men of First Battalion were coddled; in fact, it often meant the opposite. Gorham and the other airborne commanders believed the best thing for the men—the thing that came as close as anything could to guaranteeing they would make it home—was hard training. Everything Sayre observed about his battalion commander told him Arthur Gorham was the kind of boss he'd been hoping for when he volunteered for the airborne.

One day in the fall of 1942, Sayre overheard some of the noncoms in B Company talking about selling passes to the soldiers, a practice that was not only illegal, but repugnant. The sergeants had all the power; the men relied on them to be fair in their treatment. Selling passes was not only taking advantage of the position of responsibility; it was a violation of trust.

Passes were supposed to be given out for good performance. It was a way for leaders to reward soldiers for a good score on the rifle range, or outstanding performance at an inspection. In B Company, it turned out, passes were available to any soldier with ten dollars.

Sayre asked around the company and learned how the scheme worked. A soldier who wanted a weekend pass approached one of the sergeants who was dealing. For ten bucks, the sergeant approached the company first sergeant, who controlled all passes and privileges. Each noncom got a piece of the action, and the soldier got his pass.

Sayre went to his boss, Captain Sanders, and told him about the problem. The company commander refused to believe the lieutenant.

"I picked those noncoms myself," he said. "They're all good men. I don't believe they'd do something like that." He told Sayre not to mention his suspicion again. Sayre could understand Sanders's reluctance to throw the company into turmoil by firing its key leaders, but he felt the damage being done to the company's morale—in particular to the trust between the men and their noncoms—demanded action.

Shortly after that, Captain Sanders took a short leave. Since the unit had to have a commander on base at all times, he signed an order putting Sayre (who was the executive officer, the second-in-command) in temporary command. As soon as Sanders cleared the area, Sayre called in the sergeants he suspected and began questioning them. When they admitted abusing their positions, he gave them a choice: face a court-martial or take a bust to private. The noncoms knew Sayre would have no trouble finding privates to testify against them. Chances were good they'd end up in the stockade; at the very least they'd be sent to a straight-leg outfit. They gave up their stripes.

When Sanders returned from leave and found that his handpicked sergeants were now privates, he was furious. He called in the upstart lieutenant and said, "You've spent your last day in B Company." Then he took Sayre to Gorham's office and asked to see the battalion commander. Gorham listened as Sanders explained that Sayre had busted the B Company noncoms against specific instructions.

"I don't want this lieutenant in my company anymore," Sanders said.

But Sayre had already discussed the problem with Gorham, who had sided with the lieutenant.

"Don't worry, I'm moving him over to command A Company," Gorham told a shocked Sanders.

This was a promotion for Sayre, but it was also a challenge. The company had the highest rate of AWOLs in the battalion. A man who was AWOL for more than thirty days was considered a deserter, and in wartime a deserter could be shot.[3] Most men came back on their own when they ran out of money or had their short visit at home, and they faced the consequences. The company also had the highest rate of courts-martial and the highest incidence of venereal disease.

Sayre knew that many men had difficulty adjusting to military discipline, to all the nitpicking details of Army life. He also believed that some of the men who were discipline problems at a stateside training post would be great combat soldiers. The airborne, by its nature, attracted the high-spirited, the men most likely to stick a finger in the eye of authority—especially over what they considered "chicken shit" rules. But discipline is the soul of an army, and Sayre's job was to enforce discipline. Gorham let him handle it in his own way

Most of the courts-martial, Sayre learned, were for soldiers who had gone AWOL. He figured if he could fix that problem, the court-martial problem would go away, too. He began by calling the soldiers together and telling them there would be no more courts-martial in A Company for AWOL soldiers. The men waited quietly to hear the rest of the story, knowing that there had to be consequences.

"Instead we're going to have company punishment. If you're gone for twenty-four hours, that means you owe me twenty-four hours of training. That's four hours every night for six days, or all day on Sunday."

Sayre didn't have to say that this was in addition to the exhausting field work the men were already doing. At the end of the training day, a man detailed for company punishment fell out in full field gear, marched twelve miles to a determined point, set up his display so that one of the company officers could check that he had carried everything: weapon, shelter half, extra clothes and rations, canteen and ammunition, helmet, first aid pouch—upwards of sixty pounds. Then, after the inspection, the man would be turned around for the march back to post.

To tackle the problem of venereal disease, he let word get out about a civilian doctor in town who administered shots to treat the affliction. A man treated by the Army doctors went on report and could lose pay, his stripes, or both. The unintended consequence of this regulation was that VD was underreported, and men were getting sick. Sayre knew his method was unorthodox, but he operated on the assumption that, since it helped the men and didn't hurt the Army, it was one of those instances where it was better to act than to ask permission.

Sayre preferred this kind of commonsense leadership. His objective was to train soldiers, and that meant keeping as many men as possible present for training. Courts-martial worked against that. Sayre saw no need to sully a man's permanent record when there were other ways to get the job done.[4]

Like a coach putting together a team for a tough season, Sayre kept his eye out for good soldiers he could bring to A Company. One of the men he noticed was a young noncom named Tim Dyas, who had been, like Sayre, a sergeant in the National Guard.

Born and raised on Long Island, Dyas had faced tough times even before the Great Depression hit the country. His father abandoned the family in 1924, when Tim was four years old. As soon as he became old enough to work, Tim helped support his mother and his siblings. He still managed to become a star of his high school track team, regularly winning races even when the team traveled to tough competitions in New York City. But he was never far from the reminder of how harsh his life could be. When he failed to place among the top runners in an invitational meet in the city, a teammate asked him why, as the winning times were within his range. Dyas had to admit that he hadn't eaten in a couple of days.

Dyas was good enough to win a track scholarship to Idaho State University, but that would have meant leaving his mother. Instead, he took a job as an orderly at Central Islip State Hospital. In February

1941, Dyas learned that the New York National Guard was recruiting. It was common knowledge that the guard was a place where local politicians and the politically connected hid from the draft. Dyas wasn't interested in hiding out from anything: he was interested in the extra money the guard offered, money his mother could use to support his younger brothers and sisters. And if he did get called to federal service, New York State would pay the difference between his Army pay and his state wage, which seemed a very good deal to someone who had to think about every dollar.

Dyas came from a family with a military history. His grandfather had lost a leg in the Civil War, and Dyas remembered stories his grandmother told about when she started receiving compensation from the government: eight dollars a month, beginning in 1902. Dyas's uncle had fought in the Spanish-American War, and his father had fought and been gassed in World War I.

Dyas showed the same ambition in the guard that he had displayed on the track, studying every manual he could get his hands on, learning the technical details of his job so that he'd be ready when the chance for promotion came. By 1941, even the peacetime Army was growing so rapidly that the twenty-year-old could see opportunities ahead.

Throughout that year, he kept applying for airborne school and an assignment to the paratroops. But his regiment, like units everywhere, was trying to hang on to its noncoms, and his requests were turned down.

Dyas was sitting on his bunk at Fort Ethan Allen, Vermont, cleaning his rifle and listening to the radio, on Sunday afternoon, December 7, 1941. As the soldiers drew round and listened to the reports about the Japanese attacks, Dyas thought about his mother, and how worried she would be, about how his term of service had instantly changed to "for the duration." But mostly he thought about how he had to get out of the guard.

He applied once again for jump school, and indicated that he was willing to take a bust to private in order to attend. Persistence paid off, and in early 1942, his orders finally came through, and he headed south to Fort Benning.

By the summer of 1942, Dyas, wearing shiny new jump wings, was on his way to the new 505th Infantry. Now all the study and preparation paid off, and Dyas was promoted several times, all the way up to platoon sergeant. When B Company's First Sergeant was injured in a training jump, he was sent over to that company for a short while to fill the top noncom slot. Although he had risen quickly, Dyas was flattered when he learned that Ed Sayre wanted him back in A Company, even though it meant stepping down from the top spot. Dyas had taken his measure of Ed Sayre, and he was happy to return to A Company. For all his rank and responsibilities, Dyas was the second youngest man in the company, a fact he tried to keep hidden from the other troops.

One of the men who volunteered for the Army's newest arms had come from an arm that was disappearing. Private Otis Sampson had first enlisted in the Army in 1930 and served in the horse cavalry at Fort Ethan Allen, Vermont.

In that tiny peacetime Army, there was little money for large-scale training exercises. Commanders sought ways to channel the energy of the young men in the ranks, and organized sports offered an outlet. Sports also gave the units an opportunity to compete with one another, and a great deal of energy went into preparing the various teams. Sampson, a slight five foot six, was too small for football, but found his place in the boxing ring.

He fought as a featherweight at 128 pounds, and was lucky enough to be coached by some men who had fought professionally, or had fought at Army posts overseas and around the world. Boxing gave him something to do in the long Vermont winters, and he was proud to help his unit compete against the artillery and infantry regiments assigned to the post.

In 1932, Sampson reenlisted for another hitch at Ethan Allen. But there were changes afoot: the Army was planning to mechanize the old horse cavalry units. There were plenty of officers and enlisted men who thought the Army was being hasty (Even the forward-thinking George Patton was still assigned to a horse cavalry unit when Germany invaded Poland in September 1939). But the soldiers traded their mounts for trucks and armored cars. Sampson was destined for mechanic's school, but he wanted no part of it.

When the Army offered him a chance to buy out his contract, Sampson came up with the almost four months' salary required, eighty-five dollars, to get out of the remaining portion of his enlistment. With a recently mustered-out friend named Harry Bell, Sampson headed west on a 1930 Harley-Davidson motorcycle. When the cycle died at Kimberly, Idaho, the two former soldiers tried their luck prospecting on the Snake River. Later, they made their way north and found familiar work near Cascade, Idaho, handling horses. Although Sampson had never hated the Army, he did enjoy his new freedom, and the young man from the eastern mill towns found the big-sky country bracing. He changed jobs again, putting in a stretch as a lumberman, where he spent long days swinging an ax, or using a two-man saw to cut thirty-inch logs. It was hard, honest physical labor, and it made the former featherweight champ even stronger.

By December 1941, Sampson had found his way back to the East Coast, had married and found work in Quonset Point, Rhode Island, making some of the tens of thousands of huts the military would spread around the globe. In the weeks after Pearl Harbor, Sampson decided that he wanted to go back into the service. When he received his induction notice in early 1942, the thirty-year-old veteran had already made up his mind to volunteer.

A friend had shown him a newspaper clipping about something

new called the paratroopers, and Sampson decided he wanted to be part of the new unit. At the enlistment station, he ran into one of his former noncoms, an old cavalry veteran of World War I. Sampson, happy to see a familiar face, decided to work the system. The other veteran said he'd see to it that Sampson wound up where he wanted to go.

When Sampson said he wanted to be a paratrooper, the old horse-cavalryman said, "Now there's a suicide unit." But Sampson was determined.

He had to go through basic training again, this time as a thirty-one-year-old man. But the years of physical labor and his experience made it easier than it would have been for most men his age, and he even got a perfect score on the physical test for the paratroopers.

After he pinned on his silver wings, Sampson was assigned to E Company of the newly formed 505th Parachute Infantry Regiment. The company commander was James McGinity, West Point class of 1940, who was four years younger than Sampson. The regimental commander, now Lieutenant Colonel James Gavin, was only four years older than Private Sampson.

In those early days of the unit, there was a great need to get organized, to find men with experience. One technique for identifying leaders was for an officer or noncom to have the new men fall out and ask, "Who has twenty years in the Army?" If a hand went up, the commander would say, "You're the acting First Sergeant." The number moved backward from twenty until all the positions had been filled. The ranks were "acting," meaning that the soldier didn't receive pay commensurate with the responsibility, but the paperwork would eventually catch up. Of course, not all the men identified by this less than scientific approach proved satisfactory, and there was a constant shuffling going on. With his experience, Sampson was soon an acting sergeant, and he found the leadership role fit him.

In the cavalry he had worked hard on his marksmanship, and his rating as a sharpshooter had earned him an extra three dollars a month (experts received an extra five dollars a month, a nearly 20 percent pay increase). Now Sampson was drawn to a weapon that he hadn't worked with before, the 60 mm mortar. This small weapon—consisting of a tube, bipod legs, baseplate, and optical sight—provided indirect fire support at the company level. A commander couldn't always count on getting artillery when he needed it, but the mortars were his own resource.

The range-estimation skills Sampson had learned as a rifle marksman came back to him: he could look across an uneven landscape and rapidly determine how far away a target was. The idea was to get a round out as quickly as possible, then watch where it exploded and adjust fire from there. Speed was essential. Sampson liked the weapon, liked his ability to drop the rounds right where they were needed, liked the fact that he could handle so well one of the most important weapons in the company. He could make a real contribution to E Company's fighting ability, and he won the respect of his soldiers, the other noncoms, and the officers.

Once the unit settled into its routine, the hard training was once again supplemented by a sports program, including volleyball, baseball, wrestling, and boxing. Sampson had not boxed in nearly eight years, but he knew that the men looked up to a noncom who could handle himself in a fistfight. A sergeant had to be ready to back up his authority, sometimes with his fists.

So Sampson went back into training. The years of sawing thirty-inch logs and swinging a heavy ax all day long had added muscle—he was now fighting as a lightweight at 134 pounds—and given him a devastating punch. Early in 1943, he was matched to fight "Sailor" Robinson, also known as "the Pride of the 504th," the 505th's sister unit and rival in all sports contests. Sampson knocked the man out in the second round.

There were so few fighters on the bill in the lightweight class that Sampson's name appeared on the fight card again, just a short time later, with Robinson. Sampson decided he hadn't climbed back into the ring for the sheer joy of getting punched in the head. He had done it to win honors for himself and his regiment, and he had accomplished that; there was no need for a rematch.

When his company commander appealed to him, Sampson said no. Even Gavin, spotting him on a field problem, said, "I sure wish you'd fight that man again."

"I don't see why I have to lick a man twice," Sampson answered, and Gavin let it go. The sergeant told the regimental commander he'd rather spend the training time with his men, as the war was getting closer.

In his entire career as an amateur Army boxer, which spanned nearly twelve years, Sampson had been knocked down only once and had never been defeated. He also had his priorities right, and Gavin knew that better than he did.

Berge Avadanian, the former Howard Johnson's trainer, had signed on with the airborne out of a sense of adventure, and he was a good fit in the regimental intelligence section. Shortly after the 505th joined the Eighty-second Airborne Division and moved to Fort Bragg, Avadanian was injured in a training jump, and the regimental surgeon told him to sit out the next one. Instead of parachuting with the headquarters troops in the next training exercise, Avadanian was issued a large-format camera and sent up in a plane to take photographs of the drop zone from above, to record how the troopers were distributed over the area. In this way, commanders might make adjustments to the aircraft formations to get a tighter drop pattern.

Avadanian enjoyed the mission, because he had a vantage point—high above the jump planes—that he had never enjoyed before. He also got to land in an airplane. Up until then his experience was limited to takeoffs.

After the mission, Avadanian convinced his boss that the Signal Corps photo lab at Fort Bragg was too slow. The resourceful intelligence sergeant knew a place off post, in Fayetteville, that would develop and print the photos quickly. The plan gave the ambitious Avadanian a chance to impress his boss, and get some extra free time in town. Armed with the pass, he put on his dress uniform and headed into Fayetteville, dropping the photos off first. Even if the lab put a rush on things, he had a few hours of precious free time to himself.

When the lab operator developed the prints, he became suspicious. They were obviously photographs of a training exercise, and the young man who had dropped them off was clearly in a hurry. He wondered if he was looking at the work of a spy. The newspapers that year had been filled with stories about the eight German saboteurs who had come ashore in the United States from submarines, with plots to blow up industrial sites. Six of the eight had been executed. The public was constantly being exhorted to keep an eye out for Axis spies, and the people who lived around the big training bases, such as Fort Bragg, were asked to be especially vigilant.

The photo shop owner called the military police.

Avadanian was surprised to find the MPs at the photo lab when he returned. It was a long ride back to the post stockade, where Avadanian waited for his boss to explain things. What had looked like a good deal turned into a lot of trouble for a few hours of freedom.

By the end of 1942, Gavin was beginning to pull together all the elements he would need to make the massed combat drop possible: airborne artillery, engineers, and medical support. A continuing shortage of aircraft made the big drops difficult to stage, so when aircraft were available in small numbers, the regiment sent individual battalions and even companies out on independent missions. The small-unit operations were a critical part of training. In the airborne, more than in conventional units, it was critical that every man understand the scope of the mission, the big picture. A paratrooper might land by himself, cut off from his buddies, his equipment, and his leaders. Paratroopers were expected to figure out where they were and get on with the job. Every soldier had to be able to find the objective so that, even acting in small groups, they could still carry out the mission.

Gavin was building more than a unit. He was creating an entire culture. He wanted his men to believe that they were the toughest characters around. He encouraged them to think of themselves as hell-raisers. A unit that was designed to jump behind enemy lines had to be made up of men who believed in themselves, men who would act when the time came, who wouldn't stand around waiting to be told what to do. He wanted—needed—aggressive soldiers. Once, while the regiment was at Benning, this cultivated aggressiveness led to a riot.

The Cotton Fish Camp was a low-rent bar in Phenix City, Alabama, where soldiers went for cheap drinks and fights. Phenix City had a reputation as a rough town, a poor relation to the city of Columbus that sat hard on the Georgia side of the Chattahoochee River.

One Friday night, a trooper came back from a night of drinking claiming that he had been insulted and mistreated at Cotton Fish. As the story made the rounds through the regiment, it took on different shapes, getting more dramatic with each retelling. By the following night, several dozen men had decided that justice could best be served if they cracked a few heads over on the Alabama side of the river. It was the only way to teach those civilians proper respect for the paratroopers. Berge Avadanian, always up for an adventure, joined the group of angry troopers intent on setting things straight.

As they approached their target, the men spread out in the brush, deploying in a skirmish line. Then the infantrymen began to move forward, just as they had learned on all those field exercises amid the Georgia pines. But word of their plan had reached the Alabama side earlier in the day, and as the cocky GIs closed in on their objective, they ran into a squad of Alabama state troopers.

It was too late to pull back, and the men of the 505th began mixing it up with the billy-club-wielding police. When Avadanian saw the cops hauling down GIs—no doubt intending to lock them up—he jumped over a railing to avoid capture. A state trooper chased him, club raised, and Avadanian said the first thing that came to mind.

"Do you know who I am? I'm the governor's son!"

Avadanian didn't think the ruse, delivered in his Massachusetts accent, fooled the cop, but it did make him hesitate a second or two, long enough for Avadanian to clear the railing and head into the darkness.

Their tactics had failed, but they were learning the importance of secrecy. Obviously, word of their plan had gotten to the Cotton Fish Camp ahead of them. The men headed back to Benning knew the story would travel just as fast back to the Georgia side. Some of them dared hope Gavin would let this one slide.

Gavin was no prude, and while military discipline was important to him, he believed it was important for the men to see him as human. The troopers believed—rightly—that Gavin understood their situation better than most officers, as he had started out as an enlisted man himself. He sometimes showed up at the bars the men frequented, joining them for a drink, even loosening his tie or removing his jacket so that he would be out of uniform (as many of them were). The message was clear: I may be the commander, but I'm a man like you.

Gavin had a track record of sticking up for his men. When a trooper was arrested in Phenix City, charged with public lewdness for having sex with a young woman on the lawn of the courthouse, the post commander demanded to know what Gavin was going to do about this behavior. Gavin said, "Well, in view of the fact that that young man will be asked to give his life for his country in the next few months, I suggest we give him a medal."[5]

But the Cotton Fish Camp was a different matter: there were too many men involved, and even the most tolerant commander couldn't let his men brawl with the police.

The morning after the fight, Gavin found twenty-seven of his troopers in the Fort Benning guardhouse. He pleaded with the provost marshal to turn the men over to him for punishment, promising that he would handle the matter personally. He didn't want the incident reflecting on his regiment, his men, or especially on his new command. Commanders were relieved for less.

The provost was reluctant to agree—there were definite rules governing these things in the Army. But Gavin argued that paratroopers were a special kind of soldier, and so needed special attention. He made the point that paratroopers were always taught to be more aggressive than your average soldier, that they were taught to rely on their imaginations and to support one another. They were not just GIs, but fearsome warriors trained to be dropped behind enemy lines to wreak havoc with the enemy. The provost was persuaded, and he released the men to their commander.

Gavin marched them back to camp and told the entire regiment to get ready for a field problem. It was Saturday, and men who'd been counting on a pass that night and a chance to sleep in on Sunday morning knew the plans had changed.

Gavin, who was in superb physical condition, took the regiment on maneuvers through the tall grasses and marshes bordering the Chattahoochee River. All through the night, he and his officers maneuvered one battalion against the other two. They slogged through the darkness and across wet ground, lugging their full field equipment and heavy weapons. For the machine gunners, this meant weapons and tripods and ammunition. The mortar squads had to carry their tubes, as well as the heavy baseplates for their weapons. It was a group punishment, and a clear message from the regimental commander: what members of the group do affects the entire regiment. It was more than a lesson about living on a stateside post—it was a lesson for combat.

At daylight, Gavin's men were resupplied by parachute drop (another technique the 505th was developing), and they kept up their maneuvers all through the next day, Sunday, their usual day of rest and recovery from the long week. On Sunday evening, Gavin marched them back into camp, keeping up the blistering pace he was known for throughout the regiment.[6]

Gavin was satisfied that he'd made his point about discipline without crushing the unit's spirit. That evening, he saw quite a few troopers, showered and shaved and turned out in pressed uniforms, waiting at the bus stop that would take them into town. At the end of a week of training and a weekend of maneuvers, Berge Avadanian still had the energy to put on a dress uniform and head for his favorite Greek restaurant.

The hell-raising wasn't confined to the enlisted men; Gavin's officers were full of themselves, too. One of their favorite pastimes, after a few hours of drinking, was to start jumping off high platforms, like the balcony over the dance floor of the Officers Club. One evening, when the leaps from the second floor balcony onto the dance floor started to look tame, an enterprising young officer suggested that the window of the second-floor bathroom was about the same size as the jump door on a C-47. The line of men in dress uniforms, mercifully limber due to the alcohol, was soon piling out into the night air, practicing their parachute landing falls on the club lawn.

Such behavior shocked the prim and proper old-Army types, who were used to officers behaving like gentlemen. Gavin, who was old Army himself, was more concerned that all his men truly believed that they were the toughest sons of bitches around. He figured it was his job to strike a balance, to enforce discipline without breaking a man's spirit.

Gavin tempered his decisions with compassion; he always kept the good of the unit foremost in his mind. Ed Sayre learned that beneath the soft voice and concern, the commander had a steel edge.

Gavin had seen an A Company sergeant named Anderson headed into the barracks carrying beer. This was expressly against the rules, and it was especially bad for a noncom, who was supposed to set an example for the men. Gavin explained to Sayre that a commander who establishes rules and then does not enforce them undercuts his own authority. He told Sayre that Anderson had to lose his stripes.

Inspired by the stories of how Gavin stuck up for his troopers, Sayre explained what a good man Anderson was, and how he probably just wanted to escape the post exchange, which was filled with loud, tipsy troopers raising hell. Anderson, Sayre went on, was on the quiet side and probably just needed a little time away from the noise. Finally, the only people he shared his beer with were other noncoms, who drank in the privacy of Anderson's room in a corner of the barracks, away from the younger soldiers.

"He's a good man, sir," Sayre said, proud of the case he'd made. "And I don't think I should bust him."

Gavin looked at Sayre evenly. "Do you think your replacement as A Company commander will have any trouble busting him?" he asked.

Sayre saluted and left the colonel's office. He had spoken on behalf of his man, and Gavin had made things perfectly clear. Sayre told himself that he could help Anderson get his stripes back if he stayed in command of A Company. The former sergeant soldiered on and, after two months of hard work, Sayre put him up for promotion. When the papers came across Gavin's desk for signature, the regimental commander did not hesitate to sign them.

Even as Gavin built the unit and the culture, he worked to keep the pipeline full of good men. The airborne commanders were already using every incentive they could think of, from jump boots to silver wings to patches on the overseas cap to the fifty-dollar-a-month bonus. It was a sales job, and Gavin got some unexpected help when a man by the name of Barney Oldfield showed up with orders for the 505th.

Oldfield, a former newspaperman and Hollywood press agent, reported to Gavin in the summer of 1942.

"What the hell am I going to do with a newspaperman?" Gavin wanted to know.

Oldfield, who was anything but shy, said, "You're going to need good publicity, sir. One day you'll come home in victory and you'll need a press agent."

In spite of his suspicions, Gavin put Oldfield in the intelligence section of regimental headquarters. Oldfield immediately went to work getting the story of the airborne, and of the 505th in particular, out to the public. Oldfield made sure that the press was invited to anything dramatic, especially the photogenic daytime jumps.

Since so many of the stories in the national press concentrated on jumping, more than one recruit arrived in the 505th with the mistaken notion that paratroopers flew everywhere, and that they didn't do as much walking as the regular infantry. They were soon disabused of this notion and learned that Gavin made sure his troopers could outmarch any other unit in the Army.

Besides legitimate newspaper stories, Oldfield was behind some public relations efforts that were only slightly removed from gimmicks. When a sister unit adopted a Hollywood starlet as a "Regimental Sweetheart," Oldfield decided that the 505th needed one, too. When the actress Frances Farmer walked into a Hollywood police station dressed in nothing but a fur coat—which she removed—the 505th promptly adopted her. She had, the troopers agreed, just the right attitude for the airborne.

Early in 1943, Army commanders were being encouraged to support the sale of war bonds among the troops. It quickly became a com-

petition, and the post commander at Fort Benning told Gavin he expected the 505th to do its part. Gavin sent Oldfield to a staff meeting
at headquarters, where the former newspaperman learned of the post
commander's plan for an Easter morning breakfast, when soldiers
would be encouraged to buy war bonds. Oldfield didn't think breakfast
with a bunch of officers and their matronly wives would have the right
amount of appeal to separate young men from their hard-earned
money.

During his time as a Hollywood press agent, Oldfield had gotten
to know many stars and entertainers. He counted among his friends
Gypsy Rose Lee, a nationally known burlesque dancer who was appearing in a New York show called *Star and Garter*. Oldfield said he'd
ask Lee to come to Fort Benning after her Saturday performance. He
suggested they move the breakfast to the post gym to accommodate
the crowd they were sure to draw. Before Lee appeared on stage, she
would take off her clothes, and someone—presumably Oldfield—
would cover her from top to bottom with war bonds, the highest priced
bonds being placed in strategic locations on her body. Soldiers would
then be allowed to buy bonds, which would be removed as they sold.
In 1943, a quarter century before the sexual revolution, this was pretty
racy stuff. Suddenly everyone at the meeting was awake and enthusiastic, eager to do their patriotic duty by selling bonds.

Oldfield called Lee, who accepted the invitation. Soon the word
was around the post, and as the day approached, soldiers were making
plans to get up early for a seat in the post gym.

About a week before the event, the post commander got wind that
his plan for a dignified breakfast had been scrapped. Apparently, he
didn't think it appropriate that a striptease artist would be entertaining
the troops on Easter morning. A disappointed Oldfield had to call Lee
and tell her that the mission was off.

THE ALL-AMERICANS

While Gavin and his commanders worked hard to get the 505th to fighting trim, the United States prepared for its first land battle against the Germans in the November 1942 invasion of North Africa. The campaign was cobbled together, a compromise among competing views. FDR needed to get America into the war. General George Marshall firmly believed that the only way to defeat Hitler was to attack Germany across northwest Europe, the sooner the better. Churchill, keen to preserve his forces, insisted on fighting at the periphery.

Marshall was dispirited, as he believed the invasion of North Africa would only delay the important invasion of northern Europe (which proved to be true). Later, he came to appreciate the position Roosevelt was in as the leader of a democracy: he had to signal to the American electorate that America was in the war. In short, Roosevelt had to lead.

Eisenhower, who commanded the invasion, code-named Torch, thought the plan strategically unsound, as it diverted resources from the invasion of mainland Europe, which was the only offensive that could actually topple Hitler. Roosevelt's subordinates were upset, but, like good soldiers, they offered their advice, then confined further concerns to their diaries.

The plan behind Torch was simple enough. The Americans would land in western North Africa and push eastward, while the British forces pushed west from Egypt. If the design was simple, the preparations were not. The convoy system in the Atlantic had to be retooled to get troops from the mainland United States to Algeria. Soldiers preparing to fight in northern Europe had to be retrained and equipped for desert warfare. The forces already built up in England, as well as thousands of tons of supplies—everything from gasoline cans to artillery shells to toilet paper and bandages—had to be moved again to the ports, reloaded on ships, and sent south.

Though the British and Americans were separated by nearly twenty-five hundred miles of desert, the landings did put the Germans between two large Allied forces. Erwin Rommel, known even in the Allied world as "the Desert Fox" for his aggressive tactics and battlefield success, was forced to withdraw before the powerful British offensive that began on November 2, 1942. After U.S. landings in Morocco and Algeria on November 8, Rommel positioned his forces in the mountains of Tunisia and waited for the inevitable American move east. Facing Rommel was Dwight Eisenhower, an untested commander who had never heard a shot fired in anger.

The Americans quickly learned that their tanks, much more lightly armored than their German counterparts, could not stand up in a shoot-out. The German panzer troops, veterans of nearly three years of armored warfare, were experts at using every advantage offered by the terrain. At Kasserine Pass in February 1943, GIs were routed by determined German attacks. Eisenhower relieved the corps commander, and turned to a fiery old horse-cavalryman turned tanker named George Patton.

After some initial successes, Rommel's Afrika Korps was rocked by coordinated Allied offensives. Resupply over the vast distances involved became almost impossible, especially as Allied air and sea power came to bear on the Mediterranean theater. On March 9, Hitler pulled Rommel, one of Germany's most beloved fighting generals, out of the theater. Most of the Afrika Korps—with its thousands of veterans and hundreds of vehicles and tons of weapons—was abandoned to capture by the Allies.

When Roosevelt met Churchill in Casablanca in January 1943 to discuss the war, the British were still intent on delaying the cross-channel invasion from England. They arrived in Casablanca with a huge staff of military and naval advisers, supported by sophisticated communications. The American delegation, by contrast, was underserved and understaffed. Worse, American air chiefs were beginning to make noises that an air campaign alone would be enough to defeat Germany. The British suffered from no such divisions in their ranks. They knew what they wanted; they presented a unified front and argued their points. The conference turned into a meeting chaired by a superbly prepared British staff who showed up with a clear vision. The Americans were no match for them. "We lost our shirts," one senior U.S. Army planner admitted.[1]

At Casablanca, the Americans reluctantly committed to more fighting in the Mediterranean, beginning with an invasion of Sicily.

Allied planning for Operation Husky, the code name given to the invasion of Sicily, was troubled from the start.[2] The British, who had years of experience fighting the Germans, felt they should have the leading roles, and that the American forces, which had not acquitted themselves well in North Africa, should provide support.

The Dwight Eisenhower who commanded the Allied forces in 1943 was not the same Eisenhower the world would see less than a year later, in firm command of Operation Overlord and the invasion of Normandy. When Hitler invaded Poland in 1939, Eisenhower was a lieutenant colonel who had spent years as a staff officer, little time with troops, and no time in combat. Now he was in command of men who had long outranked him, who had more experience, who had seen combat. And he was being asked to put together and fight with a coalition force, which meant he had to function as a soldier in a politically charged relationship.

As winter gave way to spring in North Africa, the British and American staffs, unused to working together and not at all comfortable with each other, dickered back and forth as the weeks ticked by. Eisenhower's orders were to invade Sicily by July, yet as late as April commanders on both sides were still wondering whether the invasion was even a good idea. The problem, as with nearly all amphibious operations launched by the Allies in World War II, was not lack of manpower, but lack of shipping to move the manpower. The invading force had to hit the assault beaches with enough mass to gain a foothold, and to do that a large body of troops had to land all at once. A million men in North Africa could not take the island of Sicily if they had to be ferried across the sea a few thousand at a time.

In May, at a high-level planning session in Algiers, British Field Marshal Montgomery presented his plan for Sicily: the British would strike the southeast corner of the island, with Siracusa as their main objective. The Americans, two divisions strong, would land near Gela and Scoglitti to capture key southern airfields (denying them to the Germans and making them available for the Allies) and protecting the flank of the British Eighth Army.

George Patton, the imaginative and aggressive corps commander who was quickly becoming Ike's key battle captain, would command the U.S. invasion forces, consisting of the First and Forty-fifth Infantry Divisions. In order to seize the inland airfields for use by Allied aircraft, and to block German counterattacks during those first critical hours, Patton turned to the newest weapon in the Allied arsenal: the airborne. The paratroopers would get a chance to show what they could do.

*   *   *

After a stint at Camp Gordon, Georgia, training draftees for duty in the Pacific, Jack Norton was promoted to captain and became a company commander in the Fourth Infantry Division. In late 1942, Norton's orders for airborne school came through, and he reported to Fort Benning in January 1943.

Norton wrote to his father about his decision to volunteer for the paratroops. Augustus Norton had seen a good bit of combat as an artilleryman in France during World War I, and he did not try to hide his disappointment with his son's choice. The paratroops, the senior Norton said, were little more than "suicide troops." Dropped behind enemy lines, with no heavy weapons, they were destined to be cut off and annihilated, if they weren't killed off by antiaircraft fire and alert sentries before they could even hit the ground.

Jack Norton saw things differently. He looked around and saw men who had volunteered for hazardous duty with an untested arm of the service. They withstood the most punishing training the Army could dish out, and along the way they developed a valuable esprit. In Gavin and some of the other leaders, Norton saw men who were not only bold and original thinkers, but who were willing to lead from the front. Since paratroopers were to be dropped behind enemy lines, any man—colonel or private—could wind up fighting as a rifleman. There was no such thing as a "rear echelon" in the airborne.

"The leaders aren't just talking about it, Dad," Norton wrote. "They're the first ones out the aircraft door."

On February 12, 1943, Gavin's 505th Parachute Infantry Regiment moved to Fort Bragg, North Carolina, and became one of two parachute regiments in the Eighty-second Airborne Division. (The division also had two regiments of infantry that would arrive on the battlefield in towed gliders. The division, which had fought in World War I as the Eighty-second Infantry Division, was nicknamed "the All-Americans," as its soldiers came from all over the country. To the square red, white, and blue shoulder patch, showing a double A, the paratroopers added an arched tab with the legend AIRBORNE.)

In a welcome speech to the newly arrived troopers, division commander Matt Ridgway addressed the troops—correctly—as the "men of the 82nd Airborne Division." Some of the 505th soldiers, used to their autonomy and fiercely proud of their unit, began to call out to their new commander, "No, no. Five-oh-five, five-oh-five!"

Like all good commanders, Ridgway understood the psychology of the men he commanded. He didn't want to take anything away from them; he wanted to give them something. And that something was an additional identity: the 505th Parachute Infantry Regiment was now part of the Eighty-second Airborne Division.

"When we win this war—and we will win," Ridgway continued, "and you come home and people say 'Who'd you serve with?' you'll be able to say, 'I was with the Eighty-second Airborne Division,' and that will be a proud moment."[3]

Gavin delivered a well-trained and motivated regiment to the All-American division. The 505th was selected to provide an honor guard when a gaggle of VIPs came to Fort Bragg to see what the paratroopers were up to. George Marshall and Hap Arnold, the chief of staff of the Army Air Corps, were the ranking Americans. British Foreign Secretary Anthony Eden also attended. After Eden had inspected the troops, he took Gavin's hand, looked directly into his eyes, and simply said, "Good luck."[4]

Eden's directness and the slight touch of emotion in his voice scared Gavin a bit. The foreign secretary knew that the paratroopers, green as they were, would invade Sicily before the summer was over. Gavin didn't know it yet, so Eden said all he could in his heartfelt wish.

Shortly after that visit, Gavin's regiment was chosen to make the first-ever regimental-sized jump. One hundred and thirty C-47s dropped the troopers on three separate drop zones near Camden, South Carolina. Although the exercise was a success and showed that Gavin's and Ridgway's ideas could work—at least in daytime and without enemy fire—there was a frightening note. One C-47 lost power and then altitude, plowing through the tight formations of paratroopers. Three men died horribly in the spinning propeller blades, a grim reminder to all the troopers of the hazards they faced.[5]

Another problem faced by the entire division was the constant reshuffling of cadre as leaders were taken to staff new airborne formations. Later, Ridgway would say that no unit "had been torn up and put back together so frequently."[6] This turmoil, which kept some units from developing bonds with their leaders, led to problems, even in Gavin's 505th.

G Company, in particular, had been plagued by AWOLs since arriving at Bragg. One morning report in early 1943 showed an astounding thirty-two soldiers missing, more than 25 percent of the company. The commander was relieved and replaced by First Lieutenant Francis Joseph Myers Jr., known as "Joe." Myers, a West Point classmate of Jack Norton's, saw his first task as instilling discipline, and he decided the situation called for draconian methods.

As the AWOL soldiers returned, Myers turned them out of the barracks and had them set up their pup tents in an open area along the company street. Each man was allowed only a single GI blanket, though the nights were still cool.

Up to this point, Myers wasn't inventing anything new. Mark Alexander, executive officer of the Second Battalion, had done something similar at Fort Benning when he was sent down to F Company to get a handle on the AWOL situation there. Alexander had contacted the sheriffs and chiefs of police in the hometowns of his AWOL soldiers and got them all picked up and sent back. When they arrived, they found that they'd been moved out of the company barracks and would now be living in a makeshift stockade in the company street, a barbed wire enclosure with straw for the men to sleep on.

Alexander then played his trump card: he told the men that if they went AWOL again, he'd have them shipped out of the paratroopers. He also put a guard on this stockade. Though the guard carried a weapon, he had no ammunition. It wasn't the threat of an unarmed guard that kept them in place, but the thought of being stripped of their prized jump wings and the extra fifty dollars a month. Alexander and F Company had no more problems with AWOL soldiers.

At Bragg, Myers's approach wasn't so sophisticated. He told the men that they were not to leave the pup tents during the night. He posted an armed guard over the tents and told the guard that he was to shoot any man who left his pup tent. This guard had ammunition.

To two men who shared a tent and the same last name, Dalton L. Morris and Jack A. Morris (who were not related), Myers's orders must have seemed, if not a joke, certainly not something to be taken seriously. It was almost laughable that the lieutenant would even give such an order, which was not legal and was, in all likelihood, unenforceable. After all, what paratrooper—guard or not—would shoot his comrades for climbing out of a pup tent at night, in the safe confines of Fort Bragg?

So it must have seemed to the two soldiers. Even if they had given up some of their rights in order to become soldiers, it wasn't as if they were prisoners of war. They were just out for some good times over the fence, a little of the fun-loving behavior the paratroopers were known for. Besides, whether they admitted it or not, the officers thought it showed a good spirit that the men got into fights and pushed the rules. Of course, the troopers had to take their punishment—the story of the Cotton Fish Camp and the brawls with Patton's tankers at Fort Benning had already become legendary. But it was all part of the rough-cut image of the paratrooper.

The soldier on guard, a private named Charles Hall, wasn't thinking along the same lines when the two AWOLs came out of their tent. He shot them both dead, right in the middle of the company area.[7]

Bill Blank was asleep in his bunk in the barracks closest to the tents when he was awakened by the shots. He jumped to his feet and joined the stampede of soldiers headed outside. There, he was surprised to see Hall standing over the bodies, his rifle in his hands. The stunned men were quickly herded back inside the barracks. Minutes later, Hall, who shared the other half of a two-tier bunk with Blank, came in and began packing his gear. He was being moved to another unit, he said.

Blank was surprised to see that the shooting didn't seem to affect Hall all that much. The other troopers were in a mild state of shock, although no one made a move to do anything to Hall. Hall's only comment, as he packed his gear, was, "I had to back up to shoot one of 'em." Blank took that to mean that the men had been approaching him, or that he shot one and the other rushed him in a defensive move, and Hall had to step back in order to bring his long rifle to bear. Hall did not say why he didn't shoot to wound the men, and Blank didn't think to ask.

Wheatley Christensen, another G Company soldier, was awakened by the ruckus that followed the shooting. Men hurried in and out of the barracks, amazed at what they saw outside. By the time Hall's name got around, the soldier was already packed and gone. The troopers turned their anger toward Lieutenant Myers.

Although it was wartime, they were not in a combat zone. The bond among paratroopers, especially those in the same company, was strong: they were supposed to look out for one another, the noncoms constantly told them. Even the newest recruit could see that those bonds would sustain them in the combat ahead. Myers had not only violated that pact; he had shown something else, something dangerous. The whole incident seemed to point out that Myers didn't value his soldiers' lives.

Morale in G Company plummeted after the shooting, and the men felt betrayed. If their lives were that cheap at Fort Bragg, what did that say about how this particular set of leaders would take care of them in combat? Their company commander was supposed to shield them—not be part of the problem.

Major Mark Alexander, the executive officer of Second Battalion, heard about the shooting when he returned from the rifle range. He was shocked that Myers had given such an order, and surprised that the soldier on guard had actually gone through with it. Alexander was not surprised that it had happened in Major Ed Krause's battalion.

Krause, a former highway patrolman, was what his junior officers called a "shitstorm artist." Wherever he was, there was liable to be a disturbance. Krause was blustery and loud, given to public histrionics: yelling and cursing at the men, sometimes even at officers and non-coms in front of their subordinates. Where Gavin believed in toughening his soldiers through hard training, Krause seemed to think he could accomplish the same thing through capriciousness. The way Alexander looked at it, Krause's leadership was at least in part responsible for the low state of morale that led to so many AWOLs in G Company in the first place.

At the next meeting of the Second Battalion officers, Alexander and the others were told by their commander, James Gray, that they were not to make a lot of noise about the shooting, that it would be investigated by the proper authorities. Alexander took this to mean that the regiment was going to continue its mission: with deployment surely coming soon, with combat imminent, the emphasis was on getting the men ready. There would be no distractions. There was too much to do, too much for the soldiers to learn. It was best to close ranks and continue with that mission.[8]

* * *

A little more than three years earlier, Alexander had been a graduate student at the University of Kansas, working on a master's degree in education with the intention of becoming a professor. While there, he befriended another young man whose father happened to be the head of the Army's Reserve Officers Training Corps, or ROTC, detachment. Alexander was invited to the family's home for dinner one evening, where the colonel persuaded the young visitor that the war, which had already engulfed Europe and much of Asia, would eventually pull the United States in. He also convinced Alexander that he would be better off having a commission as an officer than getting drafted.

"How do I do that?" Alexander asked.

"Enlist in a local National Guard unit. Then I'll give you the manuals to study, and you'll take the test."

Alexander listened to the old soldier and enlisted as a private in the 137th Infantry of the Kansas National Guard, on October 26, 1940. His sponsor was as good as his word, providing the young Kansan with the manuals and regulations he needed to pass the written test for a National Guard commission. When the Thirty-fifth Division was called to federal service, the unit expanded rapidly, and Alexander was promoted to second lieutenant.

Soon after mobilization, a colonel from the regular Army (a lifelong professional soldier, as opposed to the volunteers, usually designated as Army reserve officers, now swelling the ranks) was assigned to the Thirty-fifth Division to help buck up its training. The colonel watched Second Lieutenant Alexander lead a physical training formation one day and had the young officer called up to the office of the G1, or division personnel officer. Alexander thought that perhaps he had done something wrong, but the G1 told him that the colonel had recommended him for promotion to first lieutenant. Here the rapid growth of the Army gearing up for war ran smack into the old ways of doing things in the guard, where promotions were a matter of longevity and nepotism.

Alexander was promoted ahead of another lieutenant who happened to be the company commander's brother. The jealous brothers, one of whom outranked Alexander, saw to it that Alexander got the worst details and duties they could give a junior officer, such as overseeing the KPs or the soldiers detailed for extra training. The jobs weren't onerous, but they weren't preparing him for the kind of close combat he expected to see as an infantry officer. He had an additional concern: training in the division was poor, and Alexander began worrying that he might go into combat with a unit that was far from ready to meet an enemy that had already overrun much of Europe. He figured his chances of survival were better with an elite outfit. It meant harder training, but also a higher degree of competence. When the chance came to volunteer for airborne training, he took it.

After completing airborne school, Jack Norton arrived at Fort Bragg in early March, 1943, and was sent to the 504th Parachute Infantry Regiment. Less than a week later he was shuffled to the 505th regimental area, where Major Al Ireland, the S1 (personnel officer), told him to report to Third Battalion. The battalion commander, Major Ed Krause, was waiting for a new commander for H Company. Norton's fortunes seemed to have turned. He was finally where he wanted to be: in an airborne unit, as a commanding officer, with at least some time to get ready for combat. More than that, he had wound up in Jim Gavin's unit.

Except that Gavin wasn't Norton's immediate boss; Ed Krause was.

Instead of spending his time working with his new company, Nor-

ton spent much of his day running back and forth to battalion headquarters for meetings with Krause. There was not even enough time
between the meetings to brief the first sergeant on the last "To Do" list
before Krause was handing out more instructions. And much of what
Krause wanted the battalion to work on had little to do with combat
training and more to do with inspections and parades and spotless barracks. Norton knew that those aspects of military discipline were important, but they were all secondary to the business of soldiering that
the men—most of whom had been civilians just a year or two earlier—
had to learn before they faced the enemy.

Men who had expected to risk their lives jumping out of airplanes
and training with live ammunition felt instead that they were in danger of being inspected to death by their own commander. Every day
seemed to bring an astonishing new example of poor leadership. Near
the end of one road march at Fort Bragg, the order came down to pull
the companies into tight formations, solid phalanxes of men moving
along as if on parade. (The troops usually moved along the road in parallel files, with wide spacing to protect them from air attack.) Norton
stood at the head of H Company and watched in amazement as
Krause began yelling at the G Company commander, the luckless Joe
Myers. The assembled company of soldiers looked on, some of them
embarrassed, some of them mesmerized. Then, incredibly, Krause
kicked Myers in the rear, hard enough to knock him down.

Suddenly Krause was moving in his direction. Norton got ready for
him. When the major pulled his leg back and swung it at the much
taller captain, Norton reached down and—without a word—grabbed
Krause's foot, yanked it upward, and sent the old man sprawling. Not
only did Krause walk away without another word, he left Norton alone
after that.

The incident caused another round of griping among the junior officers. They were under the control of a petty tyrant, but they consoled

themselves with the knowledge that Krause, trying to gain stature by belittling his officers in front of the troops, usually succeeded in making himself look ridiculous in their eyes.

The Third Battalion men seemed to have an inexhaustible supply of Krause stories. Lieutenant Bob Fielder, the Third Battalion communications officer, talked about a battalion formation in which Krause was standing out front when a soldier in the rear rank let out a low, singsong whistle. Predictably, Krause went running around the back of the formation, yelling, "Who did that?" The reaction inspired another soldier, this one in the front rank, to whistle, which brought the commander scurrying back around front. The soldiers enjoyed the short-lived spectacle of their commander racing in agitation, like a Charlie Chaplin character. Krause quickly figured out he was never going to find out who had disrupted his formation, and he stopped. Wisely, the troops didn't push the game to extremes.[9]

What the officers couldn't figure out was why Gavin put up with Krause. The Third Battalion commander seemed the antithesis of everything Gavin represented. Where Krause yelled and swore at his men on a daily basis, Gavin was so soft-spoken that his subordinates used to joke that he did it on purpose so they'd all have to shut up to hear him. Krause was theatrical; Gavin could often be seen walking in the regimental area, head down, hands folded behind his back as he puzzled through some problem. Gavin had a quick mind; Krause had a quick temper.

Finding the right leaders was just one among many problems Gavin faced as he pieced his regiment together from scratch. The Army was going through a tremendous expansion; experienced leaders were in short supply. Add to that the fact that the airborne required more of its leaders—namely the arduous jump school itself—and the pool of talent was limited.

As they lingered over coffee after evening chow, looking over their shoulders to see who might be listening, the junior officers could only speculate as to what Gavin was thinking. Gavin's fans, Jack Norton among them, did not want to believe the old man was unaware of what was going on. It had to be a conscious choice to stick with Krause, either because there was no one else available, or because the frequent drafts—especially of noncoms—to fill other units was already causing too much turmoil in the command.

There was another possibility, too. There were no combat veterans among the leadership of the 505th, so no one could say for sure exactly how a man would perform. Perhaps Gavin believed that Krause would be an asset in battle.

Of course, the junior officers could only speculate about the difficulties caused by relieving a senior officer, especially on the eve of battle. Gavin had to consider what was fair to Krause, who would have been disgraced if Gavin had sent him packing. Many men never recovered from that kind of blow. Gavin also knew that too many changes, especially if the men saw the changes as capricious, could ruin unit morale. Of course, his ultimate responsibility was to ensure that his soldiers had the best leadership possible when they went into combat.

Whatever his reasons, Gavin suffered through with Ed Krause, who did not inspire confidence among his men. Gavin relieved other officers who disappointed him too many times. Krause survived.

The tough training schedule did not leave the men a great deal of free time, but they could earn weekend passes. Many married men brought their wives to Fayetteville to have them close. Housing around Fort Bragg was already tight, with young wives living in rented rooms, some little better than chicken coops. Many of the junior officers had stashed their wives at a hotel just off base called Southern Pines.

In April 1943, the division was put on notice that it would be moving to a point of embarkation for overseas movement. Although this did not come as a surprise to the men, the way it was handled was shocking to a unit that prided itself on taking care of soldiers. The men were told that they had only twenty-four hours until they would be restricted to the unit area. This left little time for those who were married to say good-bye, much less to make travel arrangements for wives and families who now had to make their way home.

When Arthur and Corinne Gorham heard that the men were about to be confined to post, they decided they would do what they could to make things better. The Gorhams opened their quarters to the young wives who lived off post, so they could still see their husbands when the men came in from the field. They set up cots throughout the house, and couples took turns sharing the otherwise empty bedrooms, which afforded a little bit of privacy.

Some of the junior officers, who saw Gorham as somewhat aloof, thought that this must have been Corinne's idea, but Corinne was just going along with her husband's suggestion. She knew this side of him. These young men were about to be taken away from their wives, perhaps for years, perhaps forever. Arthur thought the intrusion a small inconvenience for what the couples were getting in return. If her husband wanted to let the men think it was her idea, that was his business.

The majority of married men were not as lucky as the few from the First Battalion who moved their wives into the Gorhams' quarters. All over Fayetteville, the news of the restriction set off frantic planning and anguished good-byes. Although the men did not know exactly where they were headed or when they would leave, they knew they were going into the war zone. Even the most optimistic realized that some of them would not come back.[10]

Harold Eatman, who lived outside Charlotte, North Carolina, was able to make it across the Tarheel State by bus on some of the weekend passes. At twenty-seven, Eatman was considerably older than the other PFCs in the outfit, and he had a wife and baby daughter in the western end of the state. Eatman had already served one enlistment in the Army.

In 1936, after a year of riding the rails with other men displaced by the Depression, he and his partner were on a train headed into Virginia when his friend said, "Let's join the Army when we get to Richmond."

Eatman, who was tired of being hungry and homeless, agreed. The two men celebrated their decision by splurging on a meal at a roadside rest stop, where the blue-plate special cost them twenty-five cents each. They showed up at the recruiting office in Richmond with fifty cents left between them.

Eatman was sent to Schofield Barracks, Hawaii, where he served in the Thirty-fifth Infantry Regiment. Things moved at an almost leisurely pace during those last years of peace: there were sunset retreats for visiting movie stars, with the officers in their polished boots and Sam Browne belts, complete with swords. Officers spent the afternoons riding (West Point required cadets to take six hours per week of horsemanship until 1940). The bored troops were left to the noncoms, though there was little money for training maneuvers. Eatman left the service after his first hitch.

When the war came in 1941, Eatman was twenty-six, married, with a child, an honorable discharge and a defense-related job: five things that would have kept him out of the draft. His prior service certainly would have allowed him to hold his head up. He had done his part for this country, and he could have rightly claimed that he was too old, just by a few years, for the young man's game of being an infantryman. But Harold Eatman didn't feel right about staying home in North Carolina while other men fought. He didn't even have to bring it up with his wife, Billie. She told him, "I know how you feel," and that was the end of the discussion.

Eatman volunteered for the airborne, because he didn't want anyone to be able to say that they were in a tougher unit than he'd been in. The extra fifty dollars a month would be useful to a family man. He noticed that all of the soldiers in his jump school class who had prior service—and thus could be expected to adapt more quickly to Army life—had been sent to the Eight-second Airborne Division. He took that as a sign that the unit would be one of the first to ship out.

In April 1943, he'd been with the unit just about a month when he returned to Charlotte, where Billie was hospitalized with an infection. By late Sunday afternoon, Eatman was looking at the clock and worrying that he might miss the bus that would get him back to Fort Bragg before his pass expired. With tightened travel restrictions, there was always a chance that the bus would be full.

Fortunately, Billie's family was with her, though it was still difficult to tear himself away. Her physician made it harder. As the time came for Eatman to leave, the doctor pulled the paratrooper aside in the hallway and told him they were fortunate they already had a daughter, as it looked as if the infection would preclude Billie from having any more children. The news was a shock, and it was going to be hard on Billie, but the thought of going AWOL did not cross his mind. He said his good-byes, kissed his wife, and left.

The woman in the bed next to Billie's, who had overheard the family conversation, cried most of the night for the young couple.

In the morning, Eatman was at chow with his H Company squad when the battalion commander, Major Krause, came into the mess and jumped up on a table.

"We're locked down," Krause told the men. "From this point on there will be no leaving the post, no telephone calls to your families. For those of you who have families in the area, the Red Cross will help them move back home."

Krause went on to detail the precautions the division would take to mask its movement. Not only were the soldiers not allowed to tell anyone what was happening, but they had to remove their shoulder patches and the airborne patches from their hats, take off their jump wings, and unblouse their trousers to hide their jump boots.

Eatman was consumed with worry about Billie, who was not only in the hospital but would surely be concerned when she didn't hear from her husband. Later in the day, he went to the chaplain and recounted his wife's situation: her illness, the news about her condition, and the fact that he had left her without saying good-bye. The chaplain told Eatman that there was nothing he could do. Eatman consoled himself knowing that Billie would read the newspapers and figure out what had happened to the unit. He went back to his duties.

On April 20, 1943, the 505th boarded trains at Fort Bragg and rode through the spring countryside to Camp Edwards, Massachusetts. The men were told that every effort was being made to keep their movement secret. Although the troopers griped about the fact that they looked like straight-leg soldiers again, it made sense that they didn't want the deadly German U-boats to know anything about their departure for overseas.

For Berge Avadanian, the arrival at Camp Edwards, Massachusetts, was bittersweet. He was not far from his home, and he knew his mother was suffering from cancer and probably would not recover before he ever saw her again. But no one was allowed a pass, so Avadanian got no closer than the fence around Camp Edwards. Outside the fence, American military police patrolled to make sure none of the paratroopers tried to get out for one last stateside fling.

The Eighty-second left Camp Edwards a week later, on April 28, and began embarking on the SS *Monterrey* late that same day. The troops on board had been issued cold-weather equipment—overshoes, long underwear, and woolen overcoats—to fool any Axis spies working in the port of New York.

Captain Jack Norton was made the berthing officer. It was his job to divide the available space among the units within the regiment. Space was so tight on the ship that no one was going to be satisfied, and Norton had no friends in the regiment by the time he finished his task and listened to the complaints.

It had been two years since Augustus Norton had missed his son's graduation from West Point because of his duties in the port of New York, and his responsibilities had only grown since 1941. The piers were lined with shipping, and the harbor was packed with more ships at anchor, waiting to be loaded or waiting for their convoys to form. Huge stocks of supplies were delivered every day by railroads that stretched into the heart of what FDR had termed "the arsenal of democracy." All the ten thousand accoutrements of a modern army—everything from tents, bandages, and bullets to locomotives and air-plane parts—passed through this portal. There were thousands of men to be housed and fed and put on board the right ships at the right time and in the right sequence. Augustus Norton was in the middle of this whirlwind.

Perhaps it was this status that made Jim Gavin agree to a request from Augustus Norton just before the *Monterrey* was to sail. It may have been a personal fondness for Jack Norton, who had quite literally followed Gavin from West Point's parade ground to this troopship; or perhaps it was Gavin's own feelings as a father. But when the elder Norton approached Jim Gavin with a special request that was com-pletely outside the rules, Gavin said yes.

Once the *Monterrey* was loaded and had moved to its anchorage, Captain Norton was told to report on deck, where he watched as a tug pulled alongside the big steel sides of the *Monterrey*. Norton was going to spend the night ashore. The little boat took him to the Brooklyn waterfront, where his father waited for him. The two soldiers rode to the family home near the Brooklyn Navy Yard, where they had a late dinner.

It was a tough night for the old man. Augustus Norton, the artilleryman who had been shelled repeatedly on the battlefields of the last great European war, knew better than anyone else in the house what dangers lay ahead for his son. The strapping young paratrooper in front of him was determined and hardworking, but like the other men spending their first night crammed on the *Monterrey* as she swung at anchor nearby, Jack Norton was mostly unaware of the horrors he would soon see. But his father knew, and he also knew that his son was trying to live up to an example he'd set for the young man.

Years earlier, Augustus Norton had written his son from France, when Jack was a baby and Augustus was unsure of whether or not he would survive to see the boy grow to manhood. The letter talked about Jack's duty to his family, to his mother, to his name. Although it was addressed to a child, it was intended to be a life guide. Jack had kept the letter, and he wanted his father to be proud of him.

Augustus told Jack he had a gift for him, and produced a holstered pistol.

"I carried this pistol all through the Great War," he said, showing his son the M1911 issue pistol, commonly known as a "forty-five" for its .45-caliber barrel. The father had recently had the gun refurbished, and it gleamed steel blue in the light. The holster, the traditional leather model with the "U.S." on the flap, had also been worked over with saddle soap. It was worn, but solid. For all the concerns swirling in his head—not the least of which was the urgency of getting back to the ship—the moment was not lost on Jack Norton. In another age, his father might have passed him a sword; the symbolism was the same.

Long before dawn, Jack Norton stirred himself from the couch, put on his uniform and buckled on his new pistol. He hugged his mother and father and went out into the darkness to meet another tug waiting to take him back to the *Monterrey*, to his comrades, to the waiting war.

Norton's parents watched the lean young man they had raised disappear into the predawn darkness. Like other parents all over the country, the parting was difficult and tearful, but the worst was not knowing if this would be the last sight of their son they would have in this world.

When the *Monterrey* passed the Statue of Liberty on the way out of New York Harbor, some of the troopers gathered on deck, where they sang a doctored version of the World War I patriotic tune "Over There." The song was about spirited American soldiers going abroad to fix things up in old Europe. The original version ended with the words, *And we won't be back 'til it's over, over there.*

But the young men gathered on the deck of the *Monterrey*, watching the great city disappear off the stern, belonged to a new generation. Many of them had volunteered for the Army and all of them had volunteered for the airborne. They would do their duty, but they also knew that many of their fathers' generation had died horribly in the trenches on the western front, had wasted away from sickness, had been shelled and shattered. And while they were hardly experienced soldiers, they did not hold the same illusions as did the men who had sailed from the same harbor in 1917. Avadanian and his friends ended their song abruptly. "And we won't be back . . ."

They let the last line hang in the air, graveyard humor, and in it, some sort of defense mechanism. Perhaps they felt smarter for acknowledging it. Even so, there were few men along the rails who were prepared for death. But that would change in time.

TWO STEPS BACK

The crossing took twelve days. The troops amused themselves by organizing boxing and wrestling matches and even staging a few variety
shows on deck. The ship's library had a supply of the new "pocket"
books with paper covers, designed so they could be printed cheaply,
packed easily, and left behind for the next GI. Many of the men had
never seen the ocean before, and spent hours at the rail, staring at the
other ships in the convoy. One of the more enjoyable—if frustrating—
rumors passed around was about a contingent of Army nurses on
board another ship in the convoy; some men strained their eyes for a
glimpse of a feminine form—an arm, a leg, long hair, anything that
might remind them of gentler times.

Once the ships were at sea, the regimental intelligence section
put out an issue of the unofficial "newspaper," *The Static Line*. The
mimeographed sheet announced that the convoy was bound for
North Africa, ending speculation among the troops. Of course they all
knew they were headed for the war zone, but it had been a kind of
abstraction. Now they knew where they were going, and seeing in it
print proved troubling for some. The regiment's two chaplains,
Captain Matthew Connelly, a Catholic priest, and Captain George B.
Wood, a Protestant minister, began seeing more men who wanted to

clear up some trouble, rekindle a forgotten spiritual life, or simply talk.

The *Monterrey* made landfall in Africa on May 10, 1943. The storied dark continent first appeared as a brown shoreline, and eventually the men could make out white buildings. Soon the loudspeakers crackled with Navy commands preparing the ship for docking in Casablanca, and the GIs joked about finding the fictional bar from the Humphrey Bogart–Ingrid Bergman movie, which had been released in late 1942, just in time for the troops to see it before they left.

Replacement Bob McGee volunteered to stay behind and help clean up the berthing areas while the rest of the division set out on foot for the bivouac. As a reward, the men on the detail were given the Coca-Cola that remained in the mess supplies. McGee stuffed his duffel bag with as many bottles as it would hold. The winter uniforms came in handy, and he wrapped the bottles carefully in the woolen underwear, stuffing more bottles inside his overshoes. Once the work was done and the detail loaded trucks to ride to the bivouac area, McGee produced a bottle. Another soldier, realizing that they wouldn't be seeing any consumer goods for a while, offered McGee fifty cents for the nickel bottle of cola. McGee decided to keep his stash a secret.[1]

Otis Sampson, mortar sergeant in E Company, was sent ahead by truck some four and a half miles south of the city to set up the division camp. After twelve days on board the rolling ship, Sampson was eager for exercise and would rather have walked with his company.

The glimpse of Africa from the trucks was enough to excite the imagination of these youngsters, many of whom had never left their home state before joining the Army. Even Sampson, who was well traveled in the United States, was fascinated. He spotted a Moroccan soldier, on guard in a doorway, wearing a robe that stretched to the ground and holding a rifle topped with a long bayonet. Sampson figured the bayonet was mostly for show, and he had to admit it looked intimidating.

Sampson and a few other noncoms supervised the unloading of trucks, which contained tents and other equipment for the camp. Using a map of the bivouac area, he saw to it that his tents were pitched in the right places, with sections, platoons, and companies aligned in neat rows. It wasn't long before aspiring merchants and traders found the camp, and Sampson warned his men that the Arab boys could use their robes to hide articles stolen from careless troopers. There had been GIs in the area since the November landings, so the children were already used to American generosity. They begged cigarettes and chocolate, calling out "Joe! Hey, Joe!"

The troopers had been confined since leaving Fort Bragg, so once the camp was established, the command gave out passes for the men to visit Casablanca. There was a considerable U.S. presence in the city, and merchants had already become adept at separating GIs from their money. Everywhere the men went they were accosted by traders selling cheap knives or camel skin purses or shoe shines. Sampson was drawn to a street with a sign, obviously posted by the provost, that read OFF LIMITS TO ALL MILITARY PERSONNEL.

Sampson and Harry Pickles, one of the men in his mortar section, stood at one end of the street, staring down and trying to see what might be so dangerous. Arab men in nearby doorways smiled at the troopers. The locals obviously knew that the sign was part of the attraction, but Sampson had no way of asking what might be in the forbidden zone. But the fighter in him saw the narrow street as a good place for robbers to attack any troopers foolish enough to enter. Besides his natural caution, Sampson felt his responsibility as a sergeant. He could hardly flout the rules, then expect his men to follow them.

He could take care of himself, but he was mature enough that he didn't feel the need to prove it. As he stood there, an MP walked up and solved the problem by telling them to clear the area.

The regiment spent two nights at a bivouac site just outside of Casablanca, before beginning the four-hundred-mile trek to Oujda, near the border between French Morocco and Algeria, and some thirty miles from the Mediterranean. A lucky few went by truck, but most were loaded on French boxcars called "forty and eights" for the numbers stenciled on the wooden sides: the cars were designed to carry forty men or eight horses.

There was nothing to do as the trains lurched along, except stare out at the flat brown country and dream about a cool drink of water. At one rest stop, the troopers got a glimpse of the German "supermen" they'd been hearing about for years, and whom they'd eventually face in combat. A trainload of Afrika Korps prisoners, headed for the coast and ships that would take them to camps in America, stopped at a siding near the Americans. The German veterans, tanned and tough looking, peered out of the same kind of cars the GIs were in, which had a certain irony. One English-speaking prisoner called out to the GIs, "Where do you Americans think you're going?"

"To Berlin," a paratrooper shouted back.

"Well, that's fair enough," the German answered. "We're headed to New York."[2]

If the troopers were relieved that the vaunted Afrika Korps was at least made up of mere men, not everything they heard was as reassuring. The command had made a big deal of the secrecy of the division's move: the men had been confined to Bragg and Camp Edwards. They had switched uniforms and shed their wings, patches, and beloved jump boots. Mail was strictly censored; any mention of the deployment was excised.

Yet before they left for Oujda, Berge Avadanian and others heard a broadcast from "Axis Sally," the English-speaking propagandist whose programs were aimed at Allied troops.

"Welcome to Africa, Matt Ridgway and your bad boys."

If Sally knew the Eighty-second was in Africa, it was a safe bet the German high command knew.

Oujda was the low point for the regiment.

The 505th drew a dusty, shadeless bivouac area near a French-built airfield. The troopers set up their tents in neat company streets, just as they had been doing since basic training. But here the tents were spaced farther apart, and the men dug trenches in the hard ground for protection from the occasional German fighter plane that made it this far. The desert winds blew a fine grit into everything—clothing, weapons, writing paper, equipment—there was no escaping. The dust scratched their throats, coated their skin, and peppered the food dished out in the chow lines. There were no shower facilities, and with daytime temperatures climbing above one hundred degrees, what little water that was available was used for drinking and cooking, rather than bathing. The daily ration of water was so heavily chlorinated that it was hardly a relief, even for men doing heavy physical labor in a hot dust bowl.

Then there were the flies: big and black and seemingly as numerous as the grains of sand. They swarmed back and forth between the mess tents and the latrines, which were just trenches surrounded by canvas screens. The men ate with one hand and used the other to fan flies away from their mess kits, but the technique was never entirely successful. It wasn't long before nearly every man in the regiment was suffering with some degree of dysentery. Men who had been in peak health before leaving the States were now losing weight and strength. They carried toilet paper with them everywhere, and frequently had to stop in the middle of some task to run for the latrine—a condition called "the GI trots." Often they didn't make it and their suffering became public. Dysentery threatened to make the 505th ineffective as a fighting unit, and there was pressure on the doctors to keep the men in the field. Only the most severe cases were excused from training.

In spite of their afflictions, Gavin pushed the soldiers hard. When the temperature climbed over one hundred degrees, training started just before dusk and lasted until dawn. The training in infantry tactics was new to many of the citizen soldiers of the 505th. Once they got assembled on the ground, the paratroopers would fight just as other light infantry units in the Army fought, but they could not be resupplied as units with a logistics pipeline were. Until they could link up with ground units, the paratroopers had to live off what they carried, what they could scrounge from the land, and what could be dropped to them. They were even trained to use captured enemy weapons and ammunition in the event their own supplies ran out.

Major Ed Zaj, the regimental supply officer, was always trying to improve techniques to get bullets, food, and water to the men, no matter where they found themselves. In putting together his supply section, called the S4, Zaj cast a wide net for men with any sort of applicable experience. His search led him to Joe Jockel, a former student at St. John's University in New York who had joined the Army in February 1942.

At a time when college experience was a rarity, Jockel had several semesters under his belt. Perhaps more important, he also had work experience that could be useful to the supply section: Jockel had been a clerk for the Brooklyn Union Gas Company, working the night shift, balancing the books and keeping track of the cash. Jockel had experience, brains, and a solid work ethic.

He was told to report to the regimental headquarters, where he was surprised to find himself talking to a major, who took the time to explain that the whole concept of resupplying a force by parachute drop was completely new. They were making up the doctrine as they went along, experimenting with various techniques, but they did not have all the time in the world. It was not revealing any secret to tell the young soldier that they would soon be in combat, and the time to figure out how to do things was now.

Jockel was reluctant. He had not joined the Army to be a clerk, even one with heavy responsibilities such as resupplying the entire unit in combat. But Zaj was serious about manning the S4 section with the best men he could find, and Gavin backed him. There could be no fighting without resupply.

"If you take the job, it'll mean fast promotion for you," Zaj offered.

For Jockel, who had struggled to pay his way through school and who intended to return to school someday, the temptation of a big pay raise proved enough. Zaj was also smart enough to flatter the young trooper, telling him that he could make a big difference for the whole command from a position in the S4 shop, that Gavin himself was interested in what happened there. Jockel agreed, and in one heady day, Gavin promoted him through four pay grades: from private to private first class, to corporal, to sergeant, to staff sergeant.

Airborne doctrine called for the troops to be dropped at night, when the big transport planes would be less visible to antiaircraft gunners, and the troopers wouldn't be targets as they floated down. Of course, darkness also meant that it would take longer for the men to assemble, to gain enough mass to attack an enemy. Gavin and the other commanders knew that the more the men rehearsed moving at night, the better and faster they'd become.

They spent days and nights on compass courses in the hills around Oujda, sometimes starting with a small group, sometimes alone. Driven into the trackless, dusty hills, they had to find their way to a point noted on a map. The first task was always to answer the question: Where am I? During daylight hours, soldiers accomplished this by terrain association, comparing the landscape around them to the map, which showed features such as hills and gullies At night, everything was more difficult.

Like many of the experienced noncoms, Sampson measured the young officers in E Company, many of whom had been in the service no longer than the privates. Evaluating officers wasn't a mere idle. The decisions made by a lieutenant or captain could determine whether or not the men survived their first battle.

Sampson thought E Company had drawn good officers. Among them was Lieutenant Waverly Wray, a dark-haired, sturdily built platoon leader from Batesville, Mississippi. The troopers respected his physical strength; he often relieved staggering soldiers of some piece of heavy equipment on the long road marches. Wray was also an accomplished outdoorsman and a crack shot, claiming that he had "never missed a shot in his life that he didn't mean to." But the lieutenant was not a typical paratrooper: he didn't drink, smoke, chase women, or gamble. When angry, the worst he might utter was "Jod Brown." The men called Wray "the Deacon," though not to his face. Whenever someone asked him about his unusual ways, Wray simply said that he tried to "walk with the Lord."

One night E Company had dug in a defensive position near the bottom of a hill. The men were supposed to take turns watching for the "enemy," but Sampson knew the young soldiers would probably go to sleep once they were hidden by darkness. They would face the same temptation in combat, where lack of vigilance would cost lives. The sergeant's job was to break them of bad habits.

After the company was in position, Sampson gave the men time to settle in. When things grew quiet around him, he slipped out of his own hole and crawled along the platoon line. Soldiers who had fallen asleep got an unpleasant surprise when Sampson pinned them to the ground and mimed stabbing them. He slipped into one position and found the same thing he had in the other holes, a sleeping form. This one, however, was large; it was Lieutenant Wray. Sampson knelt over the sleeping lieutenant and drew his finger, like a knife blade, across the man's throat. Wray say bolt upright, shocked and embarrassed that he'd been caught asleep. Sampson had made his point quite clearly: if he had been an infiltrator, Wray would be dead. Worse, the enemy might have slipped into the paratroopers' lines, exposing other men to the danger.

"Just practicing," Sampson whispered to Wray before moving away quietly. He looked back after he'd gone some distance, and he could still see the startled officer sitting up, relieved that his mistake had been in a training exercise. Sampson would not have to mention the incident; Wray was too mortified to make that mistake again.

All across the regiment, junior leaders like Sampson were working hard to teach their troopers the skills they'd need. Young men who'd been in high school classrooms or company stockrooms a year earlier were now learning how to field-strip weapons in the dark, how to move in small teams and assault trenches and bunkers. They threw hand grenades, practiced with the bayonet, made a few practice jumps, and continued their physical fitness regime.

Their physical toughening included water discipline. Big canvas bags, hung from wooden tripods at the end of each company street, were filled with stale-tasting water that had been treated with chlorine. In the morning, troopers pulled the liner from their helmets and filled the inside of the steel pot with water. From this they had to fill their canteen, shave, wash and rinse out their socks. While the other parts of their uniform were allowed to get dirty, it was especially important, in the heat and dust, to keep the socks as clean as possible to prevent blisters.

The men settled into a routine and did their best to cope with the sickness, the foul water, the sand-flecked and fly-infested food. Oujda offered few diversions, a couple of tiny bars and shady whorehouses. It wasn't Manhattan, or even Fayetteville, but the dusty little town at least offered a view of something other than more GIs.

Berge Avadanian quickly tired of walking or hitchhiking to Oujda, so he bought a bony horse from an Arab. He tied the horse near his tent and intended to keep him handy for riding into town. He figured he could even rent the horse to other footsore soldiers, which would at least pay for the animal. On his first night as a horse owner, Avadanian tethered the horse near his tent and went to sleep. In the morning, the animal was gone. It was possible the horse had gotten free, but Avadanian considered it more likely that the original owner had recovered it to sell again.

At Oujda's French-American Soldiers Club, GIs could sit and drink *vin rouge* and eat hard-boiled eggs in the company of the exotic-looking troops of the French Foreign Legion.[3] There were some well-established brothels, but the command, concerned that soldiers might be robbed or even killed in these tough neighborhoods, set up Army-supervised brothels. Private William Tucker pulled guard duty at one of these, La Rue 63, and was surprised to find that the regimental surgeons pulled tours of duty there, presumably to ensure that the men used prophylactics. Tucker's job was to keep out civilians who might prey on the GIs, but he spent most of his time breaking up fights between troopers and trying to keep the bored doctor sober.

Gavin was determined that every paratrooper who went into combat have the skills to fight and defend himself. Since the men would be dropped behind enemy lines, the battlefield would not be arranged neatly, with front lines and rear echelons where support troops and staff types could avoid coming face-to-face with the enemy. Cooks and drivers and medics found themselves doing the same physical training the infantry did. The medics, although prohibited by the Geneva Convention from carrying anything but sidearms, trained on the rifle ranges. Even Gavin jumped carrying a carbine, a lighter, smaller rifle than the standard M1 Garand carried by most soldiers. (Gavin quickly traded his carbine for the heavier and more reliable M1, which he carries in nearly every wartime photo.)

The paratroopers had another concern: their uniforms were different from the standard issue for U.S. forces. Where the straight-leg infantrymen wore olive-colored fatigues that were cut like conventional workclothes, the paratroopers wore baggy pants—which they tucked into their beloved jump boots—and oversized jackets. The pants had pockets on the sides, which the troopers stuffed full of hand grenades, food, cigarettes, anything a man might need in a hurry. The paratroopers' blouse hung down like a long shirt, which they wore untucked. The patch pockets were sewn on at an angle, and even the collar of the shirt was different. It was not beyond imagining that an infantry soldier coming across the beach might mistake a paratrooper for something other than a U.S. soldier. Gavin wanted no friendly-fire incidents if he could help it, so he sent a squad to visit the units of the First and Forty-fifth Divisions to showcase the paratrooper uniform.

Gavin knew that tough training meant the 505th would field skilled, physically hardened soldiers, and he kept up the pace in spite of the problems with dysentery. There was another benefit, too. One of the great strengths of the 505th, or of any unit that went into combat after a long period of training together, was that the men knew each other. They knew whom they could rely on and who might be a little shaky in a tough spot. More than that, as they went through the annealing process provided by hard training, they formed strong bonds that would carry them through the fight.

The veterans would quickly learn that a man's willingness to fight, to take risks, rested on these very personal bonds. It wasn't thoughts of home or the cause or patriotism; when it came down to the hard business of combat, the only reason a man performed under fire—the only reason he would get up and move when the safe, smart thing to do was to climb into a hole and stay there—was that each soldier knew that the next guy was counting on him.

But combat meant there would be casualties. As the war went on, the old hands became increasingly reluctant to get to know the replacements, a reflex action that protected them from the pain of losing someone else close to them. Ironically, these same veterans also knew that it was just those bonds that made their unit effective—and increased their chances of survival. Neither the 505th nor the U.S. Army in World War II handled the replacement issue well.

James Rodier, a twenty-year-old private from northern Virginia, had been looking forward to a ten-day furlough when he finished jump school in April 1943. But as he pinned on his wings on a Friday afternoon, he was told that furloughs had been canceled. The soldiers went back to the barracks to pack their gear. By Sunday, Rodier was on a train for New York, where he was dumped into a pool of replacements and berthed on board the *George Washington*. Although assigned to the Eighty-second Airborne Division, he did not belong to a regiment, company, or platoon. The replacement troopers had no noncoms to look out for them, no experienced hands to show them the ropes. They did not share the comforting confines of a squad or a platoon or company; they were little more than cargo. Even the designation "replacement" had an ominous ring to it. For any of the young men who considered it, the fact that the Eighty-second Airborne Division was heading off with a large contingent of replacements was significant. Whom, after all, would they be replacing, if not casualties? A man need only look at the long lines in the holds to see how many troopers the Army expected to lose—killed, wounded, captured, or missing—in the upcoming campaign.

Rodier had a lot in common with the other division soldiers. He had seen an article in the newspaper about the paratroopers, and had told his mother that was what he wanted. He enlisted before he ever got a draft notice, taking the oath in the bus terminal in Washington,

D.C., and immediately boarded a bus headed south. Rodier did his initial training with F Company of the 501st Infantry, an outfit that eventually became a part of the 101st Airborne Division. He learned early on that the Army was a collection of teams that worked together, ate together, struggled together, and suffered together. The team was both family and workplace. That reassuring identity had been taken away from Rodier when, instead of returning to the 501st after airborne school, he was sent as a replacement to North Africa.

Rodier was stuck in the replacement detachment, shortened in GI slang to the "repple depple," while the 505th trained in the North African heat. The replacements did not receive further training, but endured the heat and boredom in a state of suspended animation, knowing they could be called, but until then unsure of their fate. By late June, Rodier had lost some of the confidence he'd gained as a result of his basic training and his completing the rigorous course at airborne school. Though surrounded by hundreds of men, he felt utterly alone. (The historian Stephen Ambrose wrote, "Had the Germans been given a free hand to devise a replacement system for the [European theater], one that would do the Allies the most harm and the least good, they could not have done a better job.")[4]

In late June, the 505th conducted a training jump in high winds that injured many of the paratroopers and even resulted in a few deaths. The call went over to the replacement detachment to send up some troopers; James Rodier and two others went to the headquarters of the Second Battalion.

The men arrived with all their gear, and stood sweating in the sun outside the headquarters tent, waiting to learn what would become of them. They did not know, of course, that combat was only days away, or that their objective would be Sicily. But in the replacement camp and the division headquarters there was no shortage of rumors and speculation. Preparation had reached a high pitch, and the men got themselves worked up into a frenzy of speculation.

Now the moment had come for Rodier to finally join a unit. He had volunteered because he wanted to make a difference, and he felt he had something to contribute to whatever squad he landed in. He was relieved to be moving again.

Finally, a tall captain came out of the headquarters tent, and in a thick southern accent, started to berate the sweating replacements.

"You're not soldiers," he told them in a tone that made it sound like it was their fault, as if they had shown up here by accident, or out of some malicious intent to defraud the Army out of fifty dollars a month. He railed and whined in the same tone, castigating the men and letting them know that, as far as the troopers of the 505th were concerned, they were next to worthless. Then he sent them away.

Rodier was shocked. He had volunteered to serve his country, volunteered for the paratroops, had made it through all the training and endured virtual imprisonment in the replacement detachment, and instead of being welcomed or challenged or even thanked, this captain seemed intent on belittling him.

Rodier managed to get his pup tent put up in the Headquarters Company area; then he reached into his bag and pulled out the small New Testament he'd been carrying since he left home. It had been a source of comfort to him, and he needed something familiar. He was at the edge of a desolate continent, on the verge of going to war beside men he didn't know and who—based on the most recent evidence— thought little of him. It was too much for the young soldier. Instead of reading, he took out a pen and wrote in the fly leaf of the Bible: "If you find this Bible on my body, please return it to my mother." He wrote his mother's name and address back in Vienna, Virginia, and was suddenly overwhelmed by a terrible fear and homesickness that had not visited him to this point. All seemed lost.[5]

In addition to the night maneuvers, Gavin tried to tailor the training for the upcoming mission. He knew, from studying aerial photos, that many of the roads and intersections in Sicily were guarded by domed pillboxes and fortified positions, so he had full-scale mock-ups built for rehearsals.

Nick Kastrantas, of the regimental S2 section, was one of those responsible for building the models of the target areas. Kastrantas was born in Pittsburgh, Pennsylvania, but had moved back to Greece with his family as a small boy. There he attended a technical school and learned cartography, producing maps for the Greek army. He returned to the States before the war and volunteered for the Army and the paratroops. He already spoke Greek and French, and that, coupled with his experience as a mapmaker, made him a natural fit for the intelligence section.

In order to get the scale of the models right, Kastrantas measured the shadows of the trees in the photographs, and he noted the time of day the photo was taken, which gave him the angle of the sun. From there it was a simple trigonometry problem to determine the height of buildings and trees around the drop zones. Using these detailed measurements, the intelligence troops oversaw the building of full-sized mock-ups, including the ubiquitous pillboxes.

The units maneuvered against the targets using live ammunition, the men moving forward while their own machine guns fired over their heads at the enemy. They learned that weapons sound one way to the firer, but sound completely different downrange. They learned to distinguish American from enemy weapons. They learned to keep their heads down and hug the earth, and they learned to move forward when told. And since the tendency for green soldiers is to fire all their ammunition rapidly, leaving none for the final assault, the men of the 505th were taught to use their ammo wisely.

In one live-fire exercise, Frank Thompson, of the First Battalion's mortar section, was shot through the shoulder. The bullet entered from behind, traveled through the meaty part of his shoulder and exited cleanly from the front. Although it hurt and burned, the medics who treated him did not seem alarmed. The company medic stanched the bleeding and sent him to the aid station, where a doctor examined him, cleaned the wound, and announced that he'd be fine. The doctor saw to it that Thompson was given a pass to rest for a day. On his day off, Thompson and another trooper talked themselves into the use of a jeep, which they drove to the coast for a refreshing ocean swim.

Thompson joined his unit for training the next day and quickly learned that he had a problem: he could barely lift his wounded arm above his head, which meant he would not be able to steer his parachute. He would simply fall, like an equipment bundle, onto whatever was below him.

But he had not trained this long and this hard to be left out of the assault, so Thompson hustled and grimaced and did his job in spite of the two holes in his shoulder. His buddies and the medics went along with the charade that he was well enough to fight. After training, Thompson checked the bandages: they were filthy with sweat and dust. He went to the aid station, where a medic cleaned the wound and asked no questions about Thompson's strength or abilities. When the procedure was finished, Thompson was anxious to leave; the medic offered him a single bandage.

"I think I need two," Thompson said, indicating the entry and exit wounds. The medic handed over another and the young soldier hurried out of the tent.[6]

THE HOUR
UPON THEM

Some weeks before the invasion, the division staff became concerned that Sicily's rough terrain and poor roads, combined with the paratroopers' lack of motorized transport, would make it difficult to move food, water, and ammunition forward. There were also concerns about getting the wounded to the evacuation station on the beach. The dirt-poor farmers of Sicily had very few, if any, trucks that could be commandeered. Some planners thought the airborne should turn to that old Army standby, the mule, which was already in use in the rough terrain on some Pacific islands. If the men could parachute in, maybe the mules could, too.

Major Mark Alexander, the executive officer of Second Battalion, was given the mission to test the concept. There were no mules available, so he purchased two small donkeys from local merchants and got hold of several large parachutes used to drop bundles of weapons and ammunition. He convinced Tommy Thompson, executive officer of the Sixty-fourth Troop Transport Group, to go along with the scheme.

On the morning of the test, Alexander and four soldiers from his battalion headquarters section—a Sergeant Gavin (no relation to the regimental commander), Sergeant Berge Avadanian, and Corporals Bale and Freeland—blindfolded one of the donkeys and led him up a wooden ramp into the belly of a C-47. The animal balked when its feet struck the aluminum deck of the airplane, but the pilot kept the plane's engines shut down, and with four men pushing and pulling the animal, the paratroopers were able to get the reluctant beast into the cargo area.

When the engines roared to life, the donkey, now thoroughly terrified, began braying and straining to get free. Alexander tied the donkey's lead to one of the aluminum ribs of the aircraft, and he had the other troopers, all of whom were wearing parachutes, hook their static lines to the overhead cable, just in case one or more of them should fall out the wide door.

By the time the plane reached altitude, the donkey, still blindfolded, had determined that he didn't like where he'd been led, so he lay down to keep from being taken anywhere else. The four troopers clambered around the animal as they tried to get a good grip; they pulled the lead rope and pushed the donkey from behind as the plane circled the drop zone and the Air Corps pilots looked back in amusement from the cockpit. The men threw themselves into the battle, pushing, straining, slipping on the aluminum decking. Slowly the protesting donkey began to lose ground; the men, sweating and red-faced, pulled harder. Finally, the donkey lost its footing and stumbled toward the big door, sliding the last few feet and knocking the paratroopers down like bowling pins. When the animal finally slid out the door, Mark Alexander found himself on the animal's back.

When Alexander's chute opened, he managed to put a little distance between himself and the terrified animal. The donkey's chute opened without a hitch, and the cargo parachutes proved large enough to slow him down. Unfortunately, the jury-rigged harness slipped, and the donkey started to slide loose. Unlike the paratroopers, who were taught to bend their legs to cushion the impact, the donkey hit the ground with its legs straight. Alexander rolled out of his chute and ran to the animal, which had three broken legs and was braying in pain.

Alexander declared the experiment a failure, and Berge Avadanian used his pistol to end the animal's misery.[1]

The Second Battalion training and operations officer, Captain Paul Woolslayer, decided that the animal's body shouldn't go to waste. The men could use it to learn what it would feel like to sink a bayonet into real flesh.[2]

Woolslayer, a big man who had been an intercollegiate boxer was, like Ed Krause, very loud and very public about his bellicosity. Alexander thought that perhaps Woolslayer was all talk, but he was willing to endure him if it helped his soldiers prepare for the hard work ahead.

Woolslayer had the soldiers drag the donkey to the latrine area, where they removed one of the canvas screens surrounding a straddle trench and, using the wooden poles that had held the screen, strung the body upside down over the fetid hole. The dead animal was already beginning to reek in the heat. The slit trench, of course, smelled terrible, and had thousands of attendant flies. Gathering most of the battalion there might have seemed a good idea to Woolslayer, but the men thought otherwise.

They lined up by squads, their bayonets fixed to the end of their rifles, and at Woolslayer's urging the men came forward and delivered a butt stroke, swinging the heavy heel of the Garand into the flesh, then bringing the rifle down and stabbing straight into the donkey. After several dozen stab wounds, the donkey's insides began to spill out, falling into the stinking trench. After a hundred or so men had stabbed it, there was little recognizable about the animal. Soon the blood, the shredded flesh and gore, the smell, and the thousands of flies sickened some of the men, which pleased Woolslayer. He wanted to inure them to the horrors they'd surely see in combat.

Alexander understood Woolslayer's intention, but he didn't think much of the exercise. In fact, he didn't think much of Woolslayer. The former boxer had once booby-trapped Alexander's desk with a flare. When Alexander opened the drawer, the flare burst into flame inside the drawer, burning his hand. Woolslayer was in the room, and it looked to Alexander like he'd been waiting for the trick to play out. The captain was pretty amused.

Alexander was Woolslayer's boss and could have handled the situation through formal channels, but he doubted that would have any effect on the boxer.

"Whoever did this can meet me out back of the mess hall," Alexander said.

Alexander considered himself a pretty good fighter, and he was angry enough to hand out a beating. Even if he took one, he'd feel better than he did now. Alexander left the office and walked over to the wooden mess, circling around the back where the slop pails were lined up neatly.

No one showed up. Nor did anyone mention the incident again. Woolslayer didn't own up to it—that would have meant admitting that he hadn't wanted to fight Alexander. By heading out behind the mess hall, even with a burned and throbbing hand, Alexander had established that he was in charge of the staff, including Captain Paul Woolslayer. The operations officer remained marginally insubordinate, dragging his feet and letting Alexander know that he, Woolslayer, had been around longer and probably had better ideas on how to run things. But he did what he was told.

By this point the troopers were using V-mail (V for "Victory"), which saved tons of shipping space. The men were given forms, and they had to keep their message inside the preprinted lines. The forms were reduced in size photographically, then enlarged when they arrived back in the States.

There was a circle in the upper left corner for the censor's stamp: mail had to be read by an officer who checked to make sure the soldier wasn't giving away information that might be of use to the enemy, such as the exact location or mission of the unit, or even special training. The writing tended to be about upbeat topics that would neither alarm the folks back home nor bring down the wrath of the censor.

On May 25, while the regiment was at Oujda, Art Gorham picked up one of the forms and wrote a note to his parents back in Bellevue, Ohio.

"Dear Folks," he began. "Just a few lines to let you know I'm alive and well, having made the 'cruise' without incident. Received the Mother's Day card. Passed it around the Bn—to all the boys from all the mothers.

"Don't worry about us," he continued. "If the African sun can't kill us, Hitler won't be able to either."

"Join the Army and see the world at government expense," he wrote from the hot and dusty camp that seemed to most of the paratroopers like the edge of hell. "Tell those 4F's to quit striking and put out for those of us over here with no Coca-Cola."

The note ended simply. "Write. Love, Art"[3]

On June 9, Gavin and several of his battalion commanders, along with some air group commanders from Troop Transport, flew a reconnaissance mission in British aircraft over the targeted drop zones. They had picked a night when the phase of the moon was the same it would be on D-day, and they found all the checkpoints and key terrain features, just as they had memorized from the aerial photos. On the way back, Gavin watched the moonlight on the water and the aircraft wings, thinking to himself that the next time the moon was in this phase, he and his men would be on their way to war.[4]

All the planes returned safely, and only then did it become widely known at higher headquarters that Gavin had flown over the objective. There was much discussion at higher levels about whether officers who knew so much about an impending invasion—Gavin knew dates, times, and targets—should fly above enemy lines, with the possibility of getting shot down and captured.

Gavin had learned, within days of arriving in North Africa, that Sicily was the objective and that only one airborne regiment would make the initial assault, because of the perennial shortage of aircraft. Ridgway selected the 505th. By the time of the June flight, Gavin's battalion commanders knew most of the details, though they were constrained from telling anyone else. As the weeks went by in June, the number of headquarters people included in the planning grew, and the regiment's plan took shape.

The assault force would take off from multiple airfields in Tunisia and fly due east, over the island of Linosa to Malta, which was controlled by the British. Malta would be lit as a beacon, and the pilots would turn left, and come over Sicily's southwestern shore.

Gavin's command would be supplemented with airborne artillery, engineers, and medical support, as well as an additional battalion of infantry from the 504th Parachute Infantry Regiment. Assembled and configured for the mission, the command was dubbed the 505th Regimental Combat Team, and consisted of: Gavin's three infantry battalions, plus the Third Battalion of the 504th PIR; the 456th Parachute Field Artillery Battalion, which consisted of three howitzer batteries armed with the 75 mm pack howitzer, as well as an antiaircraft battery armed with 50-caliber machine guns; B Company of the 307th Airborne Engineer Battalion; as well as detachments from the Eighty-second Airborne Division Signal Company and the 307th Medical Detachment. A handful of U.S. Navy officers and sailors would also make the jump; their job was to call for fire from the ships offshore.[5]

Gavin's mission was to capture the high ground inland from Gela, disrupt enemy attempts to counterattack the beachhead, then assist the First Division in capturing the airfields at Ponte Olivo. Army Air Corps fighters, using this field, would be able to spend more time in the air over Sicily, thus providing more continuous air support.

The regimental headquarters section, the First and Second Battalions, as well as batteries A and B of the 456th Field Artillery, were to land in a large drop zone north and east of Gela, the coastal town that was the target of the First Infantry Division's beach assault. Once on the ground, this force would be just a short hike from a key road junction, called "the Y" in all briefings, connecting Gela to the inland towns of Niscemi, Biscari (Acate on modern maps), and Vittoria.[6] They were to seize the Y road junction and block expected German counterattacks from the inland hills. Third Battalion of the 505th and C Battery of the 456th were to drop south of this road junction and seize the high ground that overlooked it. Whatever units the Germans had on the island were probably inland, out of range of the naval guns. In order to attack the landing beaches, they'd have to use these roads. The intersection was a choke point and the paratroopers would control it.

Third battalion of the 504th was to drop south of Niscemi and cut the roads leading from that town toward Gela. In addition, the regimental demolition team was to drop about five miles east of the main drop zones and prepare the road and rail crossings of the Acate River for demolition. Captain Bill Follmer's I Company was to attack an enemy strongpoint on the high ground overlooking Gela and light a huge bonfire that would serve as a beacon for the fleet headed toward the beaches.

Gavin had gotten the word, shortly after arriving in North Africa, that the 505th would get the airborne mission. There was simply not enough air transport to drop the entire Eighty-second Airborne Division.

A shortage of aircraft wasn't the only problem: the transport pilots were nowhere near where they needed to be in terms of training. Formation flying in the daytime was hard; formation flying at night proved even more difficult, and often the pilots couldn't find the right drop zones. Navigating an airplane across a great distance in the darkness, without the benefit of electronic aids and under a strict radio silence, was also a huge challenge.

Even though the 505th had priority for aircraft, jump training also lagged behind where Gavin wanted it. The drop zones around Oujda were plagued by high winds, and their surfaces were rock and hard-baked dirt. On a training jump on June 5, winds blew over the drop zone at thirty miles an hour and more, easily twice what was considered safe. Training jumps were usually canceled when the wind reached fifteen miles an hour.[7]

But there was tremendous pressure to keep training—there were new replacements being assigned to the unit every day. Ridgway and Gavin had to weigh the advantages against very real costs to the unit. Of the eleven hundred men who jumped on June 5, two were killed and fifty-three suffered fractured ankles or broken legs.[8]

On this jump, Wheatley Christensen of G Company was surprised to look down on the drop zone and see rocks as big as soccer balls. Although he managed to land in one piece, his platoon sergeant suffered two broken legs. Such shake-ups in the leadership so close to the combat jump worried Gavin and Ridgway. Gavin's 505th made only one nighttime training jump as a regiment, and the troops were badly scattered.

As the early days of June ticked by, all the months of training became focused on a few pieces of terrain and a handful of missions. There was a great sense of urgency in the headquarters, and Gavin looked carefully for anything he might have missed in his preparations.

There was one personnel problem eating at the regimental commander: he did not believe the Second Battalion commander, James Gray, was up to leading his five hundred paratroopers in combat. Gavin later wrote that Gray was "a nice, personable, genial man who liked to play poker, and he didn't belong in the airborne."[9] Mark

Alexander, Gray's executive officer, and other officers in the battalion knew that Gray drank, and even kept a bottle under his bunk.[10] Gray had shipped a case of whiskey overseas with some of the battalion's equipment, but when the shipping crates were unloaded in North Africa, the liquor was missing.

In June, Gray went to observe a night drop by the Fifty-second Troop Carrier Wing and hear the critique of the operation at headquarters, then flew to Tunisia to see the departure airfields that would be used on D-day. According to Gray, he left word with Gavin's adjutant, Major Al Ireland, as to where he was.

Over the course of several days, Gavin asked Alexander once a day, "Where's Gray?" Each time, Alexander was unable to answer. Finally, when Alexander once more said he didn't know where Gray was, Gavin responded with, "You're the battalion commander."

Alexander asked, "Don't you want to hear his side of it?"

"Too late for that," Gavin replied.

Alexander thought that perhaps Gavin had used the incident as an excuse to relieve Gray. For the new commander, the point was moot: Gavin had made his decision, and there was no going back. Now it was up to Alexander to make sure he was ready, and that the unit didn't suffer because of the turmoil. He had to find someone who could step in as executive officer and keep things running smoothly Knowing that his weakness was administration, Alexander wanted someone who could help keep all the detailed work in hand. The commander's job was to focus on combat training and, after D-day, combat. He told Gavin he wanted the best captain in the regiment for his exec.

Gavin turned to Jack Norton, his protégé from his days at West Point, who commanded H Company, part of Krause's Third Battalion. Gavin called Norton in and told him he was about to become Mark Alexander's second-in-command. Norton was not happy; he wanted to take his company into combat, and he told Gavin so.

"I'm sorry," Gavin said in his soft-spoken manner. "But I'm moving you."

"This is my company," Norton persisted. "They need me."

Gavin understood how Norton felt. They were on the eve of an invasion, and Norton had spent years preparing for just this event. But Gavin was not just Norton's mentor; he was the commander who had to keep the best interest of the entire regiment in mind.

"You have your orders, Captain," he said. Norton saluted and left. Alexander had his executive officer.

Jack Norton was in a huff when he left Gavin, but he knew better than to show it. He was the greenest company commander in the regiment, having taken over H Company shortly before the regiment left the States, but whoever took over his company would be greener still. He wanted to stay with H Company because he believed he was the best man to led them in the coming fight, and because he knew that, for a captain, the ultimate test was to lead a company into combat. There were plenty of other officers in the regiment who would make good battalion execs, many of them senior to him; but, good soldier that he was, he packed his gear at H Company, headed over to Second Battalion, and introduced himself to the staff, including the operations officer, Paul Woolslayer. Norton knew Woolslayer's reputation: he was the tough-talking former Golden Gloves champ who had been a favorite of Gray's. He didn't expect any trouble from the operations officer, and he quickly went to work getting to know the battalion and keeping things moving as the men prepared for combat. None of them knew it yet, but the invasion was a little more than a week away.

Norton's job was to take the administrative burden off of Alexander's shoulders so that the new battalion commander could concentrate on stepping into his role as the combat commander. Norton oversaw all supply and administrative details with his usual energy.

One of the men who was impressed with the hardworking new executive officer was Staff Sergeant Tommy Gore, a Texan who worked for Woolslayer in the operations section. As a senior noncom in the operations section, it was his job to keep the command post running, updating maps with intelligence reports, helping to disseminate orders from Alexander down the chain of command.

Gore had enlisted in 1937, and so had more experience as a soldier than most of the officers he worked with. The seventh of nine children, he had joined the Army as a way to ease the burden on his family, which had been hard hit by the Depression. He had never been much of a student and didn't see school as a way out of Texas, so he followed his older brother's example and became a soldier.

Gore worked closely with Woolslayer every day, and he thought the man was all grandstanding and showmanship, with little substance. Gore had more confidence in Norton and Alexander. Those two were operating under a considerable handicap in terms of experience, but they were unflappable and willing to listen.

For his part, Alexander was a little surprised to be commanding a battalion. He looked around at his peers and sized himself up in comparison.

As far as he could see, he didn't have much in common with Ed Krause, the Third Battalion commander. As June drew to a close, Krause encouraged his men to shave their heads like Mohawk warriors, with a single strip of hair running down the center of the scalp. He suggested that the entire regiment adopt the style, to invoke something from those fierce Native American warriors, and perhaps to add something to the psychological kit bag of his troopers, something else to make them feel invincible. Gavin turned him down.

Alexander's first impression of Art Gorham was that the West Pointer was a bit aloof, but the more he got to know the man, the more it seemed that Gorham was just as nervous about his role in the upcoming battle as anyone else. Gorham may have been trying to maintain some distance between himself and his men, not an uncommon practice for a commander who might have to send some of those men to their deaths.

That thought weighed heavily on Alexander, who was eager to become a combat-ready battalion commander. Although he didn't know the exact date of the invasion, it was clear from the increasing pace of preparation that it wasn't far off. In the meantime, he had to learn how to handle a five-hundred-man unit in combat, establish himself as the commander—a man different from Gray but still in keeping with the regiment's culture. He had to get to know, in a way he hadn't as second-in-command, the company commanders and their key leaders. He had to figure out who was going to perform and whom he had to watch closely. He had to gauge his own abilities. Mercifully, all of his concerns about not letting his men down crowded out any concerns he might have had for his own safety. There was a battle coming up; his men were depending on him to get them through it and accomplish the mission. Gavin thought he could handle it; Mark Alexander had some lingering doubts.

He called the troops together for a simple speech.

"I'm the new commander," he told them. "I'll do my best, and I expect you to do yours."

Mark Alexander had been in the Army for two years and eight months.

In June, George Patton, whose invasion command would include the Eighty-second Airborne Division, assembled the men for a talk.

"No son of a bitch ever won a war by dying for his country," he told the men in what would become his trademark speech. "You win wars by making the other poor son of a bitch die for his country."

Patton, a keen student of military history, wanted to impress upon the soldiers that they were following in the footsteps of great soldiers in history. He told them, "You're pissing through the same straw as Caesar." Patton, the old horse-cavalryman, was talking about stable straw in encampments that included cavalry horses. His audience, a generation of men who were more familiar with Coca-Cola than horse stables, mistook his meaning and thought of drinking straws.[11]

On July 1, the regiment began its move from Oujda to Kairouan, Tunisia, where Army engineers had constructed dirt airstrips that lay much closer to Sicily. The heat was terrific, with daytime temperatures driven past 120 degrees by the desert siroccos. But in the 505th's camp, the men generally thought conditions were better. Oujda had been a flat, featureless landscape. In Kairouan, the men set up their bivouac in the orchards, under pear and almond trees, to hide the tents from prowling German aircraft and the sun.

On July 5, Gavin wrote to his nine-year-old daughter, Barbara, who was living in Washington, D.C., with her mother. As he sat in the stifling heat of the headquarters tent and typed the V-mail sheet (he could fit more on the form than if he used his large, looping handwriting), Gavin knew the regiment's first combat action was only days away.

"I suppose by the time you receive this you will be a bit concerned for my well-being. I will be, I am sure, in the best of health."

Without naming the place, he continued his unedited missive. "It is a bit hotter where I am now [Kairouan]. Much hotter, which I hardly believed it could be. Besides the camels are vicious, They are big and mean and stand in the runways and wont let the [aircraft] land, stand in the roads and wont let cars go by, bite anything including jeeps that come in reach of their long necks and generally make a nuisance of themselves."

After a few more chatty sentences, Gavin wrote, "I saw the loneliest sight in the world yesterday. Driving along a dirt road in the desert I came to a lone Britisher's grave marked with a plain cross and a rusty helmet."

Whether for her benefit or his, he doesn't dwell on the experience, but swiftly shifts to his soldiers.

"The 505 is doing well . . . [a] wonderful bunch. They are going to do very well. Their morale is unusually high. I have lost a half dozen or so over here from assorted injuries but what remains is tops . . . Love, Pappy."

During that last week, the supply lines for bringing in food broke down, and for a few days the entire division lived on marmalade and Spam. Gavin wrote to Barbara, "Many of us are beginning to have sore gums . . . from eating all canned soft food."[12] By this point the troopers were so lean and angry and had been living in hell so long that they would have jumped into Berlin to get out of Africa.

On July 6, the Regimental Combat Team had a birthday party for the 505th. Gavin convinced some of the officers to turn over their gambling winnings to help finance the big meal, and the money bought some bulls and sheep for barbecue. There was also some local wine and even some beer, which the troop transport pilots chilled by flying it up to high altitude.

The troops who stood in the chow lines that night had come a long way from the loose collection of brand-new GIs who had gathered in the Frying Pan at Fort Benning a year earlier. The unit had filled out, and although some of its members were untested and fresh from the repple depple, on the whole the regiment was trained and ready. The young men had a lean, tough look about them. They had been hardened by difficult training in terrible conditions. They had brawled and marched and fired tens of thousands of rounds; they had attacked mock objectives and maneuvered across a harsh landscape. But up to this point it had all been practice.

Now the hour was upon them.

On July 8, Captain Ed Sayre called A Company together for a "bull session," at which he talked about what the unit would do, and what they could expect.[13] Sayre believed in telling his men as much as possible about what was going on: not only did it ensure that each man knew the mission (and could carry on if the leaders were killed or wounded), but it helped reduce anxiety. The bull session was also a chance for the men to draw on each others' confidence, to look around at the circle of young faces and hardened bodies and reassure themselves that everything their commanders had been telling them for months was true: they were the best trained, toughest fighters in the world, and nothing was going to stop them. When Sayre was finished, the men started betting on their destination. Some thought they were going into France, some guessed Italy or Sicily, and a few men even believed they might be headed for Germany.

By the afternoon of July 9, the heavily laden men were in high spirits as they assembled beside the dark green aircraft. They would jump just after midnight; the long-awaited D-day was July 10, making this their last dusk in Africa. They were getting away from the heat and the flies and, they hoped, the dysentery that had laid so many of them low. And even the ones who were frightened could admit that they were happy the preparation was over: no more planning and pretending and wondering if they had what it took to defeat the Germans and Italians. Come what may, they were going to find out.

As far as Sayre could see, the big machine that was the 505th was working well, meeting the precise timetable for load-out. If everything went according to plan, the last paratroopers to jump would be on the ground a half hour before moonset plunged them into total darkness, shortly after one in the morning.

Although Sayre could see only a few score planes, he knew that there were more than two hundred assigned to carry the 505th to Sicily. The Troop Carrier Wing was spread out over twelve departure fields[14] to keep them hidden, as much as possible, from Axis aircraft. Even if German pilots spotted a few of the fields—and they tested Allied air superiority often—it would be difficult to learn the exact size of the invasion force from a few scattered planes glimpsed from the air.

Around seven in the evening, Sayre moved from planeload to planeload for a final talk with his men. Corporal Armstrong F. Cannady noticed that Captain Sayre was wearing what Cannady thought of as a big Texas smile. Whatever the young captain was thinking, whatever concerns he had, he managed to conceal them from his men. There was no bluster about him, just a calm, infectious self-confidence.

When Major Mark Alexander, the former Kansas National Guard private, climbed aboard his C-47, he had been in command of the Second Battalion (D, E, and F Companies) for less than two weeks, and his total military experience amounted to two years and nine months. Now, he was taking his five hundred men into combat. Like most of the officers who had almost daily contact with Jim Gavin, he was confident in his boss. He was sure of his company commanders, even though they were, like him, untried. If Alexander had doubts about anyone, he was unsure of himself.

Like many of the leaders, he would come to realize later that the burden of command was a blessing in disguise. All the worrying—about the mission, the plan, the preparation, the men—not only ensured that they were ready as they could be; it crowded out any thought of his own vulnerability. Alexander's attitude toward the possibility of getting wounded or killed was simple. He called it the "small-bullet, big-sky theory." With all this space, the odds were with him.

Across the half-dozen airfields, junior leaders made the rounds for another check of weapons and equipment. After the sweaty work of loading the aircraft and wrestling the heavy equipment bundles onto the drop racks, the men stretched out in the dusty shade of the wings and tried to rest. Amid the noise of taxiing aircraft and shouted instructions, few were able to sleep.

Some of the soldiers prayed; others sharpened the safety knives used for cutting away a failed chute; still others sharpened bayonets. They broke open the boxes of rations and packed the smaller containers in pockets and musette bags. Some of them read their Bibles.

Every one of them, from Gavin down to the newest private, squeezed himself into a tight parachute harness and buckled on all the heavy equipment. All around them sat the boxy C-47s, heavily weighted with bundles of equipment slung beneath the wings.

Richard Knopf, a twenty-one-year-old from Rochester, New York, was amazed at how much he had to carry. Knopf weighed 155 pounds in his boxer shorts, and he strapped on almost that much extra weight. In addition to the troopers' standard load—of helmet, main and reserve parachutes, rifle, ammunition, trench knife, hand grenades, rations, canteen, entrenching tool, gas mask, flashlight, first aid kit—Knopf carried land mines, wrapped in paper and cotton batting, in the cargo pockets of his trousers. In the slant pocket of his blouse he carried detonators, packed tightly in more cotton.

Just before he started struggling to get this giant version of himself up the narrow steps of the jump door on his C-47, Knopf was handed a small slip of mimeographed paper. Everyone around him was reading.

Soldiers of the 505th Combat Team

> *Tonight you embark upon a combat mission for which our people and the people of the free world have been waiting for two years.*
>
> *You will spearhead the landing of an American Force upon the island of SICILY. Every preparation has been made to eliminate the element of chance. You have been given the means to do the job and you are backed by the largest assemblage of air power in the world's history.*
>
> *The eyes of the world are upon you. The hopes and prayers of every American go with you. . . .*
>
> *Since it is our first fight at night, you must use the countersign, and avoid firing on each other. The bayonet is the night fighter's best weapon. Conserve your water and ammunition.*

The term "American parachutist" has become synonymous with
courage of high order. Let us carry the fight to the enemy and make
the American Parachutist feared and respected through all his ranks.
Attack violently. Destroy him wherever found.

I know you will do your job.

Good landing, good fight, and good luck.

James M. Gavin[15]

So it was Sicily. That was one mystery down, and a million unanswered questions to go. Some of the men crumpled the paper and tossed it away. Knopf folded his carefully and tucked it into a pocket, the one without the detonator. He thought he should keep it.

DOVE PALERMO?

DOVE SIRACUSA?

At 1930 hours, the first of the workhorse C-47s lifted off and circled the airfield. Prop wash from taxiing planes churned up a huge dust cloud that climbed like a brown thunderhead. Inside the aircraft, men tried to balance the heavy loads on their laps so their legs wouldn't fall asleep in transit. The planes quickly piled up, forming three-plane Vs, with those Vs drawing themselves into even larger Vs. By 2030, the entire regiment was airborne, and the lead planes of the 226-aircraft formation turned their noses east, toward the darkening horizon and the Mediterranean beyond. Captain Ed Sayre, seated by the open jump door, watched as brown Africa gave way to the sea.

In spite of the noise and the tension, some men slept on the three-hour flight. It was cooler in the aircraft, the first time they'd been cool since arriving in Africa. Others rehearsed their missions, calling to mind the details of sand tables and briefing maps they'd studied so hard. Closing his eyes, Sayre could picture the big Y road junction and the high ground above Ponte Olivo. As the company commander, he was responsible for everything his unit did or failed to do. His concerns ranged from whether his men would find the mortar tubes and machine guns dropped in bundles from the wings of the aircraft, to whether the most inexperienced private would remember to pull the pins on his hand grenades before tossing them. His biggest fear had nothing to do with the possibility that he would be dead before sunrise; he was much more concerned that he might fail in his mission, that he might make a mistake that would get men killed.

Malta, the landmark for the pilots, was supposed to be well marked with lights, but the time to sight it came and went with no island in view. By this time, around ten o'clock, Sayre's plane began bucking the strong winds coming across their flight path. The planes carrying First Battalion commander Art Gorham, Sayre, and two platoons of Sayre's A Company managed to stay in a relatively tight formation, despite the threat of midair collision and the lack of plane-to-plane radio communication. Sayre, watching through the open door, could see the dim lights marking the wingtips of the other planes.

As minutes slipped by, Sayre experienced the same shock other commanders felt: Through the open jump door he spotted antiaircraft fire coming up on the left side of the aircraft, meaning they were coming in on the wrong side of the island. If they missed Malta, he reasoned, maybe they missed the turn altogether and had overshot the southern tip of Sicily. The planned hard left turn now had them flying north along the eastern coast of the island, far from their drop zones.

Sayre made his way slowly to the front of the aircraft, waddling under the burden of his hundred pounds of gear. The pilot, a former commercial flier, wasn't surprised, nor was he rattled by this latest wrinkle.

"Do you want to jump here or try to find the right spot?" the pilot asked.

"Let's go where we're supposed to go," Sayre replied.

The pilot very calmly turned the plane back out to sea for another shot at finding the right drop zone. Back at the jump door, Sayre was happy to see the other planes in his group follow their lead and execute the same turn. He might be lost, but at least he still had his company with him.

Sayre checked his watch. Every minute they spent drilling holes in the sky meant another minute behind schedule, another minute closer to moonset. Landing in pitch blackness was more dangerous, and assembly would be more difficult. For the moment, at least, there was nothing to do but go along for the ride. He trusted the pilots and figured it was better to arrive late to the right spot than to arrive on time and lost.

The minutes stretched into a long hour, but finally the lead pilot sighted the landmark he was looking for, the long lake, il Biviere, that lay just inland from the beach some six miles southeast of Gela. As the formation crossed the coast, Sayre saw antiaircraft fire flare below them, the tracers like long fingers of light arcing up. He was relieved to see that very little of the fire was reaching the aircraft, and that there was no sign of antiaircraft artillery, which fired large-caliber shells timed to burst among the formations of thin-skinned airplanes. Still, the ground fire made some pilots skittish, and the tight formation began to slide apart. Every foot of distance between the bucking aircraft meant a greater dispersion of troopers on the ground, and could easily translate into hours before the company could assemble.

An anxious Sayre stood in the doorway of his C-47, hands grasping the aluminum skin of the plane, peering out onto the moonlit countryside. Above his head, the red light came on, the signal from the pilot that they were close to the drop zone. The men struggled to their feet, and Sayre put them through their prejump commands, screaming to be heard above the deep rumble of the engines. The troopers pressed into a tight mass, eager to get free of this big target, which the enemy had clearly sighted. Only the red light and discipline kept them riveted in place.

Ed Sayre looked at the dark forms in front of him, all of them ready to follow him into the unknown. He was, as always, a little awed by their faith and courage. He said a simple prayer.

"Lord, let Your will be done."

*   *   *

Bob McGee, who'd found the stash of Cokes while cleaning the ship back in Casablanca, was already exhausted when he was pulled up the narrow boarding ladder in the belly of a C-47 on the evening of July 9. He and the other demolition man assigned to regimental headquarters had spent the long hot day rolling bundles of land mines. The disks, weighing about ten pounds each, were laid on their edges and wrapped in blankets. These cylinders were then braced with long pieces of wood before everything was tied up with padded canvas. The finished bundles weighed about a thousand pounds, and the men spent hours wrestling these heavy containers to the bellies of the aircraft.

After he finished this work, McGee began his own preparations, packing his M1 rifle, ten pounds with five pounds of ammunition, hand grenades, food, water, spare clothing. The demo men also carried blasting caps wrapped in cotton batting. When he'd finished, McGee had added an additional hundred pounds to his body weight and had to be pulled up the narrow aluminum stairs that hung below the jump door.

The plane carrying McGee and other men from the regimental headquarters section was so heavily loaded with troopers and equipment bundles that the pilot could not get it off the ground. When he reached the end of the runway, he aborted the takeoff and merely taxied cross-country—the land around the runway was as flat and hard as the runway itself—to come around for another try. The copilot came back and asked some of the troopers to move to the cockpit, and the rest to slide as far forward as possible along the seats. The trick worked, and the plane was soon airborne.

When McGee settled in his seat, trussed up in his heavy gear, the butt of his rifle case was right in front of his chin. He could not lower his head to sleep. When he saw other troopers unhooking their reserve

parachutes—worn slung across the belly—to relieve some of the pressure for the long flight, McGee unhooked his, too. He pushed the butt of his weapon away from his teeth and was soon asleep. Soon he was awakened by the sounds of the men around him, shifting their gear and buckling their reserve chutes into place. McGee tugged on the chest strap of his harness, which buckled easily. The second buckle of the reserve chute, which went around his rifle, wouldn't budge. The web straps, made tight on the ground, had no leeway, almost as if he'd grown or the harness had shrunk during the flight.

Now McGee was worried. His reserve was unhooked, his rifle case loose. If he couldn't get ready, he could throw off the timing of the entire stick, or simply be shoved aside and have to return to Africa, humiliated and probably facing court-martial.

The first jump command came back. "Stand up and hook up!"

The jumpmaster on McGee's plane was Lieutenant Colonel Herbert Batcheller, the regimental executive officer. While the other troopers struggled to their feet and hooked their static lines to the overhead cable, McGee fumbled with his reserve. All around him, the other troopers were ready. He lagged behind, a threat to the integrity of the team.

"Sound off!" Batcheller yelled over the sound of the engines.

McGee had seen jumpers hesitate before; he had even seen men refuse to jump. They were washed out of the paratroops, sent away in disgrace.

This, he thought, *will be worse.*

The men would think he deserted them in the face of battle.

When it came his turn to sound off, McGee said, "Not ready!"

"What's the matter?" Batcheller yelled.

"I can't hook up my reserve."

"This is a hell of a time to find out, McGee," Batcheller said. Then, to the man in front of McGee, Batcheller said, "Fix it." The

paratrooper in front of him was huge, 225 pounds without his equip-ment. He turned, lifted his knee to McGee's chest, and pressed in all his weight. The buckle snapped into place, the big man removed his knee, and McGee breathed again.

Relieved, McGee closed up the stick. Batcheller was looking out the door; everyone else in the stick had his eyes on the lights.

The red light came on, then, moments later, the green light.

But Batcheller did not move. He could see that they were still over water. The green light stayed on for a long minute, then went back to red as a sheepish pilot realized his mistake. Batcheller, unfazed, stayed at his post.

McGee could see, in the darkened plane, only the red light, and the dim silhouettes of his buddies. Occasionally, something lit up the frames of the aircraft windows. Even if he wanted to bend over and look out the window, he wouldn't have been able. Stuffed into his parachute harness, saddled with heavy equipment, squeezed between the man in front and the man behind, his rifle like a big splint on his chest, he just wanted to get clear of the aircraft.

Then the red light turned to green, and Batcheller went out the door, followed quickly by the others. The stick moved almost as a sin-gle organism, and McGee was merely a part of it. Shuffling to the door wasn't so much an act of will as an act of surrender.

They'd been told that the jump altitude would be around four hundred feet. McGee was surprised, when his chute opened, to see that they were at least a thousand feet up. At least, he noted, they were over land. That high up, McGee felt exposed, almost naked. The big sky was brightly lit with tracers and flares; in the glow, the other parachutes looked like big mushroom tops. When he dipped below the horizon, the light suddenly disappeared, and McGee's eyes couldn't adjust fast enough to see how fast the ground was coming up below him. He even lost sight of the other paratroopers; then he hit the

ground, hard. He could hear the war over the next ridge, a distant *pop pop pop* of rifles and machine guns, but all around him was silence. McGee rolled onto his back and unsnapped the tight harness, then quickly yanked his rifle from the padded container. He jammed the pieces of the weapon together, checked the action and the safety, and fixed his bayonet. He had arrived. All the long months of training, all the road marches and endless field problems, all the sacrifice, had brought him to this point. He took a step toward the sound of the guns. Then he fell hard, facedown. His leg was broken.

McGee lay still in the darkness, listening for sounds close by. There was plenty of noise and light over the ridge, but around him, in what seemed to be some sort of valley, there was nothing but darkness and lonely silence. He looked around, saw olive trees, felt that the ground beneath him had been plowed, although the deep furrows were baked by the Sicilian sun until they felt like concrete ridges. One of these furrows had broken his leg.

After a few minutes, his leg began to throb, but he caught his breath when he heard rustling in the undergrowth nearby. Then silence. Then rustling again, closer and right in front of him.

McGee hoped that whoever was in the bushes knew the challenge and countersign. He readied his weapon, pointed his rifle at the noise and yelled, "George!"

"Marshall!" came back out of the dark. Then "Marshall!" again, and again and again. The area was full of troopers, each one waiting for someone else to make the first sound. When a flare rose over the ridge, McGee saw that for all the answers he got to his challenge, the noise in front of him was made by a dog sniffing around in the grass.

After dawn, a medic attended to McGee's leg, which was broken low. The medic removed the boot and fashioned a splint out of McGee's bayonet scabbard. When the medic left, McGee realized he could not move with the makeshift splint, so he pulled it off, put his boot back on and laced it up tight. He would have to hobble, and it was going to be painful, but he was going to get himself to an aid station.

When the green light blinked on above Colonel Jim Gavin's head, he leaped through the door, followed at split-second intervals by the rest of the stick. The last man in the line was Jack "Beaver" Thompson, the bearded journalist from the *Chicago Tribune*. Thompson had made one other jump: into North Africa with a battalion of the 504th Parachute Infantry Regiment. Thompson was armed with a typewriter.

Gavin landed hard, collapsed his chute, slid out of the harness, and checked his weapon. More planes rumbled overhead, but in the darkness it was difficult to see what was happening on the ground. Gavin began moving in what he believed was the same line the plane followed, the accepted technique for "rolling up the stick," gathering the paratroopers who, presumably, have also landed more or less in a straight line. When he saw the outline of a man, Gavin raised his weapon, braced himself for what might come, and gave the challenge.

"George."

"Marshall" came out of the dark. Gavin hurried forward, glad for the company of Major Ben Vandervoort and Captain Al Ireland, both of the regimental staff.

None of the officers recognized the area from their many hours of map study. Even Gavin, who flew over the objectives in a reconnaissance flight a month earlier, was stumped. Since the prevailing winds were out of the northwest, the men speculated that they had probably dropped too far to the southeast. They checked out their compasses. Some wore luminous versions on their wrists, like oversize watches; others carried World War I–vintage models in leather pouches. After checking his bearings, Gavin decided they'd head northwest in the hopes of finding the right drop zone. Before setting out, he looked around him in the dark; he was now in command of five of his thirty-four hundred men.[1]

It was slow going over the rugged and rocky countryside and Gavin, in the lead with Vandervoort beside him, stuck to the shadows as they hurried through olive groves, climbed over stone walls, and darted across moonlit roads. Along the way, the group picked up another fifteen or so troopers. They could hear firing around them, but so far, none of it was close.

An hour after landing, Gavin heard a voice close by, but couldn't tell if it was English. Signaling for his men to take cover, he hurried to the shelter of a stone wall that paralleled a dirt road. Gavin had been a soldier for nearly twenty years, but this was his first face-to-face encounter with the enemy. The colonel lifted his head just high enough over the wall to see and raised his carbine, and there, hands thrust deep in his pockets, was a lone Italian soldier walking down the road, singing happily to himself.

"*Alto,*" Gavin said aloud, freezing the man in his tracks.

Just then Ben Vandervoort rushed onto the road through an opening in the wall, a .45-caliber pistol in one hand and a knife in the other. "I'll take care of him," Vandervoort said.

Gavin was not sure what his operations officer meant, but he told the aggressive major to get the prisoner off the road. *Here is a chance,* Gavin thought, *to find out exactly where we are, if we are even in Sicily.*

The solitary Italian was suddenly surrounded by six threatening forms. He could make out their foreign uniforms and the distinctive bloused boots worn by paratroopers. He and his comrades had been told by the German propaganda machine that American paratroopers tortured and murdered their prisoners, that they were all long-term convicts of the worst stripe who had gained their freedom by volunteering for hazardous duty. This image was fueled by the hairstyles some of the troopers favored: shaved heads or Mohawk cuts.

"*Dove Palermo?*" Gavin asked, but the soldier was too frightened to answer.

"*Dove Siracusa?*" Gavin said. He named the major city on each end of the island. All the soldier had to do was point, and Gavin would at least know he had landed in the right country. But the man was in his own nightmare, on a deserted road, surrounded by armed men he couldn't speak to, who had come to kill him.

A frustrated Gavin didn't want to stand around waiting for an enemy patrol to discover his tiny group; he needed to get to his objective. But they could not simply abandon the prisoner, who would spread the alarm. Gavin reluctantly decided they must take the Italian with them.

Vandervoort said he'd learned, in a course on handling prisoners, how to keep the man from running: remove the prisoner's belt and cut the buttons off his fly so that he'd have to hold his pants up. Vandervoort holstered his pistol and poked his big trench knife against the Italian's chest, just to let the man know he meant business. The terrified soldier could only mutter, "*Mamma mia, mamma mia.*"

Vandervoort made his move. He grabbed the man's trousers as moonlight glinted off the knife blade. This was too much for the prisoner, who clearly thought the Americans were about to castrate him. Although he was unarmed and outnumbered six to one, he fought. Screaming, he grabbed the knife blade with his right hand and pulled the Americans down on top of him in a kicking, wailing tangle of arms and legs. Then, incredibly, he got away. One minute the paratroopers had him surrounded, and the next he was gone.

"What in the hell did you think you were doing?" a furious Gavin asked Vandervoort. Wisely, the major did not answer.[2]

Gavin was less than two hours into his war. He did not know where he was or where his objectives were. He did not know where his men were or where the enemy was. He and five of the toughest fighters the United States Army had produced had just been given the slip by an unarmed, terrified Italian soldier. Finally, as the group pressed on, something went right: the men saw shellbursts on the distant horizon. Following a maxim he had learned as a cadet at West Point, "march to the sound of the guns," Gavin led his group westward.

Gavin's fears about the lack of pilot training proved well founded, as many of the pilots had become lost over the Mediterranean. Many of them even missed the landmark of Malta. Of course, even if they had been allowed all the training they needed, the stiff crosswinds still would have scattered the formations.

All but two of the lead group of thirty-nine aircraft carrying Ed Krause's Third Battalion found Malta and turned onto the proper course, but by the time they identified the drop zones north of Gela, only nine of the aircraft were on target. The rest were scattered along the southern coast of Sicily. The next group found Sicily and even Gela, but were unable to locate the drop zone through the dust and smoke churned up by the preinvasion bombing. Some planes turned back out to sea for another run, and some troopers landed within three miles of the DZ, but most were dropped some fifteen miles to the east, near Vittoria. The third group, carrying Arthur Gorham's First Battalion, was scattered early in the flight. Gorham and part of Ed Sayre's A Company landed close to their drop zone, but a large percentage of the troopers landed fifty miles away, in the British invasion sector. The group carrying Gavin was the most widely scattered, with some troopers dropped up to sixty miles from the DZ. Gavin landed some thirty miles from where he wanted to be. The fifth group managed to stay together, but they got lost together and dropped Mark Alexander's Second Battalion twenty-five miles from their DZ. Three pilots, in direct violation of orders, refused to drop their troopers and brought the angry men back to Africa rather than simply dumping them into the darkness.

The whole jump was over in about an hour, and the pilots turned around and headed back to Africa. In their debriefings back at the air-

fields, the aircrews were overly optimistic about their success rate, es-
timating that 80 percent of the troopers were dropped on the proper
drop zones. In fact, only one unit, Bill Follmer's I Company, was
dropped intact on the right DZ. Gavin later estimated that only 12 percent of his troops actually landed as planned.[3]

Gavin and his troops had worked hard to prove that a mass jump
of this size was possible, yet much of what they had accomplished was
undone before any of the 505th's soldiers even saw the enemy. Instead
of landing on a handful of tight drop zones, the GIs were scattered
over nearly a thousand square miles of Sicily. Gavin's experience was
not unusual, as men found themselves in small groups or even alone.
Fortunately, Gavin had trained his men that the most important thing
was to get on with the mission, to attack the enemy wherever he could
be found. It would take an unprecedented display from the junior
leaders and from individual soldiers, but there was a chance the paratroopers could still succeed.

All through the night move, Gavin and his staff officers consulted their
maps at intervals, hoping to recognize some landmark that would tell
them where they were. When the column halted, the troopers knelt or
stood, facing outward, watching to see if they were being followed,
their eyes straining against the darkness for enemy patrols.

But the long hours of being awake took their toll. At some point, a
tired trooper failed to notice that the man in front of him, the only one
he could see, had moved off. The little column was then split into two
elements, but the leaders and most of the men weren't even aware
there had been a break. This kind of thing happened regularly in training, but every sergeant and corporal in the regiment guarded against it
by constant vigilance.[4] The officers, unaccustomed to doing a noncom's job, weren't as attentive. Soon Gavin and the first few men in
the column were no longer head of a group of twenty; by daylight the

commander's patrol had been reduced to six men, including Ireland and Vandervoort.

The paratroopers approached two farmhouses, but the locals were too terrified to communicate with the Americans, so Gavin and his tiny patrol pushed north and west. As they crested some high ground, there was a burst of small-arms fire, and the lead trooper went down. Gavin hit the ground, pressing himself to the earth as the rounds struck close enough to spray dirt in his face.

The instinct in this situation was to take cover. Through training, the soldiers had been taught to immediately return fire, forcing the enemy to take cover so the GIs could move. Put enough accurate fire on an enemy position, and he might even stop shooting.

Gavin raised his carbine and began firing, but the lightweight weapon, which was proving unreliable all over the island, jammed. Vandervoort, six feet to his left, was having the same trouble with his weapon. Then Gavin saw something remarkable: an Italian officer, standing no more then fifty yards away and observing them through field glasses, as if watching a training exercise. The officer's head and shoulders were partly hidden by low hanging branches, but his leather puttees and reddish brown trousers were clearly visible. Al Ireland saw the officer, too, and fired a burst from his tommy gun. The Italian crumbled to the ground.

Gavin could see that the trooper who had been on point had fallen almost in the enemy position; the man was dead. The enemy firing increased, and then Gavin heard an explosion that might have been a mortar round. He decided that they had run into an enemy platoon, at least, and that he should pull back and go around. Gavin shouted at the others to move, while he provided covering fire with his uncooperative carbine. The troopers backed up, then made a wide circle to avoid the enemy position. They'd had a close call and suffered one man killed, but they were still moving.

Early on July 10, Gavin saw something that gave him pause: a

destroyed German scout car, the kind used by the reconnaissance elements of a panzer division. He got a sick feeling in the pit of his stomach:
there were not supposed to be German armored units on the island.
When he was briefed on the enemy situation just before D-day, Gavin
and his division commander, Matt Ridgway, were told that the only combat units they would run into were Italian, although there might be a few
German "technicians" on the island, advising their allies.

In fact, Allied headquarters knew that two German tank divisions
had moved to Sicily.

Throughout the campaign in North Africa, Allied intelligence was
privy to the highest levels of German communications, thanks to the
work of the code-breakers at Bletchley Park, outside London. There
the British government brought together a team of highly intelligent, if
sometimes peculiar, characters with expertise in everything from
mathematics and cipher systems to crossword puzzles. Their success
in breaking the codes used by enemy high command—code-named
Ultra—meant that the Allies knew the big picture of German troop
deployments.

The more the Allies used Ultra intercepts, the more they came to
rely on this source of information, the more paranoid they became lest
the Germans learn that their codes had been compromised; thus
Ultra's effectiveness was limited. The Allies could not simply act on
every bit of information; doing so would show their hand. It was one
thing for the Allies to know what the Germans were doing. It was another for the Germans to know that the Allies knew.

As if this weren't enough to worry about, Allied planners were concerned that someone who knew about Ultra would fall into German
hands. Paratroopers, because they dropped behind enemy lines, were
more likely to be captured than regular infantry. Gavin's aerial reconnaissance of the invasion area drop zones a month before D-day had
alarmed Allied intelligence officers. If they had told Gavin about the
presence of the panzers, and Gavin had been shot down in June or

captured on D-day, this precious resource provided by the years of hard work at Bletchley Park might have been compromised. Although it was an agonizing decision for the highest commanders, it was a deliberate one. The paratroop commanders—Gavin and Ridgway—were not told of the presence of German armored units on Sicily.[5]

The airborne commanders weren't the only ones operating in the dark. Communications between the Germans and Italians, who were supposed to be working together, were poor and got worse in the first hours of the invasion. The Germans did not put much faith in the fighting abilities of their allies, and their defensive plans took this into account. Major General Paul Conrath, commander of the Hermann Goering Parachute Panzer Division, was responsible for the section of the southern coast considered the most likely target for the Allied invasion. Conrath's study of the terrain convinced him that the most likely landing beaches were in the area of Gela and Scoglitti. He positioned his forces far enough inland to be out of the range of U.S. and British naval guns, but close enough to rush to the attack once he determined where the main enemy effort was. The bulk of his division was held near Caltagirone, roughly twenty-five miles from the invasion beaches of the First Division at Gela and the Forty-fifth Division at Scoglitti. Gavin later wrote that if Conrath "had known the details of the Allied plan, he could not have picked a better location to assemble his division."[6] The Germans were so sure that Gela would be a target that the defenders had conducted a map maneuver exercise just days before the Allied invasion. The commanders and staffs were familiar with the road networks they would use to launch their counterattacks. Fortunately for the Americans, the Fifteenth Panzer Division, which played a crucial role in the defensive exercises, was shifted to the western part of the island just after the map exercise to protect the Sicilian capital, Palermo.

Conrath organized his forces into two battle groups, called *Kampfgruppen*. His plan called for the right battle group to attack through

Niscemi, across the plain surrounding Ponte Olivo airfield, and over the mass of hills called Piano Lupo, to hit the Allies near Gela. Conrath's left thrust was aimed from Biscari along a low ridge at the beaches near Scoglitti.

Conrath got his first warning of the Allied move around 10:00 P.M. on July 9, when a German reconnaissance flight spotted the huge fleet heading toward southern Sicily. Conrath immediately ordered to his commanders to prepare to move once the Allied main attack was identified. But thanks to the poor state of communications and the island's primitive infrastructure, some of Conrath's subordinate units received no orders at all, and Conrath had no communication with either his own corps headquarters, or the Italian units in his area of operations.

To make things worse for the defenders, even the smallest bands of paratroopers scattered over the island set out to create as much chaos as they could. Men moving cross-country cut phone lines where they found them. More than once, a German or Italian commander sent out a courier on a motorcycle or bicycle, only to find out later that the courier—and the dispatches—disappeared, the victim of a hasty ambush. The entire southern part of the island was thrown into chaos. Reports reaching headquarters claimed that thousands of paratroopers had dropped into the area through which Conrath hoped to advance. (Reports at the headquarters of the Italian defenders ran as high as thirty thousand paratroopers.)[7] The Germans had no way of knowing that the airborne units were tiny and disorganized.

This disruption, of course, had been part of Gavin's plan all along. In fact, it was just this kind of small-scale fighting, aimed at confusing and alarming an enemy, that early proponents of airborne warfare saw as the paratroopers' biggest potential contribution to the fight.

One of the junior leaders who understood and acted on Gavin's intent was Lieutenant Peter J. Eaton of the Third Battalion, 504th PIR (one of the units attached to the 505th to make it a regimental combat team). Eaton landed two miles northwest of Biscari (present-day

Acate) and immediately went to work, gathering some thirty-six troopers from three different aircraft. Once he had his patrol organized, he determined that he wasn't far from his original objective, the high ground south of Niscemi. His entire battalion of nearly five hundred men had been given the mission to block the road and bottle up any enemy units in or north of the town. As he pointed his men toward Niscemi, which was miles away across hilly, enemy-held terrain, Eaton had no way of knowing how many other 3/504th men were headed to the fight. But Gavin's instructions had been clear: the biggest mistake a leader could make on this night was to sit and wait for further instructions.

When the sun came up on D-day, July 10, Eaton's point man signaled: enemy in sight. The lieutenant moved forward quickly and saw, on a dusty road just below them, two small Italian trucks towing antitank guns. The paratroopers went into their practiced drill, moving quickly into firing positions that covered the road, checking their rifles and grenades and bayonets. On Eaton's signal the patrol opened fire, riddling the trucks and kicking up dust on the roadside. Some of the Italian soldiers never knew what hit them; those who tried to return fire were cut down, and a few managed to dive for cover and scramble away through the low brush.

Eaton's men stepped out into the road carefully. The lieutenant and his sergeants examined the guns and load of ammunition, which had not been damaged. Suddenly the paratroopers were much more heavily armed and felt more confident that they could handle whatever came down the road next. They went to work quickly, hauling the guns to the sides of the road, where they prepared concealed positions. They removed the Italian dead and pushed the trucks out of sight, then posted observers on the hillside where they had a long-range view. Other paratroopers unwrapped the small antitank mines they'd been carrying in their pockets and set them up on the road. They used their machine guns and captured antitank guns to cover the minefield: anyone trying to remove the mines would be under the guns.

Then they waited, being careful to stay out of sight, as the sun climbed and the day grew hotter and even the insects slowed down.

About twelve-thirty, Eaton got word that an enemy column was moving toward them on the road from the direction of Niscemi. When they came into view, the lieutenant estimated that he was facing a battalion of Italian infantry—several hundred men—accompanied by a small tank. But Eaton had picked his site well, just as he'd been coached on countless field problems back at Benning and Bragg and in North Africa. The hills channeled the infantry, meaning the enemy could only approach on a narrow front (thus reducing their advantage of numbers). When the GI gun crew destroyed the tank, the enemy infantry lost interest in trying to force the position. Eaton's band, smaller than a full-sized platoon, drove the enemy back.[8]

This kind of action was repeated all over southern Sicily. Reports reaching enemy headquarters tended to exaggerate American strength— no infantry battalion commander would willingly report that his move was blocked by a double handful of stubborn GIs. German and Italian commanders, both those cut off back at headquarters and those in the field, assumed that the paratroopers were executing a bold, deliberate plan. In fact, the ad hoc units thrown together by various junior leaders kept the enemy off balance and guessing. The defenders had never encountered an airborne assault before, and as Gavin, Ridgway, and others had predicted, they did not know how to react.

8

SMALL BATTLES

Dean McCandless, First Battalion's communications officer, had slept on the flight from North Africa, arms crossed on his reserve, head bobbing. He figured it was his body's way to avoid worrying (one he would re-create on each of his combat jumps for the remainder of the war). He landed without getting too banged up, and quickly located one of his men, Ott Carpenter, after clearing his parachute. They couldn't find their radio bundles, but they were soon joined by a half-dozen other troopers, and the group began moving along a road in a direction McCandless thought would take them to the battalion objective.

They hadn't gone far when an enemy machine gun, sighted on the road, opened fire, scattering the invaders. McCandless immediately hit the ground and crawled for cover. When he stopped moving, the only trooper still with him was Carpenter. They moved away from the machine gun, and though they were down to two, it was easier to move quietly with two men than with eight. Shortly after they began moving, they heard voices, which McCandless guessed was another enemy outpost covering the road they'd been following.

Gavin had told his men that the hand grenade was the weapon of choice in the darkness, and now McCandless and Carpenter prepared to throw a couple of grenades in the direction of the voices they heard.

Before they pulled the pins, it dawned on McCandless that some of the other half-dozen missing troopers might be nearby, and that their grenades might hit some of their scattered comrades. The two communications men pulled back and made a wide circle around the enemy. As the sky lightened in the east, they spotted a hilltop that offered a vantage point. If they couldn't see their comrades, perhaps they could at least figure out where they were.

The terrain here was almost as empty of vegetation as the treeless flat of North Africa, but with hills. If a fold in the ground didn't block his view, a man could see for miles. The hills—brown in the summer sun, hard-baked, and smelling of burned grass—were covered with a patchwork of rocky fields and stunted orchards, bordered by stone walls or fences made of rows of cactus. The whole scene was capped by a dome of clear, china-blue sky. A dirt road crossed the hilltop they chose, with a shallow drainage ditch and a low hedge between. McCandless and Carpenter scraped shallow holes in the rocky soil at the bottom of the ditch. When the sun was fully up, they saw a welcome sight: the invasion fleet lying offshore. Small landing craft bustled back and forth to the larger ships, disgorging more combat power onto the island with each trip. Although they weren't in contact with any other Americans, McCandless and Carpenter knew they weren't alone on the island.

McCandless was carrying code books, as encoding and decoding radio traffic was part of his job as communications officer. Now, isolated and cut off from the battalion, with the chance of being captured, he worried about the code books falling into enemy hands. He moved along the ditch, dug a hole and covered the books.

Their little hilltop outpost offered a vantage point, but it also limited their movement. If they moved along the road, or tried to strike out cross-country in search of the battalion, they could easily be spotted from a distance. The two men lay low during the morning hours, watching things develop around them.

The Navy was in the fight, and the two men saw the muzzle flashes on the big ships lying offshore, and then, seconds later, heard the big shells cutting the air overhead, like trains passing by. The firepower was reassuring, even though there was no guarantee the Navy wouldn't shoot at their hilltop. Both men wished they were in closer contact with other GIs.

About midday on July 10, McCandless and Carpenter heard vehicles on the road. The hedge between the ditch and the roadway gave them some cover, and they pressed themselves deep into their foxholes as three German tanks clanked up the road. If the tankers spotted them, the paratroopers wouldn't stand a chance. Carpenter suggested that they might have to surrender, a prospect neither of them relished. Then they figured that there was no room for prisoners inside the vehicles.

"They'd probably just shoot us," the men agreed.

The lead vehicle stopped just on the other side of the hedge from where the two paratroopers lay in the ditch. McCandless looked up from his hiding place, through the hedge, and saw the tank commander just a few yards away, looking through field glasses at the invasion fleet below. Fortunately for the paratroopers, the sight of the fleet kept the German's attention, and he never looked at the ground around his vehicle. McCandless and Carpenter remained frozen in place, with violent death close by, trying not to move or breathe too loudly, hoping none of the tankers dismounted to relieve himself beside the road. For a few agonizing minutes, the big tank above them belched fumes, the ugly snout of its main gun pointed menacingly toward the beach. The tanks couldn't hit the Navy ships, but they could make quick work of a couple of infantry soldiers lying in the open. Finally, the German commander called down to his driver, and the lead tank lurched toward the beach, with the others following. McCandless and Carpenter breathed again.

While the fight raged on around them and huge Navy shells passed overhead, Carpenter spotted a herd of cattle grazing peacefully

in a field below them. McCandless noticed that when they were looking at the cattle head on, the silhouette looked like that of a man.
Maybe they could use this fact to their advantage, McCandless
mused, passing through the herd toward the American beachhead.

Carpenter didn't think this was such a great idea. In fact, he
pointed out, the cattle looked so much like people that perhaps there
were already people down there. While McCandless considered this,
the two men saw an enemy patrol of some seven or eight men moving
across the field where the cattle were grazing, heading right toward the
two Americans. The paratroopers had already escaped detection by the
tank commander; how much longer would their luck hold out?

The GIs checked their weapons. Carpenter had a tommy gun,
while McCandless was armed with a carbine and a pistol. They
crouched close to each other in the ditch and watched the patrol move
toward the base of the very hill they occupied. Carpenter said he
would start shooting at the soldier farthest to the right and work his
way toward the middle. McCandless would start with the soldier on
the left. It was about as detailed a plan as two lone men could come
up with on short notice. The odds weren't good, but the troopers
would have surprise on their side.

As the small patrol drew closer, the rise of the hill soon hid them
from view. Carpenter and McCandless tensed and got ready for the
enemy to crest the hill right in front of them. The two Americans lay
like that—fingers on their triggers, hearts in their throats, for what
seemed like hours. McCandless's imagination worked overtime. Had
the enemy spotted them? Were they even now sneaking up on the two
Americans? Were they going to come from the side? From behind?

The patrol never appeared. Finally, McCandless and Carpenter
accepted the fact that the enemy had bypassed the high ground, and
they relaxed a bit. They decided to wait for sunset before heading for
the battalion objective.

Then–Lieutenant Colonel Jim Gavin inspects soldiers' field equipment, Fort Benning, Georgia. (*Photo courtesy Barbara Gavin Fauntleroy*)

Above: British foreign secretary Anthony Eden visits the 505th at Fort Bragg, March 1943. Gavin later wrote, "He knew that we, green as we were, in four months' time would take on the battle-seasoned Wehrmacht by spearheading the assault onto the island of Sicily." *(U.S. Army photo, courtesy Barbara Gavin Fauntleroy)*

Right: Arthur Gorham as a lieutenant. He would become the first commander of the First Battalion, 505th Parachute Infantry Regiment. *(Photo courtesy Bruce B. G. Clarke)*

Otis Sampson in the horse cavalry, Fort Ethan Allen, Vermont, 1930.
(Photo courtesy Otis Sampson)

Sampson in Sicily, 1943. Sampson and Mark Alexander found the same studio photographer, who favored this pose. *(Photo courtesy Otis Sampson)*

Major Mark Alexander, Second Battalion commander, Sicily. "When Major Mark Alexander, the former Kansas National Guard private, climbed aboard his C-47 on the evening of July 9, he had been in command of the Second Battalion for less than two weeks, and his total military experience amounted to two years and nine months. Now he was taking five hundred men into combat." *(Photo supplied by Mark Alexander)*

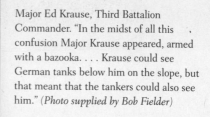

Major Ed Krause, Third Battalion Commander. "In the midst of all this confusion Major Krause appeared, armed with a bazooka. . . . Krause could see German tanks below him on the slope, but that meant that the tankers could also see him." *(Photo supplied by Bob Fielder)*

Lieutenant Bob Fielder, Third Battalion communications officer. "With his face pressed to the ground, Fielder couldn't see the enemy. But they saw him. The tank opened fire with its machine gun, stitching the dirt just beside him." (*Photo supplied by Bob Fielder*)

Second Lieutenant George Clark, I Company. To complete his independent mission on D-day, Clark walked several miles on a shattered ankle. (*Photo courtesy George Clark*)

Berge Avadanian *(right)* and Tom Michaud clean fish caught using Italian hand grenades near Trapani. *(Photo courtesy Berge Avadanian)*

Sergeant John Sabo *(left)* and Corporal Harold Eatman *(right)*, H Company. "The machine gun opened up, only yards away, and Eatman felt something hitting his legs and back. His first thought was, *This is what it feels like to be shot.*" *(Photo courtesy Harold Eatman)*

Fred Morgan, A Company medic, shown here in Normandy mid-June 1944. "When a wounded man or his buddies yelled for a medic, a medic came up. It didn't matter that the unit was under fire, moving forward, or retreating, the medics' first concern was always to take care of the wounded, and they often did so at great risk to themselves. And for this the infantrymen loved them." *(Photo courtesy Fred Morgan)*

Staff Sergeant Tim Dyas. The second youngest man in A Company, Dyas smoked a pipe to look older. *(Photo courtesy Tim Dyas)*

June 1943, Oujda, French Morocco. After nearly a month in Africa, lean E Company troopers practice "parachute landing falls" from platforms. *(Photo courtesy of John Cages, front rank, second from left)*

Jim Gavin talks to the troops days before the invasion, Kairouan, North Africa. *(Photo courtesy Barbara Gavin Fauntleroy)*

Above: Captain Ed Sayre (*right*) receives the Distinguished Service Cross from Major General Matt Ridgway (*left*) in North Africa, late summer, 1943. "Holding his map, Gorham pointed at the road junction that was the objective of the entire 3,400-man regiment. He didn't have to say that A Company would have to attempt its capture alone." (*Photo courtesy Ed Sayre*)

Right: Jack Norton (*right*) and Bill Harris photographed near Garibaldi Square, Naples, Italy, October 1943. Nearly killed by an enemy machine gun during his first hour in the war (the near misses ripped his jacket), Norton went on to make every combat jump and fight in every campaign with the Eighty-second Airborne Division during World War II.

Beaver Thompson of the *Chicago Tribune (left)* and Gavin at the railroad crossing below Biazza Ridge, July 11, 1943. Note how censors scratched out Gavin's shoulder patch. *(U.S. Army photo)*

Troops of Third Battalion moving up the gentle eastern slope of Biazza Ridge, early on July 11. Gavin sent individuals to the left, but used Krause's nearly intact battalion to hold the critical right of his line. *(U.S. Army photo)*

Mostly Third Battalion troopers at the gatekeeper's cottage below Biazza Ridge, Sunday morning, July 11. These men are minutes from joining the fight. (*U.S. Army photo*)

Regimental staff and radio operators at Biazza Ridge. Includes Major Hagan, Third Battalion exec; Captains Wall and Maress; Lieutenants Fielder, Harris, and Ward. "When Gavin drew close, Fielder said, 'We won't take off, sir.' Gavin, who knew he had problems but didn't assume that this was one of them, looked at Fielder and said, 'So what?'" (*U.S. Army photo*)

Major Ed Krause and Private Faley inspect a panzer knocked out near Biazza Ridge. *(Photo supplied by Bob Fielder)*

Krause *(left)* and Faley with one of the German field pieces that caused so much trouble for the paratroopers. *(Photo supplied by Bob Fielder)*

Matt Ridgway, who commanded the Eighty-second Airborne Division in Sicily (*left*) and Jim Gavin. Photo taken in winter 1945, when Gavin was division commander and Ridgway had moved up to command the XVIII Airborne Corps. (*Photo courtesy Barbara Gavin Fauntleroy*)

Troops of Third Battalion, after the battle, pose on a captured Tiger at Biazza Ridge. (*U.S. Army photo*)

Jim Gavin around VE Day. When he took command of the Eighty-second Airborne Division in the summer of 1944, Gavin became the youngest division commander since the Civil War. *(Photo courtesy Barbara Gavin Fauntleroy)*

The marker at Ponte Dirillo. The plaque is incomplete, and includes names of paratroopers killed in other locations in Sicily. The whole area is neatly maintained by troops from a nearby U.S. Army signal station. (*Photo by Dealyn Ruggero*)

* * *

Major Mark Alexander's flight was uneventful, and he spent most of the three hours standing in the open doorway, watching the Mediterranean glimmer in the thin moonlight. When the red light came on, Alexander began his jump commands, and within minutes, his entire stick was standing, static lines hooked to the cables overhead, the troopers all facing him in the rear of the plane. Alexander, in his position by the door, could look down and see that the aircraft was still over water.

Then the green light came on.

The troopers, reacting as they had been trained, all began shuffling for the doorway, eager to get out of the aircraft as quickly as possible. The heavily weighted paratroopers would have no chance in the water below. Alexander, horrified, did something he'd never had to do before: he blocked the doorway, with the help of the man immediately behind him, who could also see the water. The entire stick pushed against them, but Alexander had a grip on the door frame. To the men behind, he just looked like a reluctant jumper, and they all knew what to do in that situation: push harder.

Alexander screamed over the aircraft engines.

"Move back! Move back!"

Finally, the men were convinced that the major was right and the green light was wrong. When the pressure released, Alexander clumped up the crowded center of the aircraft to the cockpit, where a sheepish Tommy Thompson explained that his copilot had hit the green light too early. Cursing, Alexander returned to the jump door.

It became obvious, minutes later, when they finally did clear the coast, as a considerable amount of tracer fire climbed toward the aircraft.

Alexander had made it a point of his discussions with Tommy Thompson and Colonel Cerny, the commander the Sixty-fourth Troop

Carrier Group, that, no matter where they were dropped, he wanted Second Battalion dropped together so that they could organize quickly and fight as a unit. In a display of disciplined flying that was uncommon that night, the pilots managed to keep the planes close together, and the Second Battalion was dropped in a relatively tight drop zone, albeit far from their objective.

The planned DZ for Alexander's battalion sat at an elevation of some 120 meters above sea level. But this formation missed the planned drop zone and instead came in over taller hills, the aircraft holding a near level flight as the ground below them jumped up. Instead of dropping from 600 or 700 feet, Alexander's men leaped from airplanes that were only 350 to 400 feet above the ground. The parachutes barely had time to open or slow the jumpers' descent before the men slammed into the rock-hard Sicilian hillsides. The result was a large number of broken ankles and legs.

Alexander, moving backward as he hit, banged his head on a stone wall and was dragged by his parachute before he could fight his way free. As he rolled and struggled to gain his footing and collapse his chute, he could feel a familiar pain in his leg, which he had hurt in a training jump back in Alabama. He could stand and walk, but it was going to be painful for a while.

Alexander's landing was difficult; others fared worse. One of the battalion surgeons, a recent medical school graduate named Kurt Klee, landed in the barbed wire entanglement directly in front of an enemy pillbox. When the soldiers inside saw him struggling just a few feet away, they opened fire, killing the paratrooper before he could even clear his chute. Another man, Corporal Fred Freeland, got hung up in the same area and saw what happened to Klee. He played dead, hanging limply in the wire and hoping the enemy wouldn't fire a few rounds into him just to confirm he was dead.

Mark Alexander's leg hurt, but he could still hobble fairly well. He quickly found Richard "Teddy" Tedeschi, the Italian-American GI from the Bronx who would act as his interpreter. The two men began knocking on the doors of the farmhouses in the immediate area, with Alexander posing questions to figure out where they were. They collected a few other men, and the little group kept close to their commander. One of the GIs accidentally shot an old man who appeared suddenly, startling the young paratrooper. Hearing of this, Alexander went to that house to check on and console the distraught family of the wounded civilian.

Lieutenant Harold Thain, executive officer of D Battery of the 456th Parachute Field Artillery, was the jumpmaster of a plane with only eight men, but a heavy load of radios and a pack howitzer (so-called because it could be broken down in pieces and packed by Army mule, or—in the case of the airborne—in bundles). When the green light came on and the troopers started out the door, one man ducked by Thain, headed for the rear of the aircraft. Overcome by fear, he had decided that he would rather face court-martial than jump. Thain tried to grab the trooper, wasting precious seconds and putting a big gap between himself and the rest of the stick, a delay that would translate into quite a distance on the ground. Thain landed, alert, energized and ready for a fight, but instead found a silence that was eerie after the hours of drumming aircraft engines. He was alone on the battlefield, far away from his comrades, and he cursed the man who had refused to jump.

Thain listened carefully, and soon made out the sounds of other men moving nearby. Nervous, straining to see, his finger on the trigger of his weapon, he tried the challenge, and two troopers from the 456th emerged from the blackness. The men were not from D Battery, but their presence gave Thain confidence. The three men consulted their compasses; since the planes were supposed to fly north over the drop zone, they headed south to roll up the stick. Thain checked his watch; it was about 0100, the night black and silent.

After moving for a while, Thain had to urinate. Even though it was dark, and even though the men had been living in close proximity to each other for over a year, Thain stepped behind a tree. When he came back out, his companions were gone. He could hardly believe it; he had managed to find some other paratroopers without getting shot, and now they'd slipped away from him somehow. (He found out later that the two men had been captured by a German patrol, but they managed to escape during the night and made it to the battalion, without their weapons but otherwise unharmed.)

There was nothing to do but push on alone. By first light, Thain was exhausted and not at all sure as to where he was. He'd been up and moving for a stressful twenty-four hours, the last few in complete darkness behind enemy lines. Every noise had the potential to be an enemy patrol. Every shadow held the threat of instant death; every slight noise he made with his footfalls threatened to betray him. Worse, he was getting sloppy because he was so tired. When he spotted a small house with a light shining at the window, he simply walked up and knocked on the door. A very frightened older couple answered. Though taken aback by the sudden appearance of a man bristling with weapons, they invited him in and gave him milk and bread.

It was a bit surreal. He had seen no enemy, had found and lost some of his own men, and here he was, sitting at a farmhouse table in an enemy country—a land he and his comrades had invaded—placidly eating.

Thain showed the couple his map, and they pointed out where he was. More good luck: his drop zone was not far away. He thanked his hosts and headed out into the morning, refreshed and hopeful that he'd soon be with his unit.

Rather than walk on the road or in the open, where he could easily be spotted by an enemy patrol, Thain entered an olive orchard and moved among the trees. When he caught a glimpse of a figure in uniform, he pressed himself up against a stone fence, his heart thumping in his chest. Then Thain heard a *click* as the man flipped off the safety on his weapon. Thain scanned the orchard. He couldn't see anything, and he couldn't be sure the other guy wasn't drawing a bead on him. He had no target, so he called out "George!" and got a reassuring "Marshall" in return. Thain had finally linked up with another trooper from the 456th, and the two men headed off in search of more.

Ted Visneski, of Pittsburgh, Pennsylvania, was a demo man in B Company of the 307th Engineers. His mission was to blow up what needed blowing up: fortifications, bridges, enemy positions. Shortly after landing, Visneski linked up with five other troopers. They knew they weren't close to Gela, and, like Jim Gavin, they had an idea their planes had been blown southeast, so they headed north and west. Shortly after sunrise on July 10, the small patrol spotted what looked like a fortified house. As they watched from a covered position, a dispatch rider came out on a motorcycle, headed straight toward them. When he got close, they gunned him down. Visneski went out into the road, approaching the bloody body: the man was dead. Visneski didn't have time to contemplate what he'd just done; he wanted to get out of the open. He'd been taught to take documents and maps, which might betray an enemy's plan, so the trooper removed the leather dispatch case the rider had been carrying.

The Germans in the fortified position heard the shooting and sent out a patrol that, to the six Americans, looked like a company of one hundred. The enemy opened up almost immediately, and Visneski scrambled to get over a stone wall, hoping to put it between himself and the onrushing Germans. Just as he was clearing the wall, he felt something pound his chest. He fell to the ground on the other side and found that he'd been hit twice, once under the armpit and again on the left side of his chest. He went down heavily on the hard ground, aware that the paratroopers around him were firing, but the

Germans were still coming on. Some troopers were caught on the far side of the wall, unable to climb with enemy bullets drilling into the stone; others were on the same side as Visneski. As if this wasn't confusing enough, the Germans flanked the little patrol, and they had men on both sides of the wall, too. There was shooting in all directions. The paratroopers tried to pull back, but some enemy had cleverly set up behind them to cut off retreat. Although he was losing blood fast, Visneski managed to hold on to his tommy gun. An attacking German soldier got in among the troopers before he was knocked down; a paratrooper bayoneted the man, who screamed in terror as the blade went in.

Visneski and the others managed to extricate themselves, but his wounds pumped blood with every movement. A trooper patched Visneski up as best he could, and injected him with a styrette of morphine. Then, it seemed to Visneski, another soldier shot him with a styrette. Things started to get a little hazy at this point, although he was in a lot less pain than he had been, and he was determined to keep up with the group. Several times during the day, men tried to take the dispatch case from him, but Visneski—dazed, drugged, weak from loss of blood—hung on.

(Later, the small patrol of engineers would find the regimental command group. Visneski, who had hung on to the dispatch case through the entire fight, walked up to Gavin to hand it over. He held his tommy gun by the pistol grip, and inadvertently pointed it at the regimental commander, who calmly reached out and pushed the muzzle toward the ground.

"Get this man to an aid station," Gavin said as he took the case.)

Bill Follmer's I Company was the only unit dropped intact on the correct drop zone. Follmer, who had been given a semi-independent mission, had chosen for his company's DZ a small valley just inland of il Biviere, the long narrow lake that so many of the pilots had used for a landmark. There was a road running down the valley, and Follmer figured he would be able to see moonlight reflecting off the surface, which would help him orient himself and his company.

During the flight, Follmer made several trips from his post at the aircraft door to the cockpit of the aircraft, dragging the heavy load of his parachute and gear past the outstretched legs of the troopers seated on the bench seats.

One of I Company's squad leaders, Bill Dunfee, the last man in the stick, was "the pusher," whose job was to make sure everyone cleared the aircraft.

"You sure they know where we're going, sir?" Dunfee asked as Follmer went by again.

In the dim light, Dunfee could see the captain grin at him.

Dunfee had turned twenty-one just three weeks earlier. The Depression had hit his family hard, and Bill was between jobs when the realization came to him that he would be drafted, and sent wherever the Army wanted him. Instead, he enlisted so he could have a little control over his destiny. Since he had only ten dollars to his name when he showed up at the recruiting station, the fifty-dollar-a-month jump pay offered by the paratroopers looked good. Dunfee had taken to his role as a leader and took his duties seriously, though he joked with Follmer.

When the command came to stand and hook up, Dunfee noticed Follmer's runner, a private from the headquarters section, sit down again.

"Stand up," Dunfee said.

In the darkened belly of the plane, it was hard to make out what was happening, but the soldier clearly wasn't supposed to be sitting down.

"I'll stand up when it's time to jump."

The private sounded frightened, but Dunfee knew fear was a normal reaction. Only an idiot would not be frightened at the prospect of jumping from an airplane over enemy territory.

"You'll stand up right now," Dunfee said. The man stood.

When the green light came on, Dunfee felt the line ahead of him moving, and the men shuffling forward as quickly as they could with their heavy loads, trying to get out the door as close as possible to the man in front. He could see the dim outline of the open door, with the silhouettes of jumpers flashing through. The company runner, just ahead of him, didn't turn to the right, but shuffled toward the rear of the airplane, where there was a space big enough for a man to hide. Before the man could get past the open door, Dunfee grabbed the back of his main parachute and yanked him backward. The two men went out the door together.

When he landed, Dunfee was alone. A few seconds' lag time between jumpers in the doorway could mean hundreds of yards of separation on the ground. A full minute between jumpers would put two miles between men on the ground. An angry Dunfee went looking for the runner, but the private didn't want to be found by the only man who knew what he had done in the aircraft.

Follmer's pilots put I Company out right where the company commander asked, but the valley was narrower than Follmer anticipated. Instead of landing on relatively flat ground, he landed on a hillside and snapped his ankle. In spite of his pain, Follmer managed to gather five or six men of his headquarters section, all of whom had landed close to him. Hobbling on a broken ankle, he came across a darkened farmhouse, where one of his men found a donkey. When the farmer came outside to investigate the noise, one of the GIs tried explaining that they were going to borrow the animal so that Follmer could ride it. The farmer spoke no English, but he understood that these soldiers were about to take a valuable piece of property. He also knew that there was little he could do about it, so he quickly dressed, then attached himself to the little group of paratroopers to keep an eye on his animal.

Looking for a spot he could easily defend, Follmer, now astride the donkey, moved his headquarters element toward a small hilltop which his platoon leaders could find. The farmer tagged along. Follmer set up his command post, and throughout the night his platoons checked in, reporting on their missions, accounting for their men, and turning over prisoners rounded up in their patrols. Follmer put a guard on the prisoners, who were mostly Italians happy to be out of the fighting. As daylight glimmered in the east, Follmer sent men out to find the rest of his company and to make contact with the First Division units coming across the beach.

Twenty-two-year-old Second Lieutenant George Clark was an extra lieutenant, a supernumerary in I Company, carried on the books as an assistant platoon leader. There was something about the solidly built former high school football star from Pennsylvania that won the confidence of his superiors. Clark and ten men of his platoon were assigned a separate mission, one that had to be accomplished in his first hours on the ground. They were to set fires in the hills above Gela that would serve as beacons for the ships coming in from the Mediterranean. In addition to the gear that all troopers carried, Clark was loaded down with extra explosives to be used as incendiary devices. The big cargo pockets on his trousers held phosphorous grenades and even land mines, wrapped in cotton batting. He was to look for something that would burn and could be seen from a distance, which probably meant he'd have to set fire to a building.

The pilot of Clark's plane, who had found the right drop zone, was in a hurry to get out of the heavy concentrations of flak around Gela, and so did not slow down to the jump speed of just over a hundred miles an hour. When Clark's parachute opened, the sudden deceleration punched some of his gear through the bottoms of his pockets.

Clark landed on a steep hillside, so that the entire force of impact came down on his uphill leg, shattering his ankle. He rolled over painfully and squirmed out of his parachute harness. Hobbling and taking care not to slide down the hill, Clark rolled up his stick, finding only five of his ten men. Then he sat down and removed his boot. He didn't need a medic to tell him that something was terribly wrong; the bottom of his left heel had moved an inch or so to one side. Clark put his boot back on over the broken ankle, laced it as tightly as he could, and told his men they were moving out.

Not far away, one of Clark's men, Howard Goodson, landed inside an orchard that was closed off by a tall fence made of cactuslike bushes. Goodson heard someone land on the opposite side of the fence. Before he could issue his challenge, he saw the other man's head over the top. Trooper Joe Patrick, who stood over six and a half feet tall, looked right over the top of the fence. Goodson called him, and the two men hacked away at the prickly fence from opposite sides with their bayonets.

Although Goodson had not had a hard landing on Sicily, a jump injury from a few weeks earlier was still plaguing him. In a practice jump in North Africa, Goodson had loaded the cargo pockets of his trousers with hand grenades. When the wind across the drop zone picked him up and slammed him back down on the rocky surface of the DZ, the grenades caught beneath his leg nearly shattered his thigh. He was bruised so badly he could hardly walk. By July 9, he was able to make it to the plane under his own power, but the jump had taken a toll on him, and he was not going to be able to keep up with Patrick as the tall man set out to find Lieutenant Clark. Goodson figured he'd be okay on his own.

The medics had told him flat out that he wasn't going on the jump, but Goodson had insisted just as strongly that he was. He got his way. Now he was in Sicily and unable to keep up with the able-bodied men. The only good thing was that the paratroopers were so scattered that he was bound to run into someone else, and he didn't expect to be alone for long.

Unlike most of the paratroopers, who sought out the enemy, George Clark's mission called for him to avoid contact until he lit the beacons. Staying clear of roads and open areas, the small group moved some three and a half miles in the direction of the coastal town of Gela, which Clark had seen from the airplane. Several times they heard small arms fire close by, but they skirted the firefights and pushed onward.

Around 3:00 A.M., Clark found himself on a hillside overlooking Gela, where he was to light the fire. Moving parallel to the coast, the troopers soon found an Italian house with a six-foot pile of wood leaning against its outside wall. In the hills around him, Clark could hear the firing of the island's alerted defenders, so he set his men up in a small perimeter to keep an eye out for enemy patrols. Then he knocked on the door of the house. Inside, he found an Italian couple, wide awake and dressed. First they'd been frightened by the sounds of aircraft low overhead and the firing all around them. Now they found an apparition at the door: a large man, sweating in blackface, holding a pistol, his belt and suspenders festooned with grenades and knives. *This* was the bogeyman the Germans had warned them about.

Clark, who did not speak Italian, signaled that they had to leave. As he expected, they did not want to go. The lieutenant did not want to frighten them further; he already felt bad about what he was about to do. He struggled to keep his composure, although his ankle throbbed in hot spikes of pain and every second's delay meant that an enemy patrol might find his men and keep them from completing the mission.

"You have to leave," he said in English, pointing to the door. He pulled a phosphorous grenade from his pocket and held it up. Finally, the couple began to move. Clark knew the family could file a claim with the American command, but he had no way to convey that fact to them, and no time to worry about it. When the civilians cleared the building, Clark pulled the pin on his grenade and tossed it back inside the open doorway. Then one of his men fired the pile of wood leaning against the house. Clark stepped back and waited until the whole structure was engulfed—so that it could not be easily doused—before pulling his men out of the dangerous circle of light. Within a few minutes, the house was entirely in flames, and Clark and his men melted back into the darkness.

When his green light finally came on, Ed Sayre leaped into the slipstream and prop wash. A second later, Sayre's static line, attached to a cable in the aircraft, pulled his chute open. There was a violent tug as his overburdened body tried to continue its plunge, while the parachute pulled—in the exact opposite direction—at the harness lashed tight around his body. He slowed enough to know his chute was fully open, and he felt, more than saw, the ground rushing up below him. Then a painful jolt as he crashed and tumbled down a steep hill. Sayre braced himself, and as soon as he stopped rolling, he tore at the harness to get free of the tangled parachute. In his thrashing he felt both undergrowth and open areas, which he took to mean he had landed in a field with cultivated rows. He could make out stakes holding up some of the plants, which told him it was probably a vineyard. The moon was gone, and suddenly the Texan understood the full import of their long delay. They would have to find the drop zone in total darkness.

Sayre did a quick assessment: five or six enemy machine guns, which had been firing at the aircraft, were now traversing the area, trying to hit the paratroopers. If they'd landed on flat ground, they would have been easy targets, but the hilly vineyard protected them. For the moment, at least, it was safe enough to move around and find his soldiers.

Sayre heard men around him, thrashing among the grapevines, challenging one another in stage whispers. They were scattered over several hundred yards, and in the darkness and hilly terrain, it took the better part of an hour to round up his company headquarters element, which consisted of his first sergeant, his runner, and an Italian-American soldier from New York City who would act as an interpreter. Private First Class Vincent Calandrino's family was Sicilian, and he hoped to visit relatives when the fighting stopped. Sayre wasn't surprised to find his young interpreter alert and ready for action; the company commander had discovered, over the course of their training, that the diminutive former barber—Calandrino stood about five and a half feet tall—was fearless.

Sayre located his headquarters element, but there was no sign of the three rifle platoons. It was also clear that he was not on his assigned drop zone, though he had no idea how far off he might be. Breaking out his handheld radio, a new piece of equipment called a "walkie-talkie," Sayre contacted platoon leaders Mike Chester and G. W. Presnell, but they were just voices coming out of the darkness. The lieutenants didn't know where they were with regard to Sayre, and the captain wasn't sure exactly where he was, either.

Sayre told the lieutenants to listen for three rapid shots from an M1 rifle, which would be easy to distinguish from the machine guns. He had one of his men fire into the air; the platoon leaders now had a direction to move.

"Collect your crew-served weapons and ammunition and move towards me," Sayre told them. He knew, from his own experience in rounding up his small band, that it might take the platoon leaders quite a while to find their men, their weapons, and ammunition. He had assembled just over a dozen men—not exactly a huge force—but he wasn't about to sit around and wait for the enemy to come looking for him. He knew, thanks to their use of tracers, where the enemy machine guns were, and he remembered clearly what Gavin had told them, time and time again, during the long training period.

"If you're lost, find the nearest enemy and attack him."

It was now nearly two-thirty in the morning. Crouching low and skirting the small hills, using the grape arbors for concealment, Sayre and three of his men moved toward the machine gun positions. Since the guns had been firing steadily for more than an hour, Sayre suspected that the enemy was well supplied, and probably in fortified positions. Pinpointing the guns was a simple matter of following the arcing tracers back to their sources, and getting close enough to see the muzzle flashes.

Sayre was moving through the vineyard when he came across another paratrooper, Major Walter Winton, the First Battalion executive officer. Winton was clearly having trouble moving, and when Sayre got close he could see that Winton had badly injured his knee in a rough landing.

Sayre explained his plan—he intended to attack the guns—and Winton told him to go ahead. The Texan then crawled a little over a hundred yards back to where he'd left his headquarters element. The First and Second Platoons had not yet arrived, and no one had heard from Third Platoon, so Sayre had a force of twelve men to attack at least six dug-in automatic weapons. But he also had some advantages: the enemy wasn't aggressive. They had not sent out patrols to find and kill the invaders. Sayre could hit them when he wanted and from whatever angle he wanted, and the enemy didn't know how many—or in his case, how few—paratroopers were in the vineyard.

Sayre moved his twelve men to a sheltered spot behind one of the steep little hills and, huddling close to the sweating troopers in the darkness, he told them his plan. They would pinpoint the enemy machine guns, which were still firing steadily, then attack with hand grenades. (Direct-fire weapons, such as rifles and machine guns, have signatures in the darkness: the enemy can locate the shooter by the muzzle flashes. Hand grenades don't present that problem.)

Sayre divided the group into two-man teams, each of which would move close to a gun emplacement. The troopers would crawl as close as possible to the assigned target, find a covered position, and pull the pins from their hand grenades. Once Sayre had all his teams in place, he would throw the first grenade, which would signal the others to throw theirs.

It was too dark for him to see his soldiers' faces, but Sayre could feel the tension coming off them in waves. They had trained together for months, through some of the toughest conditions imaginable. They had entrusted their lives to one another, and now they were about to be tested. They were primed to go, and as ready as Sayre could make them.

The commander led the way again, crawling beneath the machine gun fire to where the teams could reach the targets with a good toss. He expected the enemy to open fire immediately, and that would give the troopers a clue as to what they faced. If the position was too strong, or if there were too many defenders, Sayre would pull his men back.

Around three-thirty, Sayre had all his men in place. He scuttled into his own position, removed a grenade from his pocket, pulled the pin, and lobbed it to land inside what he thought was a roofless sand-bagged position. Sayre's men threw their grenades as soon as they heard the *pop* of the first fuse.

By the light of the explosions, Sayre could see that they weren't attacking sandbagged positions, but heavily fortified concrete pillboxes. The defenders responded with a flurry of their own grenades. After a lull of a few seconds, there was a string of explosions, as many as twenty, all around the GIs. Sayre shouted for his men to pull back, and they stumbled into an empty trench, some five feet deep, that offered them temporary shelter. The trench, Sayre figured, was meant to be part of the defensive position. It was just luck that the Americans didn't drop right on top of alerted defenders.

Sayre counted heads: only one of his men had been slightly wounded, and none lost in the exchange of grenades. The group withdrew to the company command post, where Sayre had left his communications sergeant. Shortly afterward, First and Second Platoons came in. Sayre was happy to see the lieutenants doing exactly as he had taught them: they positioned their men in a defensive perimeter.

By 5:00 A.M., about forty-five men from the two platoons had gathered around Sayre, bringing with them two 60 mm mortars and fifty rounds of ammunition, as well as two light machine guns with two thousand rounds for each gun. With the eastern sky beginning to lighten, Sayre could now get a good look at what he faced.

A Company had landed in a vineyard on the hills just east of a large, two-story stone house, which he figured was the winery. The big building, and a smaller house right beside it, had been turned into a garrison, and all around it were small concrete-and-stone pillboxes that protected the main building. As with any such fortifications, the guns were laid out so they could protect each other from attack. The position controlled a road that led inland toward the Ponte Olivo airfield, and south toward the regiment's objective at the Y junction. Sayre wanted to take the garrison before the enemy could bring up more reinforcements.

By dawn, almost half of A Company had found its way to Sayre's command post. Several of the men had been banged up badly in the jump. They had also been awake for most of the preceding twenty-four hours, as had Sayre, but they were still ready for a fight. Sayre pulled his leaders in to the center of his small perimeter and laid out his plan.

He told his mortar sergeant to set up the tubes in a depression some four hundred yards east of the pillboxes. Sayre would spot the fire from the front, then relay adjustments back to the mortars. He wanted the mortars to drop shells on the smaller, outlying pillboxes.

The 60 mm shells, each packing less than three pounds of high explosive, were not going to shatter any of the concrete emplacements, even with a direct hit. But the rounds were designed to spray hot shrapnel on impact, and this would force the gunners inside the pillboxes to move away from the firing slits. While the barrage was going on, the enemy would be blind, and the troopers could move close. Sayre told the Second Platoon to hook to the right, then pour small-arms fire on the openings in the pillboxes. Once Sayre and his assault force were close, the Second Platoon and the mortars would shift fire to the big house, while the assault team covered the last few yards. They'd go in with rifle grenades, bazookas, and hand grenades.

This was when the value of all the practice maneuvers, particularly those using live ammunition, became apparent. The men in the assault team had to trust that the mortar gunners and the soldiers in Second Platoon were good enough to keep their fire on the targets. A stray round could kill a fellow GI; shrapnel from the mortar rounds would not distinguish friend from foe.

Sayre kept his plan simple, both to avoid confusion and because he trusted that his soldiers would take the initiative when needed. As he waited for his platoon leaders to brief their men and move into position, he checked his own weapon—he had picked up a rifle and grenades—and those of the men in the headquarters section.

During combat, paratrooper leaders sometimes find themselves operating a couple of levels up or down. Company commanders who collected only a squad of soldiers became squad leaders. A sergeant who found a hundred men but no officers was the de facto company commander. If he'd had all of his troopers present, Ed Sayre might have positioned himself in the center of the action, where he could control things and give commands. Instead, with just over fifty men available to assault a strongly entrenched position, Sayre joined the assault team. Besides, this early in their first fight, he thought it was important that the men see him sharing their risks.

By 5:30 A.M., it was light enough to see clearly, even though the sun wouldn't clear the horizon for another twenty minutes. Sayre confirmed that the trench system that had sheltered him after his first assault on the pillboxes was still unoccupied. Since the trenches ran nearly to the pillboxes, the A Company men could use them to get within hand grenade range without exposing themselves to fire.

The pillboxes here, and all over the southern coast, varied in size, but most stood only six to ten feet high and were fifteen to twenty feet in diameter, with a concrete dome roof and twenty-four-inch-thick walls of reinforced concrete. Two or three firing ports gave the defenders something less than 360-degree coverage.

While the positions looked ominous from the outside, there was not much comfort inside. The defenders' field of vision was severely limited, and the dome magnified sounds on the interior, so it was both difficult to see and hear someone approaching outside. The tiny space inside was claustrophobic; three men standing and watching would necessarily be leaning on one another. If all three fired their weapons, especially automatic weapons, the noise inside was deafening. On top of that, the defenders gave up the ability to move: once the attackers located the pillboxes, the defenders were stuck, while the attackers could always bring up more men, more guns, more explosives.

Maneuvering outside of fortifications, such as the pillboxes, required a much higher degree of training that most of the Italian soldiers had. With poorly trained troops—and not enough of those—the fixed fortifications made some sense. Their use was cynical: experienced officers and noncoms who put the defenders inside knew that the men were doomed in any determined attack.

The first mortar round landed right on target among the pillboxes. Satisfied that they had the range, A Company's mortar gunners began dropping rounds into their tubes. The pillboxes were raked with shrapnel, and Sayre knew that the men inside could not keep their posts at the firing slots.

Now Sayre gave an order that surprised his men.

"Fix bayonets!" he called out.

Sayre wasn't expecting to finish the fight with a grand charge. He wasn't even sure the bayonets would be useful if his men had to go inside the narrow confines of the pillboxes. But he wanted to send a clear message to his troopers: A Company had come to kill the enemy. In a close-quarters, even face-to-face fight, a split second's hesitation could mean the difference between living and dying. If soldiers were going to die in this fight, Ed Sayre wanted to ensure that they were enemy soldiers.

All along the assault line, sweating troopers reached down to their scabbards, yanked out their bayonets, and seated the steel blades on their rifle muzzles with a distinct clank. Second Platoon poured on the fire from the trenches, machine guns and grenades and rifle fire. There was little or no return fire; some of the enemy tried to run, but they were cut down.

Sayre called for Second Platoon and the mortars to shift fire, and the assault team closed the final few yards. A few GIs were hit by enemy fire as they rushed across the open ground, but a handful of paratroopers got close enough to the pillboxes to toss hand grenades into the firing slits. Within minutes, Sayre's men had knocked out the six pillboxes that had been menacing them all night. The defenders who weren't killed or wounded quickly surrendered.

Fred Morgan, a medic who had trained with A Company since Fort Benning, now went to his grisly work. The twenty-one-year-old from Edgartown, Massachusetts, had enlisted in the Army immediately after Pearl Harbor, but had found himself working as a medical orderly, which did not fit his idea of joining the war effort. He volunteered for parachute school to get out of the hospital ward. Originally, he had been assigned as a rifleman, until the unit found out that he had worked as a hospital orderly in his first months in the Army. He

transferred to Headquarters Company of First Battalion, where he and
the other medics were trained by Dr. Carl R. Comstock, a pediatrician
turned battalion surgeon. During months of intense training they had
seen quite a few injuries: broken limbs, gruesome compound fractures, even bullet wounds, but nothing had prepared them for the
sights they now encountered.

Morgan dug into his aid bag for bandages and morphine. He
talked to the wounded soldiers, determined to keep them—and himself—as calm as he could. His patients, enemy and friendly, had to be
stabilized for evacuation across the beach. One GI was wounded too
badly to wait. Morgan and another medic wanted to move him as
quickly as possible in the hopes of getting him to a hospital ship.

As Sayre and his A Company troopers consolidated their gains and
prepared to assault the winery, Morgan and his fellow medic prepped a
stretcher for their wounded man. Sayre could not spare any riflemen
to escort them. Although the Geneva Convention allowed medics to
carry pistols for self-defense, Morgan and his comrades did not. Instead, they wore white armbands with a red cross that was supposed to
keep them safe as noncombatants. (By the time of the Italy jump, in
September 1943, the command ordered the medics to carry pistols. A
crate of .45-caliber automatics arrived at the departure airfield as Morgan was loading up, the weapons still thick with the Cosmoline grease
used for packing. Morgan traded his weapon with the Air Corps crew
for cans of fruit. By the time of the fighting in Normandy, in 1944,
Morgan removed the white armband, which attracted attention, but
he did not carry a sidearm during the war.)

Morgan and his partner struck out in the direction of the beach,
keeping to the low ground amid the vineyards. The load was heavy, and
Morgan worried that the wounded man, who had stopped moving and
was making no sounds, was already dead, but they were in too much of
a hurry to stop and check. There were shells coming from the fire support ships, and Morgan worried that the U.S. Navy would kill him.

The medics heard a vehicle and looked around. A small tank appeared on an elevated roadway about a quarter mile away and just visible through the thin undergrowth. When the turret turned, it was clear that the crew had seen something moving down in the low ground. The Italian tanks were small, but the medics were unarmed, with no real cover. Suddenly, the tank's stubby gun fired, sending the first shot overhead. Morgan and his comrade hurried on, with Morgan thinking that if the man in the stretcher was dead, at least he wouldn't suffer from the jostling. The tank could not depress its gun far enough to hit the men scuttling along in the low ground, and the troopers didn't stop moving until they cleared the valley and were overlooking the invasion beaches. When they finally reached some soldiers of the First Division, their fears were confirmed. The young paratrooper they had carried all the way from A Company's first firefight was dead.

Back at the strongpoint, Ed Sayre and his men immediately went to work dragging the enemy guns to positions where they could be used to fire on the two-story winery and the smaller, adjacent house. Enemy troops inside those buildings had seen everything that had happened to their comrades in the outer ring of pillboxes, and they poured fire from first- and second-story windows in a desperate effort to keep the GIs at bay. Some of the enemy tried to break from the strongpoint, but the troopers in the overwatch firing positions cut them down in the open area around the house.

Now, using the captured machine guns, the GIs had even more firepower, and they forced the defenders away from the windows. Moving under cover of this fire, the troopers of First Platoon reached the walls of the big winery, where they crouched beneath the firing slits and armed their grenades.

Amid the confusion and deafening fire, a bazooka team jumped from the trench, knelt before the heavy wooden doors of the house, and fired a rocket, which blew the doors down. Sayre ran from his covered position, across the few yards of open ground, and hurled two hand grenades into the smoking hole where the door had been. The GIs could now hear the screams of men inside. A horribly wounded German stumbled out of the doorway, trying to hold his guts with his hands. Others were yelling, *"Kamerad! Kamerad!"* while a terrified Italian soldier called out, *"Madre di Dio!"*

Sayre yelled, "CEASE FIRE!" and the order was repeated by the noncoms and troopers arrayed around the outpost.

"Come out, come out!" the First Platoon yelled. The defenders who could still walk stumbled out of the smoking doorway, hands raised, blinking and coughing, some of them bleeding from shrapnel wounds. Sayre's men quickly disarmed them, then hustled them away from the garrison. American medics began to treat the wounded of both sides.

Sayre took stock of his situation. There were some forty Italian soldiers and ten Germans in the mix of prisoners. Four of his men were wounded, one seriously. Sayre was surprised none of his men had been killed in two sharp assaults on fortified positions (he did not yet know that the soldier carried off by Morgan and the other medic had died en route to the beach).

Sayre interrogated the prisoners, using Calandrino and another trooper who spoke German, and learned that the strongpoint was an outpost of a nearby *Kampfgruppen,* an armored battle group.

This was a shock. If these prisoners were to be believed, not only was there German armor on the island, but there was a combat team only two miles away, just outside the town of Niscemi. The paratroopers had been told by U.S. intelligence that there were no German armored forces in Sicily. Now Sayre knew differently, and he and his lightly armed men were directly in the path the panzers would take to get at the vulnerable beachheads.

The best weapon for holding off the Germans tanks were the U.S. tanks coming ashore at Gela, but Sayre had no way of knowing when reinforcements would arrive. Gavin's combat team had some howitzers from the 456th Field Artillery, and in a pinch these guns, used in the direct-fire mode, might stop a tank. But Sayre hadn't seen any of the artillerymen around. His men had bazookas, which had proved useful against pill-boxes, but the new rocket launchers had a range of only about three hundred yards, so the firing team had to get close to the target before they could shoot. When fired, the weapon shot smoke and flame out the back, which meant the enemy could spot the bazooka team. With its four-foot-long tube, the weapon was difficult to use unless the operator was kneeling or standing, which further exposed him to enemy fire.

The A Company paratroopers, far from being spooked, were energized by their first victory, and they prepared to hold off an attack by German armor. Sayre set up his two platoons (Third Platoon was still unaccounted for) in an all-around defense, then took stock of the weapons he'd captured. The winery contained twenty machine guns and an astonishing half million rounds of ammunition. Since the paratroopers had trained with all sorts of captured Axis weapons in North Africa, the men could handle the new additions to their arsenal. Sayre distributed the guns and the ammunition evenly among his platoons. He didn't have a lot of paratroopers, but he certainly had a lot of fire-power, with one machine gun for every two or three GIs. His men had definitely announced their presence on the island, and they had put themselves astride a road the enemy would have to use sooner or later. It was just the beginning of a long day.

By the morning of July 10, Gavin was torn between his intense desire to get to the objective area and take charge of the regiment, and another somewhat less glamorous but very important consideration: his tiny band was in no shape to fight their way out of another chance encounter with an enemy patrol. Still, as the sun rolled up its steep arc, Gavin pushed his luck, leading his men on a brisk, cross-country move. They stayed away from roads and trails and likely spots for enemy outposts, and they nervously scanned the surrounding hills as they darted from one bit of concealment to another. Gavin studied his map, trying to guess where the enemy patrol they'd run into earlier might be now, or where it might be headed. His job was to get to the objective; getting killed or captured in a firefight along the way wouldn't help anyone.

As he moved, Gavin kept running into individual troopers, whom he policed up. He was building his unit man by man, and was up to nearly a squad by the time he spotted Ray Kenworthy, a machine gunner from H Company.

Kenworthy had an easy, if lonely, landing in the open spaces of an orchard. After getting out of his chute, he sat beneath one of the trees and took a drink of water as he sized up the situation. In a short while, he heard yelling nearby, but since he was alone, he decided to keep still and see what developed. Two paratroopers walked by, talking loudly, as if walking on a stateside street. Kenworthy wanted to join the men—there was safety in numbers—but finally decided that the noisy pair would draw unwelcome attention. He decided to stay on his own, and let them pass.

Once he was alone again, Kenworthy headed west, his best guess for backtracking on the path his plane had taken. He was looking for the big equipment bundles that held his weapon, the .30-caliber light machine gun and its ammunition. He found a bundle, but someone had gotten there ahead of him, and the machine gun was gone. Not only could he not do his main job, which was to provide all-important automatic weapons fire, but he was still alone in enemy territory and armed only with a folding-stock carbine—a peashooter, in the paratrooper's estimation.

Just as it was starting to get light, Kenworthy moved to some high ground, to gain some perspective. It was from this perch that he spotted a small group of troopers working their way west. From all the map cases dangling at their shoulders, Kenworthy figured it was a bunch of officers. They certainly looked lonely. He set off to intercept them and found himself facing none other than Slim Jim himself.

"Who are you?" Gavin asked.

Kenworthy identified himself as an H Company machine gunner.

"Where's your weapon?" Gavin asked.

"Someone got to the bundle before me, sir."

Gavin motioned for the private to join the little column. They were a pitiful sight, armed with two carbines that jammed, one tommy gun, one pistol, and one M1 Garand. As much as it galled him to admit that he couldn't do what he wanted—reach his objective—Gavin had to be realistic. The next enemy patrol would probably get them all. Better to wait until nightfall and continue the move then.

A frustrated Gavin began looking for a hiding place too rugged for enemy vehicles and not in the obvious path for foot patrols. At mid-morning, he found some gentle hills crisscrossed by irrigation ditches. One of these was cut into the side of a hill and offered a view across a half mile of farmland, which would allow them to spot someone approaching. He picked a ditch that was dry and filled with undergrowth, settled his men, and took stock of the situation. The troopers pooled their resources: a couple of K rations and some concentrated food bars from their escape kits, a few weapons, and a chancy supply of ammunition.

"We were holed up like hunted animals," Gavin later wrote. "Tired, wounded, hungry, but too sick at heart to eat, we apprehensively scanned the countryside for any sign of friend or foe."[1]

As the day wore on and the troopers ran through their meager supplies of water, Gavin began to feel as if he'd failed on his first day in combat. He had not accomplished his mission. He could not find his men or even get to his objective. He spent most of the restless day sitting and worrying, when what he wanted to do was act. But with just a few men, and with the countryside crawling with enemy patrols, he had to wait, and waiting was difficult.

9

WRONG PLACE, RIGHT FIGHT

The first sensation was wind, and only then came falling. Sergeant Otis Sampson, the former lumberjack and boxer, kept his body tightly coiled as he waited for his chute to open. There was a sharp blow on the back of his head, which forced his helmet down over his eyes and crammed his body even more tightly into his harness. Sampson reached up and pushed the brim of his helmet back. Below him, an antiaircraft searchlight pivoted, searching the sky for planes and paratroopers. There was rifle and machine gun fire, and he could see the sharp muzzle flashes beneath his feet.

The ground below was uniformly dark, and then, in the last seconds, something darker than the background was right below him. He pulled down hard on his right side risers and crashed through branches to land on the ground, but not before a tree limb smacked him in the mouth. Sampson was half sitting, his feet in front of him, his parachute hung up in the tree above him. The two blows to his head, in quick succession, had left him dazed.

Sampson had landed in some sort of enclosure, a small olive orchard bordered on one side by a low stone wall. Just to his right was a much higher wall that he was glad he had missed. He could no longer see the muzzle flashes of the rifle and machine gun fire, but judging from the sound, the fighting was only a few hundred yards away. He unsnapped one side of his reserve chute and the chest buckle on his harness, then drew his knife. All paratroopers kept their knives razor sharp for just this moment, and he made two quick slashes where the webbing gripped his thighs. Free of the harness, he reached for the case containing his tommy gun.

It wasn't there.

Sampson searched the ground frantically, but the darkness yielded nothing. After a few seconds of panic, Sampson recalled that the harness, once free of his weight, had been pulled up into the tree. Standing quickly, he reached into the branches and found the canvas case. Reassured by the heft of the tommy gun, he quickly switched from a twenty-round to a thirty-round magazine, stashing the smaller magazine in his gas mask case.

Now Sampson wanted a look around. He climbed back into the tree he'd crashed through. Olive trees are trimmed so that they grow broad but not high, making it easier for the farmer to harvest the olives, a process accomplished by hand with rakes. Climbing would have been easy without the equipment he was wearing, Sampson thought, but he made it to the top, being careful not to make too much noise.

From the upper branches, Sampson looked up a gentle slope, at a patchwork of stone walls and dark rows of trees. As he watched, the big searchlight was shattered by rifle fire, and the light went out. Sampson checked his compass. The searchlight was almost due north, right on the flight path. He'd been on the ground just a short while—it wasn't even one o'clock yet—so anyone who'd jumped after him would still be somewhere up that hill. There was obviously a fair-sized body of enemy soldiers up that hill, and Sampson didn't want to head off alone into what looked to him like a hornet's nest.

In his immediate area, Sampson saw a stone building, which was dark. There was a high wall with a courtyard on the opposite side. He

climbed out of the tree, picked up his tommy gun case, and leaned it
against a cactus beside the wall.

Then he heard someone nearby. He had been making so much
noise that an enemy patrol might have gotten close without him hearing it. Sampson carefully pressed his back against the wall and, looking
over the sights of his tommy gun, squinted to make out forms in the
darkness. He saw nothing, but heard someone rustling in the trees to
his front. Then he heard rocks falling, probably off the top of the wall.
Someone was climbing the wall just a few yards in front of him, and
he imagined a squad of Germans closing in. He clamped hard on the
tommy gun grip, ready to fire at a shadow, a noise, an identifiable
form. But the next sound was of someone dropping to the ground on
the far side of the wall.

"George," Sampson called out, realizing, even as he said it, that he
had reacted too late. Someone had been inside the enclosure with
him, but was gone. He stepped out of the shadows and crossed the
few yards to the wall. There, next to another olive tree, he could see
the top of the wall silhouetted against the slightly lighter sky. Stones
had been knocked loose. Sampson climbed the tree and looked over.
He felt somewhat secure, hidden in the thick foliage, but he still
couldn't see anything, nor could he tell how far it was to the ground on
the far side of the wall. He had made it through the first jump of the
night without injury, and he didn't want to break his leg leaping from a
tree. He unhooked the thirty-foot climbing rope coiled on his web gear
and tried to untie it. Apparently it had been snagged in the foliage of
the first tree; the knot was pulled tight and he couldn't get it loose.

He was wasting time. Reaching out as far as he could, Sampson
grabbed a branch that hung over the wall, pushed off from the tree,
and let go.

"Relax," he told himself, just as he'd done when falling off a horse
in his days as a cavalryman. Landing safely, he once again put his back
to the wall and looked around. Nothing but the sound of his own

breathing. He tasted blood where the limb had smacked him in the face when he landed, but it would leave him with nothing more than a fat lip.

So far Sampson had been merely reacting, and he felt like a failure as a sergeant. He had no plan, no idea where his men were or even if they were still alive, and, perhaps worst of all, no idea where he was. He was sure that the pilots had not found the drop zones: nothing around him matched, in any way, the sand tables and maps he'd studied so hard back in North Africa.

He cradled his weapon and scanned the blackness.

What now? he thought.

Up the hill to the north, the rifle and machine gun fire continued; none of it was from American weapons. Sampson thought he could hear voices calling out in Italian. Where were his troopers?

It was a bad joke. Otis Sampson had left North Africa with thirty-four hundred men and had somehow landed completely alone in enemy territory. The darkness served to make him feel even more isolated and alone, even if it did provide a little bit of security. That would change at dawn.

If I had landed on the right DZ, I would have gone north, he reasoned. *Best to stick with the same plan.*

There were clearly Italians to the north, so he planned to head east for a distance, then turn north. If he hadn't found anyone before daylight, he told himself, he'd dig in and prepare to fight it out. Standing at the southeast corner of the building he'd nearly landed on, he could make out a haystack nearby. Since he could see only a few feet in any direction, he planned to move in short jaunts, from one vantage point to the next. As he stepped toward the haystack, he heard someone moving behind him.

Sampson peered into the darkness, every sense concentrating on pulling some figure out of the darkness. Gripping his tommy gun tightly, he gave the challenge.

"George."

There was no answer, though he was sure that whoever was making the noise was close enough to hear him, maybe only forty or fifty feet away.

"George," he said again, louder this time.

He crouched, straining to see into the blackness, every muscle taut.

"Damn it, answer me!"

The answer came in Italian, and Sampson knelt and fired a burst with his tommy gun, watching carefully to pinpoint the muzzle flash he expected to get in return. Instead, he heard someone moving away through the dry grass. He took a few steps in pursuit, then thought better of it. As much as he wanted to get the best of whoever had come so close to him, he realized his first responsibility was to find his men.

On the east side of the haystack, Sampson found a stone wall with an opening that led to a narrow lane. The lane was bordered on both sides by walls that were higher than his head. Looking down the narrow path, he could see that its lighter dirt would make anyone walking there visible.

What a place to be caught in, he thought. Without stepping into the lane, he scanned the far wall for an opening. He saw one to his right and ran for it. Finding himself in a wide field and comforting darkness, Sampson paused to listen and orient himself. The firing to the north had died down, and as he started moving in that direction, he came upon another stone wall, this one running east and west. He passed through an opening and continued north, uphill, still very much alone. Since he was looking up the slope, Sampson did have an advantage: anyone standing above him would be silhouetted against the sky.

He had gone several hundred yards when he became aware of a solitary figure standing to his left. For the second time in just a few minutes, Sampson had found another man in the darkness, with no idea who it might be. He held his tommy gun high and moved forward slowly, as quietly as possible. This time, Sampson didn't give the sign. He'd been the first to speak last time and had exposed himself. If he could get close enough to see if the figure was friendly or enemy, he'd get off the first shot. The other man spotted Sampson, and there was a tense moment when each was aware of the other, waiting for the other to do something first. Sampson was certain the other man's weapon was pointed right at him Then he took another step, and the two were able to identify each other. This time, it was an American.

"Why the hell didn't you give the challenge?" the GI scolded Sampson. "I almost let you have it."

"Why the hell didn't you challenge me?" Sampson shot back. "I had you covered, too."

The frightened paratrooper was from another company, and he was standing guard over two of his buddies who'd been injured in the jump and were resting against a low wall just a few feet away. One of the men had a broken leg.

Sampson couldn't stay put; he had to find his own men. He left the three GIs and headed north again, stumbling across another figure standing alone in the dark field. This paratrooper, a major Sampson didn't know, wanted the sergeant to help him.

"I'm sorry, sir, I've got men of my own to find," Sampson answered. When he left, the major stayed in the same spot where Sampson had found him, looking confused.

Finally, Sampson found an E Company soldier, Tony DeMayo, who told him about another man who'd been badly hurt in the jump, possibly a broken hip. DeMayo was rounding up troopers, and he pointed northwest, telling Sampson that the company was forming just a short distance away. A relieved Sampson headed uphill as DeMayo continued his mission.

It was still completely dark when Sampson found Lieutenant Talton Long, commander of E Company. Long was as calm as if this were a training exercise. He listened to Sampson's description of the buildings and fields down the hill to the south, and agreed with the sergeant that they weren't where they were supposed to be. They'd have to wait until dawn to get a good look around the area; in the meantime, Long had established his command post and was sending men out to gather lost troopers. As they came in, Long strengthened his growing perimeter.

"Find yourself a defensive position and get some rest. I've put Watts over against that west wall," Long said, indicating where at least one of Sampson's men was. "I've sent patrols out to help round up the strays," Long said, but he didn't know where any other men from the mortar section might be.

Sampson, happy to be back with his company, talked to a few men as he felt his way around the position. He learned there were troopers from D Company as well as E Company, and some of the airborne artillerymen from the 456th. The more he learned about their numbers, the better he felt.

The sergeant was surprised to find the men eager to talk about their jump: how hard it was or who got hurt. They'd done this in training, but Sampson thought that combat would be different, as once they landed they had to focus on much deadlier possibilities. But in the darkness around the company perimeter, the paratroopers were comparing stories about bruises and broken legs, just as they had back in the States. One thing was different. The olive grove just to the west had been an enemy strongpoint; some troopers had landed right on top of the defenders and had been shot while still hung up in the trees.

Sampson paired up with the company communications sergeant, George Clark, and the two men found a position a little downhill and some distance from the company command post. They dug on either side of a discarded parachute, which lay stretched out on the ground between them. In the hour before dawn, the men experienced something they hadn't felt in the two months they were in Africa: they were cold. The two had a small tug-of-war, with the parachute sliding slowly back and forth as first one man, then the other pulled it around him for warmth.

Before it was fully light, the two noncoms left their positions to look for their equipment and men. Clark found his radio bundle and Sampson found one other trooper, whom he pointed toward the company position.

As the light grew on D-day, the company perimeter was ragged but growing. Many of the men had been awake for twenty-four hours. In that time, they had endured hours of sitting strapped in a parachute harness and saddled with over a hundred pounds of gear; they had flown three hours, some of them through violent winds that made them airsick. They had made a night parachute jump into enemy territory, and some of them had been shot at the whole night through. Now that daybreak was approaching, there was little prospect for rest. The company had to rejoin the battalion, which had to get on with its mission.

As the eastern sky lightened, Sampson went back to the company area and found a section of the perimeter that he and his few men could occupy. He dug a hasty trench, then told Lieutenant Long where he was. He was glad to see the sun come up, and not just because it chased away the chill. When he'd watched it set the night before over Africa, it occurred to him he might not live to see it rise again. One day down.

The sun also revealed the landscape, and confirmed that they weren't anywhere near their drop zone. The hills around them were divided by neat stone walls, open fields alternating with olive orchards. On the hill below E Company's position, Sampson saw the cluster of buildings where he had landed in the darkness. He continued working on his trench, hurried on by the sound of small arms fire, which picked up as daylight revealed the paratroopers' position.

"Hell, they can't hit anything," Sampson called out to his men as the first round passed high. Then, as he was bent over, a bullet kicked up dirt right below his face. He crouched in the hole and began digging faster, putting his grandstanding aside at least for the moment. Once he finished his hole, he climbed out and found his commander.

"Lieutenant Long, can I take out a patrol and look for my equipment bundle and my men?" Sampson asked. He was a mortar sergeant, which meant he needed his men, and he needed his mortar.

"Do as you think best," Long answered.

Sampson asked Corporal Neil Curtis, another radioman, if he wanted to go on patrol. The two men had struck up a friendship before, sharing stories about sailing.

Curtis and Sampson headed south, downhill toward the spot where Sampson had landed. They kept an eye on the known enemy positions, where the firing had been coming from, and kept out of sight. As they walked, they heard 81 mm mortars go into action, dropping rounds into the olive grove to the west of E Company's position. Since the 81s were a battalion asset, the sound meant that at least part of the Second Battalion was gathering nearby (Sampson's 60 mm mortars were a company asset). The sound was reassuring; it meant that paratroopers were going on the offensive.

Sampson looked to his right and there, his head and shoulders showing above a stone wall, was an Italian soldier, running downhill, away from where the American mortar rounds were landing.

"Halt!" Sampson called as loudly as he could.

The Italian looked at the two troopers, then headed downhill and continued running. Sampson raised his tommy gun to his shoulder and called out again. The Italian put a little more distance between himself and the exploding mortar rounds before stopping. Sampson and Curtis trotted over to the wall, which turned out to border a narrow lane running north and south, with walls on both sides.

It was fairly easy to see that the Italian had abandoned his position because of the incoming fire. Sampson figured there might be others. By this time the mortar shelling had stopped, so Sampson motioned for the Italian to go back up the hill, north on the road.

As they moved uphill with the prisoner in front of them and weapons at the ready, Sampson and Curtis spotted the abandoned position. Apparently their prisoner had stayed longer than his comrades, because they found two concrete pillboxes, their abandoned machine guns pointed down the lane they'd just used to come north. The guns would come in handy in the company perimeter, Sampson thought. There was a pile of grenades in the open. Sampson was thinking how foolish a move that was, as a single stray bullet could have exploded them and killed everyone in the position. Then his prisoner picked up a grenade and turned toward Sampson.

It might have been because he had his tommy gun on the man, or it might have been because he figured the prisoner was too frightened to do anything hostile, but Sampson immediately knew that the man was simply showing the American captors where the grenades were. The move might have gotten him shot if he'd been guarded by a jumpy GI. Sampson disarmed the man, then looked up to see other paratroopers coming south on the lane. They had followed the mortar barrage into the olive grove and had swept the area clear of enemy.

Sampson poked around behind the pillbox on the left and found one of the searchlights he'd seen as he floated to the earth. Its lens had been shattered by rifle fire.

Sampson shouldered one of the machine guns, Curtis picked up the other, and the two men and the prisoner were headed for E Company when they encountered a captain coming down the lane from the north.

"Where did you get those machine guns?" the officer, who was from another company, asked Sampson.

"From the pillboxes, sir."

"I'll take them," the captain said, reaching toward Sampson's load.

"Sorry, sir," Sampson said, keeping a tight grip on his find. "You'll have to capture your own. We need these for our defense."

Before the officer could register a protest, Sampson and Curtis moved out quickly to deliver their prizes to their own Lieutenant Long. As they moved through the dense olive grove where the Italians had been dug in the night before, Sampson saw that the enemy positions had been dug under the cover of the trees at the edge of the grove and covered the fields where many of the E Company troopers had landed. Things got worse as they pressed through the grove. Sampson and Curtis saw a couple of troopers who had been caught in the trees right above the enemies' heads. They'd been shot before they could get clear of their harnesses, before they could even get their weapons out to have a fighting chance. Sampson, thinking about his first helpless minutes on the ground, and about how he couldn't find his tommy gun for a frightening few seconds, promised himself that he would never again jump with his weapon bundled in a carrier. He would go out fighting, if it came to that.

Sampson helped incorporate the two machine guns he'd brought into the defensive perimeter, sighting them for the best coverage of any routes an attacker might use to approach. Once he finished, he went back out to find his men and mortars.

Joe Lyons, with D Battery of the 456th Field Artillery, was, like the other troopers, surprised to learn that there were German tanks on the island.

Lyons's battery was armed with big .50-caliber machine guns. Theoretically, the machine guns were to provide antiaircraft protection for the howitzers. But since equipment and men were so widely scattered, not one of the three howitzer batteries managed to assemble the guns and men to function as intended. Only a few of D Battery's crews found enough bundles to piece together the big machine guns, but there were no battery formations to protect.

Lyons landed safely and gathered fifteen men by dawn on D-day, July 10. As they moved, the small patrol came across several Italian pillboxes whose crews were mostly interested in surrendering. Since Lyons did not want to be outnumbered by prisoners, even prisoners as cooperative and eager to please as these Italians, he did not keep the enemy soldiers with him. Lyons's troopers disarmed the enemy and sent them walking in the direction of the American-held beaches.

When one group of defenders refused to come out, Lyons's patrol used a bazooka to fire a rocket at the firing slit of the pillbox. The damage was slight, but the enemy surrendered, and the GIs soon packed them off toward the beach under a white flag.

When they moved, Lyons and another soldier took point. Hearing the deep rumble of a big engine, they jumped off the road and hid in a ditch, holding perfectly still as the biggest tank they had ever seen passed within a few yards. Since the crew of the tank was buttoned up (locked inside with the hatches closed, ready for a fight), the troopers felt pretty sure that they had not been spotted.

The two men did what they'd been trained to do. They let the tank pass them and checked to make sure the vehicle wasn't followed by supporting infantry, then stepped out into the road and—from a distance of only twenty-five yards—fired a rocket at the back of the tank.

The rocket bounced off without exploding.

"Let's try again," Lyons said.

They quickly loaded another round. In training, they'd been told they could disable a tank by hitting the tread. They fired at almost point-blank range, and managed to hit the tread of the tank. This time the rocket exploded, but the tread was unharmed.

Lyons and his partner had succeeded only in alerting the enemy. As the turret swung slowly around like a ponderous head, the machine gun began firing heavy slugs into the brush alongside the road. Lyons and the trooper had taken on a tank and had only pissed off the crew. They turned and ran.

Lyons had encountered one of the massive German Tiger tanks that would cause so much trouble for the paratroopers in Sicily. The Tiger Mark VI (Panzer VI Ausf H Tiger Heavy Tank to the Germans), at fifty-six tons, was nearly twice as heavy as the other panzers and outweighed the U.S. Sherman tank by twenty-five tons. Nine feet tall, nine feet wide, and nearly twenty-eight feet long, the Tiger mounted a version of the fearsome 88, one of the most deadly big guns fielded by any side in the war, along with two machine guns. No armored vehicle in any arsenal could stand up to a Tiger in a toe-to-toe fight, and the paratroopers were about to take them on.

It was after daylight that Howard Goodson—the paratrooper whose jump injury had prevented him from keeping up with Clark's patrol— ran across some soldiers from the First Division, which had come ashore at Gela. They helped him hook up with some other 505th troopers, including two I Company men: Mike Terella and Mike Caruso. Since the men had been moving almost continuously without sleep or any food beside K rations, they decided they should rest for a while on their way to the drop zone. Terella and Caruso, who spoke Italian, approached a farmhouse and asked for food. The family obliged, preparing a big pot of chicken soup while the hungry paratroopers waited outside. The farmer then produced big bowls and spoons for the seven invaders. Goodson happily dug in, but lost his appetite when he found the rooster's comb in his bowl. Apparently, nothing went to waste among these poor Sicilian farmers.

When they started moving again, Goodson's group found some paratroopers who had taken over an Italian garrison, liberating large casks of local wine. They punched holes in the barrels and filled their steel helmets with wine, but within hours, the wine brought memories of North Africa: they had the GI trots again.

The GIs who had taken the garrison had confiscated weapons from the prisoners. Sidearms, like officers' pistols, were particularly prized as war souvenirs and something to be traded with Navy men and rear echelon types for food, clothing, and other goodies. Goodson was saddened to see that the paratroopers also helped themselves to watches, rings, wallets, anything else the Italian prisoners had—which wasn't much.

10

THE ROAD TO GELA

Company F radio operator LeRoy Leslie landed hard, but missed a rock wall that would have made it worse. The twenty-two-year-old South Carolinian had the wind knocked out of him when he hit. He managed to roll over onto his left side, then heard a distinct thump on the ground very close by. There was no conscious thought, just a dread certainty: it was a grenade. Leslie put his right hand up to shield his face as the grenade exploded, sending hot shrapnel into the back of his hand and the part of his neck that was exposed. Fortunately, it was an Italian grenade, which was much smaller than either the German or American versions and didn't pack the same deadly punch.

Now he was wounded, still on the ground and still held down by the dead weight of his parachute, and whoever had thrown the grenade was obviously close by. Leslie reached down, yanked his boot knife free, and hacked off the harness of his parachute. He sensed, rather than saw, a man about thirty feet away, between him and the rock wall. There was no time to grab his weapon, and he wasn't about to wait for the next grenade, so Leslie, his neck and hand bleeding, lunged at the Italian soldier who had come to kill him. There was a brief, desperate struggle until Leslie stabbed the man in a close embrace. He was pushing the body off him when he saw someone else close by.

"Les, is that you?"

It was Mark Alexander, the Second Battalion commander.

"It's me," Leslie managed. He'd had two close brushes with death in his first minutes on the ground, and he had stabbed a man to death. As many of his comrades were learning, action was the antidote for horror.[1]

"Let's go," Alexander said.

Leslie gathered his weapon and equipment and followed the major toward the rest of the unit. When they closed on the growing perimeter, Leslie was happy to find Lieutenant Neal McRoberts, the F Company commander, and several other men from his unit. One of the troopers put sulfa powder on the wounds on Leslie's neck and hand. Since he wasn't wounded too badly, Leslie gave his morphine styrette to the medics, who had set up an aid station near the command post.

Berge Avadanian sat just a few feet from the jump door of the C-47 that held the members of the S2, or intelligence section. As the jumpmaster bellowed out the commands, Avadanian could see the streams of antiaircraft fire coming up from the ground. The sight made him want to get out of the plane quickly. Apparently, the pilot also wanted to get away from the ground fire, and Avadanian felt the plane lurch and begin a steep climb.

The interior of the plane exploded in sound. The engines, already loud, became louder as the aircraft clawed for elevation. There was the distant, dangerous popping of the weapons below them, the strangely silent arcs of tracer ammunition like bright lines drawn across the sky. When the green light came on, the men moved as one to clear the doorway. In a couple of seconds, Avadanian was out in the slipstream; his chute snapped open with a reassuring pop, and he swung beneath it and looked around.

The first sign that he was too high was that there was plenty of time to look around and see other chutes around him. Then he saw aircraft *below* him, flown by pilots who had stuck to the plan and maintained the proper altitude. Now Avadanian had to worry not only about being hit by antiaircraft fire, but about being chopped up in the propellers of an aircraft passing below him. The planes themselves were blacked out, but Avadanian could see the glow from the engine exhaust. Every once in a while he could make out the dark shape of a C-47 sliding across the lighter background of the earth below.

He landed on a hillside amid some low trees. As he scrambled to get clear of his parachute and recover his weapon, he saw a road below him in the moonlight. Then he saw movement on the road. It was something big, bigger than a man and moving slowly, deliberately, a big black shape, blacker than the surrounding fields.

It's a tank, he thought.

In his excitement, he did the first thing that came to mind: he raised his weapon and fired.

Avadanian heard yelling, in Italian, coming back at him; then he could make out the sound of horse's hooves as the driver hurried his wagon away.

Sweating and hyperalert, Avadanian knew he had to find some of his comrades. He listened carefully, moving along the hillside until he heard a rustling. There were no voices, in Italian or English, just the sense that something was nearby. Then more rustling. Avadanian decided he'd better not lead off with a few shots this time, but do what he'd been trained to do, which was to challenge anyone he encountered. Keeping low, just in case someone answered his challenge with fire, he called out in a stage whisper, "George!"

There was a lowing in answer. Avadanian moved away from the cow, laughing at himself and the stories he'd already piled up.

From a piece of high ground, Avadanian saw the glistening surface of the Mediterranean. He figured he'd do better heading for the coast: if he found any other paratroopers, eventually he'd come in contact with the units coming over the beaches. He moved carefully, avoiding the roads and trying not to make too much noise. Progress was slow, since the fields were cut by stone walls, some of them as much as six feet tall. If he didn't come across a gate, he had to climb over.

When he heard something moving, Avadanian froze in his tracks and scanned the blackness. There was a silhouette, barely visible but distinct; it looked like another paratrooper, so he gave the challenge.

"George!"

The figure stopped moving, but gave no response. Now Avadanian began to worry; he decided to give it another try.

"George," Avadanian called again.

"Washington!" came back.

It was the wrong response, but delivered in the right language and accent, so Avadanian held his fire. He moved forward and found a frustrated Dr. Lester Stein, the battalion surgeon, who angrily admitted that he had forgotten the password.

"It's Marshall," Avadanian told him.

The two men moved off together in the direction of the beaches.

Jack Norton's plane had come in low over the Mediterranean, buffeted by winds and even splashed with spray as it skimmed over the salt water. As ranking man, Norton was jumpmaster, and was in the door when the plane crossed the coast. Just behind him stood Tommy Gore, the battalion operations sergeant. Norton found the sergeant's presence reassuring, because Gore—though only twenty-three—was one of the most capable soldiers in the entire headquarters.

Norton kept waiting for the pilots to climb to a higher altitude as the land rose below them, but the craft kept on level flight, and the hills got closer. Gore, looking over Norton's shoulder, could see the faint tracks of roads below them, glowing in the moonlight. Both men had made extensive studies of the maps and terrain models of the objective area, and as they peered down, they tried to fit the pattern of roads and shape of the coastline here with the mental image they each carried.

When the green light came on, Norton shouted, "Let's go!" and pushed himself into the darkness. The plan called for them to jump from 350 to 400 feet, which would have given the jumpers time to get control of their chutes and look below them. While the parachutes were not entirely steerable, a man could slip to avoid serious obstacles, like buildings and walls. Norton did not have time for any maneuvers. Seconds after his parachute opened, he crashed into a high stone wall that smacked him on the back and shoulders. He crumpled to the ground, found his footing, and shook loose of his harness.

Must have jumped pretty low, Norton thought as he looked around, trying to pick out shapes. He could hear movement around him, the rustling of parachutes, the grunts of men hitting the ground, the receding drone of the aircraft engines. He gave his eyes a few seconds to adjust to the darkness. He was looking for a road, and he soon spotted one in the dim moonlight. Since there was no reason to believe the carrier pilots had dropped him in the wrong place, Norton assumed he was on the DZ. In fact, the Second Battalion was some twenty-five miles from their objective. The good news was that the unit, though misplaced, had landed close together.

Norton had already developed a reputation in the unit as a man who could get things—lots of things—done right, and in a hurry. It was a talent that would serve him, and the Second Battalion, well. His first job was to set up the battalion command post and figure out where they were. Then he'd make contact with the companies gathering out in the dark, and from them, gather the figures on how many men were accounted for, how many were injured, how many missing. He needed to know if the rifle companies had found their weapons bundles, with the critical machine guns and mortars, as well as the medical supply bundles. Norton's job, in short, was to wrestle order from chaos, to get a handle on everything that affected the battalion's ability to fight, so that his boss, Mark Alexander, could concentrate completely on *how* to take the fight to the enemy.

There was sporadic firing going on, much of it aimed at the airplanes overhead, some of it clearly aimed at targets on the ground. The more Norton looked around, the more he questioned, with a growing sense of dread, whether they were in the right spot.

This was not like being lost in training, which could be embarrassing, or could even lead to a man getting relieved. Second Battalion was on a tight schedule, part of a detailed attack plan that involved the entire regiment. They were one of the key parts in the big machine, but nothing was going to happen if the battalion was lost. Norton felt a tremendous need to establish exactly where his unit was, so they'd know where they had to go to accomplish their mission. He found a corporal from the intelligence section and the operations officer, Captain Paul Woolslayer.

"This is the command post," Norton told Woolslayer, indicating the spot where they'd landed. "Get it set up. I'm going to look around and see if I can pinpoint where we are." In the dark, it was difficult to gauge Woolslayer's reaction or even to see his face, but Norton thought he'd made himself clear.

Norton took the corporal and another man with him and moved west alongside the road, Norton on one side, the other men opposite him. The dirt track was visible in the dying moonlight, a shade lighter than the surrounding fields. They had gone less than a half mile when Norton heard voices, but they were too far away to make out what was being said. The executive officer also thought he could see some movement up ahead. He signaled to the others, and he and the corporal moved forward in a crouch, every sense tuned to what was in front of them. The area was full of paratroopers wandering around, looking for their buddies, and Norton didn't want to shoot—or get shot by—a jumpy GI. He also suspected that the road, and any intersection that

lay ahead of him in the blackness, was a likely spot for an enemy outpost.

Now Norton could definitely hear men talking, but the words
were still indistinct, just murmuring in the darkness. He wasn't sure
what he would find, so he pulled a grenade out of the cargo pocket on
his trousers and straightened the pin. Finally, Norton raised to a
crouch and gave the challenge.

"George!"

The reply came back in accented English.

"George, hell!"

Norton saw the bright muzzle flash of a machine gun firing directly at him and felt something pull at the shoulder of his uniform as
he tossed the grenade. Another round rang off his helmet and tore his
chin strap loose. When the grenade exploded, he called to the other
men to pull back.

There was barbed wire on the sides of the road, and Norton saw it
before he got entangled. The former Army track team hurdler pulled
his weapon high across his chest and leaped over the wire. The three
men made it back to the command post, where Norton found that a
bullet had plinked through his suspender strap and another had grazed
his helmet. The third trooper had been slightly wounded in the exchange, so Norton made sure the man got to the medics.

At some point, Norton thought, *this story will be funny. But it isn't
now.*

After he'd caught his breath, Norton went looking for Captain
Woolslayer, whom he'd put in charge of getting the command post up
and running. He found Woolslayer crouching in a shallow foxhole,
sweating, digging, muttering. There was firing in the area, but none of
it was coming anywhere near.

Norton asked Woolslayer what he'd accomplished, but the operations officer couldn't tell him anything about the status of the unit. He

had no idea what companies were in the area, how many wounded or injured. As far as Norton could see, he had done nothing except dig himself a hole.

Norton had too much to do to worry about Woolslayer. He moved around the perimeter, collected the information he needed, and warned the men about the nearby enemy position. He still did not know where they had landed, although he was pretty sure that they weren't in the right place.

Tommy Gore, who had jumped right behind Norton, was alone when he landed. He could see planes overhead, and thus knew which direction the beach lay, and he headed out cross-country. Soon he came upon a high stone wall, which he climbed with some difficulty, hauling his heavy equipment up and over. Then there was another wall, and another. The whole process was frustrating—for all he knew, there might be gates just a few yards away in the darkness. And the climbing was not only tiring, but left him exposed as he pulled himself over the top. The walls were also a clue that they had not landed at the right drop zone: there hadn't been this many walls on the maps, aerial photos, or sand tables of their objective area. Gore, as battalion operations sergeant, had studied the maps and photos and built the sand tables himself. If anyone was going to recognize the drop zone, it would be him.

He'd gone far enough to work up a good sweat when he heard machine-gun fire, and Gore huddled against a wall, trying to catch his breath and figure out where the sound was coming from. He calmed down once he figured the fire wasn't directed at him, and then realized it was a clue as to where the other troopers were. Taking care not to run into an enemy patrol, he moved slowly through the night and found the battalion command post at dawn. Gore immediately went looking for his boss, the operations officer. He found Captain Paul

Woolslayer on the ground in the fetal position; when Gore approached him to ask for instructions, Woolslayer muttered that he couldn't get killed, that he had a wife and two daughters at home who needed him.

"I've got to make it home," Woolslayer said. The captain, a brute of a man who was tough in training, who always finished the road marches and could go as far as anyone in terms of physical stamina, had fallen apart in his first hour in a combat zone. Gore was glad to see Captain Norton in the area, taking charge and getting the headquarters people focused and moving.

Gore also saw the body of the young battalion surgeon, Kurt Klee, who had been removed from the wire and laid out for the graves registration people.

Norton wasn't paying attention to Woolslayer, and he said nothing about him to Gore. Gavin had told them that every man has breaking point: some men reach it quickly, some go through years of combat without coming close to falling apart. Woolslayer had simply found his breaking point right away.[2]

At dawn, it became harder to ignore the operations officer's plight. Mark Alexander learned that Woolslayer had spent the entire night digging his own foxhole, and had done nothing to help Norton get the command post or the battalion organized. Alexander decided to give Woolslayer a chance. Maybe, Alexander reasoned, if he got up and moved and didn't die right away, he would regain some of the confidence he'd shown all through training.

Alexander told Woolslayer to pull himself together and take some men from D Company to clear one of the largest pillboxes, just to the west of the battalion perimeter. Since the pillboxes were on the side of the long slope that led down to the ocean, Alexander thought that perhaps their guns were trained downhill, making the enemy vulnerable from the rear, the uphill side.

Alexander's idea seemed to work, and Woolslayer came up with a plan. He chose Lieutenant John D. Sprinkle, the well-liked executive officer of D Company, and organized an assault on the largest pillbox, a two-story concrete dome that dominated the area around the olive grove.

Defensive positions, such as the pillboxes the All-Americans encountered in their first hours on Sicily, are not designed to stand alone. Since the men inside have limited fields of vision, the positions are mutually supporting: the blind spots of one pillbox will most likely be covered by the weapons in another.

After dawn, Woolslayer and Sprinkle led a group of twelve men, including Allan C. Barger, communications sergeant of D Company, out of the battalion position and through the small, walled olive orchards that spread across the slope. When they got close, Sprinkle set off to do a leader's reconnaissance: he'd crawl forward and assess the situation, and from that, he'd develop his plan of attack. Sprinkle told the men to stay out of sight while he and Sergeant Anthony Karmazin scouted the pillboxes. Guided by the noise of the machine guns, Sprinkle headed for the enemy, using the low growth for concealment. When he got to a point where he could see the biggest pillbox, the two-story concrete-and-stone giant, the aggressive lieutenant thought he could move all the way forward without the enemy seeing him. Once he reached the outside wall of the pillbox, he'd toss hand grenades through the firing apertures. Instead of exposing his entire patrol in a big attack, he'd take out the enemy position on his own. Sprinkle broke cover and moved forward.

Luis D. Santos, of Second Battalion's D Company, was on the opposite side of the big pillbox, unaware that other paratroopers were close.

Santos had been in a big hurry to get to the ground. The eighteen-year-old had taken full advantage of the big dinner prepared for the paratroopers before they left Africa, figuring that there was an even chance that it would be his last meal. He loaded up on chicken and beef, eating past the point of fullness. But after months of canned field rations, his body was no longer used to that much food. About an hour into the plane ride, Santos broke into a cold sweat and was hit by a wave of cramps; he was suddenly afraid he'd lose control of his bowels. Defecating on himself in the airplane would not only be embarrassing; there would be little chance to change out of his clothes for days once they were in Sicily. The private held on tight, willing his body to obey, but he watched for the red and then the green light with a good bit more eagerness than some.

Santos had come to the United States from the Dominican Republic illegally in 1941, when he was sixteen. He landed in New York, where he had family, and managed to find small jobs. When the United States entered the war and young men were called to duty by the hundreds of thousands (and eventually, by the millions), Santos learned that he could become a citizen by receiving an honorable discharge from the armed forces. The fact that the country was at war didn't deter him.

Santos was born Luis DeLosSantos, but the Army paperwork changed that to Luis D. Santos, which was easier for the Americans to pronounce. He spoke almost no English when he volunteered and was sent to Arkansas for training as a medic. The other men had a great deal of difficulty understanding his heavy accent, and with his dark skin, some assumed he was part African American (which was not an asset in the segregated Army of World War II). Santos mastered a little English as he went along, and in spite of the language barrier, managed to finish his training with a high standing.

When the word came out that the paratroopers—with their extra fifty dollars a month in jump pay—were looking for volunteers, Santos lined up, but the noncom told him his English wasn't good enough. Santos pointed out that he had managed to get through training with what command of the language he had. He finished jump school in early 1943, and on the night of July 9–10, he jumped with D Company.

Santos had landed easily and immediately unhooked his rifle from his parachute harness; then he undid the harness itself, and without even moving away from his chute, began to unbuckle his pants. When his trousers were partway down, something caught his eye. It might have been the movement, it might have been sparse moonlight glinting off the man's rifle as he aimed at the paratrooper, but Santos saw him and reacted quickly. He grabbed his own weapon, which was assembled and loaded, and fired, knocking the man down. Without even checking to see if the man was dead, he squatted for the relief he desperately needed. Then he tore his undershirt loose and wiped himself. The rifle shot was bound to attract attention, so as soon as he finished his business, Santos grabbed his rifle, yanked his pants up as high as he could, and hurried away from the area.

As the light came up on July 10 (about the time John Sprinkle and the D Company patrol were getting ready to check out the pillboxes), Santos was still alone, still in the area where he landed, and curious about the man he'd shot. He retraced his steps and found a small stone building that looked like a church, with a pillbox attached at one end. The dead man had probably come from the pillbox, but Santos couldn't be sure if the man's comrades had missed him yet or had come looking for him. The body—it was an Italian—was where he'd left it, as was his abandoned parachute. Santos sat down to watch the pillbox, then moved from one covered position to another to get a closer look. Soon he saw movement in the distance, on the opposite side of the enemy position. In a moment, he could make out a familiar figure: Lieutenant Sprinkle, the D Company executive officer. Santos waved his arms and tried to get the lieutenant's attention, but Sprinkle was looking at something else. From his vantage point, Santos could see that Sprinkle was drifting into the fields of fire of the pillbox near the church. The trooper hollered at the officer, but it was too late. There was a burst of fire and Sprinkle went down.

Santos couldn't tell if the men inside the pillbox had heard him shout, but he wasn't going to wait to find out. He had a clear approach, and the defenders inside were probably focused on their front, where they'd just killed Sprinkle. Santos hurried alongside the church and came out on the back side of the pillbox. He pulled out a hand grenade, tugged the pin out, stepped away from the wall for the angle, and hurled the grenade into the firing port. As soon as heard the boom of the explosion, he began yelling in Spanish for the men inside to come out with their hands up. He threatened them with more grenades.

Incredibly, the heavy door to the pillbox swung open, smoke curled out of the opening, and wounded men, dazed from the blast in such a tight space, began stumbling out. Some were bleeding from shrapnel wounds, others were bleeding from their ears as a result of the concussion. Santos trained his rifle on them and continued giving them instructions in Spanish. The Italians understood him, and they did everything he told them to do, throwing down their weapons and holding their hands in the air. More and more men piled out of the smoky door; when they stopped, Santos was incredulous: seventeen Italian soldiers stood before him. They had no way of knowing that they'd been attacked by a lone paratrooper; all they knew was that an American had gotten close enough to throw grenades into the firing ports, and was not going to let up until they surrendered. So out they came.

A surprised Santos wasn't sure how he was going to handle seventeen prisoners, or even what his next move should be. He had not found his company or even one other trooper, and now he was responsible for seventeen men. If they rushed him, it was likely he could only shoot a couple before they got him. But these Italians, like so many others the GIs were encountering that day, had had enough of a war they didn't want in the first place.

Fortunately for Santos, a patrol from his own company came up moments later, drawn by the sound of his hand grenade. The little band of troopers had come from the battalion perimeter, and a sergeant motioned for Santos to come along with his prisoners.

Because his English was so poor, Santos was unable to explain what had happened, or how he'd wound up with seventeen prisoners. Santos was sent with a larger batch of prisoners toward the beach, where they were eventually turned over to the Forty-fifth Division troops. He rejoined his unit three days later. By that time, the incident was all but forgotten.[3]

One of Jack Norton's duties was to make sure the dead were collected in a central location. He went about this task with the efficiency that was becoming his trademark, but seeing the bodies shook him. In the short time he'd been with the battalion, Norton had made an effort to get to know as many of the leaders as possible, and John Sprinkle had made an impression on him: the young lieutenant was competent and likable, and had the makings of an excellent soldier. Now, on the first morning of the war for the 505th, he lay wrapped in a parachute shroud, awaiting burial in a shallow grave far from home, and Jack Norton had his shocking first lesson in the realities of war.

Twenty-three-year-old Sergeant Franklin Spencer was the message center chief of Second Battalion headquarters. He landed in a tree, and although his body weight pulled him to the ground, his chute was draped over the branches, which made it difficult for him to move. As soon as his ears adjusted to the relative quiet, he heard a rustling nearby. One of the rumors the troopers had heard and passed around was that the Germans would use vicious dogs to find wounded and injured paratroopers, and that the dogs were trained to kill them. When Spencer heard the breathing of an animal, he reached for his boot knife. The grunting got louder, although it was too dark to make out any shapes. Finally, Spencer lunged at the place he thought the sound was coming from. He stuck a farmer's pig, which went squealing off into the night.

By dawn, Spencer had managed to hook up with a couple of other troopers. There were not enough of them to constitute any kind of force, so their first inclination was to get closer to the beach and link up with a larger body of American troops there. They stumbled on a pillbox, which opened up on them with automatic weapons. Spencer had a clear sight of an Italian soldier drawing a bead on him with a rifle, and then, unbidden, the thought, *He doesn't even know me and he's trying to shoot me.*

The paratroopers, perhaps because they were unprepared, or because they were outnumbered, took the worst of the fight and were driven back. One of the men went down in a heap, his stomach torn wide open. The fire was getting heavier, and the men who could move wanted to get out of there, which meant abandoning the wounded GI. The troopers were under heavy fire, and more men would be hit if they stayed.

Spencer heard someone say, "Don't leave any water with him," because they'd been taught that soldiers wounded in the stomach should not have water to drink.

Spencer was torn, but joined the small group pulling back, abandoning the wounded GI and hoping that the enemy would take him prisoner and provide first aid. A noncom told Spencer, who was armed with a tommy gun, to provide covering fire as the small unit disengaged. Spencer laid down fire as best he could, and in the few moments they were all moving as fast as they could toward the beach. No one mentioned the wounded man they'd left behind.

Private Cecil Prine of B Company climbed a high rock wall and found a road on the other side, just a bit paler than the surrounding countryside. Prine was able to make out a shape lying in the road, motionless. He approached slowly, cautiously, his weapon ready, and found a soldier from his company named Joe Garidel, who had been knocked unconscious in his landing. Prine pulled Garidel out of the road, and the noise attracted another trooper. Now there were three of them. But there was nothing else: no firing, no aircraft, nothing at all. They heard the mild tinkling of a cowbell in a field somewhere below them. It was a lonely, spooky sound.

Once Garidel came to and was able to walk, the three men set out. Soon they heard someone in the field where they'd heard the cowbell. Their challenge, "George," was met by, "Hey, I'm an American!"

"Shut up," one of Prine's companions said in a stage whisper. "You'll bring the Germans around."

Incredibly, they found twenty men in the low ground. Sergeant Harvill Lazenby, from Tennessee, was the ranking man, which made Prine feel better. The sergeant claimed to have been a professional gambler in civilian life, and he displayed all the cool one would expect of a gambler. Lazenby, armed with a tommy gun and a .38-caliber pistol he'd collected somewhere, organized the men for movement. They had no idea where they were, although it was pretty clear that they were nowhere near the drop zone. They headed toward the sea, hoping to encounter an American unit coming across the beach.

Just after dawn, Lazenby's men ran into a German patrol that was also moving, probably out looking for paratroopers. In a short, intense firefight, the Americans overwhelmed the enemy, killing more than twenty of them and capturing nine, without suffering any casualties. To Prine, the twenty-year-old private, this merely confirmed what he had been told and what he truly believed: the paratroopers were more than a match for anyone they'd meet on the battlefield. No less an authority than General George Patton had said he almost felt sorry for the bastards the GIs were going to come up against. Prine wasn't the student of military history Patton was, but he had all the evidence he needed in the bodies of the dead Germans and the stunned prisoners they led toward the coast.

The GIs and their prisoners all dove for cover when two jeeps mounting .50-caliber machine guns came up the road from the beach, guns blazing. One of the lead troopers, hiding behind a rock, waved a handkerchief and shouted out, "We're the Eighty-second Airborne!" over and over, until the jeeps stopped firing.

"We're the Forty-fifth Division," one of the men in the recon patrol said. "And this is our landing zone."

Prine and his buddies had landed at least fifty miles from their intended drop zone. They attacked the enemy where they found him, and now had to find a ride to the other end of the American sector.

Bill Bishop, a twenty-one-year-old squad leader in G Company, was the "pusher" in his stick, determined to empty his plane of troopers. He was also determined to be careful. In a training exercise an overly enthusiastic pusher had grabbed the Air Corps crew chief, who was lingering around the open doorway of the plane, and shoved the man out, thinking he was a paratrooper balking at the jump. The Air Corps man did not have a parachute and fell to his death. By the time of the Sicily invasion, Bishop saw, the crew chiefs were tying themselves to the aluminum ribs of the fuselage.

Bishop's plane was hit with flak and machine gun fire as it crossed the coast. The young sergeant from Cairo, Georgia, thought it sounded like rain on a tin roof. The only visible effect it had was to make the men strain for the door.

The pilot of Bishop's plane held his course steady as the first jumpers cleared the door, but then a sudden burst of ground fire caused him to lose his nerve. Bishop felt the plane buck as the pilot increased airspeed and banked sharply right. The deck of the aircraft was slick with vomit—many of the men had been airsick on the bumpy flight over—and the half-stick remaining in the plane began to slide and fall. Bishop clawed his way along the deck plates, glad to see that the troopers ahead of him were just as determined to get out of the plane as he was. On his belly, weighed down by more than a hundred pounds of gear, he was in no position—literally—to shove anyone out.

The C-47 banked hard right when Bishop clawed his way to the lip of the door and threw himself out. His body bumped on the underside of the aircraft, which stood nearly on its wingtip, and he had a second to think that if any of the cargo bundles beneath the plane were released at this moment, his parachute would be hopelessly tangled and he'd shoot for the ground like a stone. (Before the next combat jump, in Italy, Bishop told the pilot of his plane that if he accelerated or turned sharply to avoid ground fire, thus endangering the paratroopers, Bishop would toss a hand grenade into the cargo space as he cleared the door. The pilot on that flight held his course.)

Bishop was knocked unconscious on landing, and when he woke, he wasn't sure how long he'd been out. It was immediately clear to him that they were not on their assigned drop zone, and that they'd landed right in the midst of the enemy positions that had pounded their airplane with antiaircraft fire. A large searchlight that had been spotting aircraft for the gunners now swept the sky in lower arcs, looking for paratroopers who could be shot as they floated down. Bishop and another soldier named James Stepp set out to pinpoint the big light so they could knock it out.

As they moved through a relatively open area, the light suddenly swung toward them, inviting the enemy machine gunners to do the same. The two troopers threw themselves down, and Stepp let out a small cry. Bishop hadn't heard any rounds come close to them, but as he hugged the earth, he heard Stepp grunting and in obvious pain.

"I'm hit," Stepp said. "I'm hit."

The two were flat on the ground in the pitch dark, close to an enemy position. They couldn't stand up, and Bishop certainly couldn't use a flashlight to see what had happened to Stepp, but the man was obviously in pain and needed first aid.

Bishop opened his mussette bag and pulled out the raincoat he carried there. He crawled to Stepp so that the two lay head to head, and threw the raincoat over their upper bodies. Under this makeshift blackout shelter, Bishop flipped open his cigarette lighter to examine Stepp.

Stepp's face was covered in blood, laid open in a deep gash from his hairline to his jaw. Apparently, when the two dove to the ground almost on top of one another, Bishop's bayonet had opened Stepp's face from top to bottom. In the gloom under the raincoat, it appeared that the gash had sliced right through Stepp's eye.

Working quickly, Bishop pulled out a compress bandage and applied it to Stepp's face, tying it as tightly as he could. Then he closed his lighter, hurriedly stuffed his raincoat into the open musette bag, and held Stepp by the arm as they scuttled back toward where Bishop had left the rest of his platoon.

The young sergeant's war was off to an inauspicious start. He'd been knocked unconscious in the jump, was able to find only a part of his unit, had no idea where he was, had been pinned down by an antiaircraft battery, and had inflicted a serious wound on one of his own men. He decided to wait until daylight before moving again.

(Stepp was evacuated with other wounded troopers and was captured by the Germans before he could reach the beach. Bishop blamed himself for Stepp's capture, and he assumed that the young man had lost his eye. Years after the war, Stepp called Bishop and asked if he could visit his former sergeant. Bishop agreed, though he was nervous about facing the man he'd scarred. He was relieved to find that Stepp had not lost his eye, and he did not hold Bishop responsible for his being captured.)

After dawn, Bishop spotted a stone building with smoke coming from the chimney. There was a low wall enclosing a courtyard, so he had no view inside any windows. He had to get closer if he was going to find out if he'd stumbled across a German or Italian outpost. Bishop positioned one squad to cover him as he slipped over the wall into the courtyard, then crept up to a window. He raised his head and his rifle at the same time, pointing the muzzle into the open window.

Inside, he saw a woman holding a heavy pot, getting ready to put it on an iron stove. He could see, through the open top of the stove, her cooking fire. Before he could do or say anything, the woman saw him and screamed, dropping the pot full of food onto the stove, making even more noise. Bishop jumped, startled, but fortunately he didn't fire. The woman turned and grabbed a small baby that had been sitting on a pallet on the floor. She fell to her knees, clutching the baby, her hands clasped in prayer. She was crying and yelling, clearly terrified.

Bishop was horrified: the woman thought he was going to kill her. He made comforting sounds as he backed off, then found the door. He went into the room, telling her over and over that everything was going to be okay, everything was going to be fine.

Alerted by the woman's screams, some men came running in from their work in a nearby field. They all started yelling in Italian, and Bishop called for his support squad. He had identified those Italian-American soldiers who could help with translation, and he and his interpreter soon had the civilians calmed down and convinced that the Americans meant them no harm. Bishop's squad handed out chewing gum and cigarettes as a gesture of good faith. Convinced that they were not in danger, the Italians took a quick measure of the paratroopers and decided that these were the men who would deliver them from German occupation and the war. The men told Bishop's translator where the GIs could find a German unit nearby. Bishop thanked them and positioned his small platoon for movement.

Soon, they spotted an armored car right where the Italian farmers had told them they'd find it. They crept close, the men spread out and alert. The vehicle appeared to be some sort of antiaircraft gun, and then Bishop saw the big searchlight. The light had been shot out, but not before the crew used it and the gun to slaughter paratroopers as they descended. Now the crew was sitting nearby, with no guards posted.

Bishop's patrol gunned them down to a man.

Sam Ellis of B Company, 307th Engineers, landed on one of the chalky roads that were visible in the moonlight. His first reaction was to get out of the open area, and he dragged his gear and his parachute like a train as he scrambled behind a roadside stone wall. It was only after he was behind this cover that he took the time to unfasten his harness. He moved farther from the road, crossing a field and finding a couple of other troopers, including Lieutenant Richard Riley. Riley was intent on finding well water, or any water that wasn't tainted by the chemicals the Army had been dumping into the drinking water in North Africa.

The small band was on this mission when, in the half-light before dawn, they heard a vehicle coming down the road they were following. The GIs lay down alongside the road and watched as a German half-track armored car rattled toward them. The commander was clearly visible, standing on the passenger seat, and he waved at the troopers. In their jumpsuits, they must have looked like German soldiers to him. The paratroopers waved back and let the vehicle pass by.

Joe Jockel, the former St. John's University student who had experimented with ways to resupply the regiment by air, landed on the hard roof of a building and broke his leg in three places. He rolled off the roof and lay in blinding pain until he was found by some troopers, who carried him to a roadblock they'd set up. Like so many small groups, they had no idea where they were, but they were determined to do something. They propped Jockel up against a stone wall, put his rifle and grenades near him, and told him they were going to stop anyone coming up the road. Jockel, ready to do his part, sat and watched his leg swell all through D-day.

The next day, the healthy troopers got policed up by a noncom. They couldn't carry the badly injured Jockel, but they knew that American troops had established a beachhead and were nearby. They moved Jockel to a roadside ditch, left him with his weapon and some morphine styrettes, and told him to watch for the GIs who were sure to come up the road from the beach. He spent the night of July 10–11 hiding in the dense brush, helpless, unable to move, alone, and wondering who would come up the road in the morning.

He heard them before he saw them: vehicles on the road. Then he saw, through the brush, men walking ahead of the vehicles. They were coming from the direction he thought the Americans would come from, but they were in black uniforms. For a long, sinking moment, Jockel thought he was about to be discovered by German troops. Then he heard the men speaking English, and he yelled out the challenge.

"George!"

Jockel had been discovered by a reconnaissance element of the Forty-fifth Division, and though he was far from his drop zone, he was glad to be back in American hands. The recon soldiers called for a medic, and soon Jockel was loaded onto a stretcher and carried to an aid station. He wound up in Gela, waiting for evacuation behind the more seriously wounded. He was surprised to see that Sicilian civilians came through the aid station, giving out cheese and wine.

By this time, almost thirty-six hours had elapsed since Jockel's leg was shattered. It had swollen to two or three times its normal size, and so the doctors determined they would have to operate on one of the hospital ships lying offshore. Jockel was moved to the beach, where he lay on a stretcher next to big piles of ammunition waiting to be trucked inland. The high explosives made him nervous.

Then the air raid sirens started. Jockel, fearing an explosion amid the piles of ammunition stacked on the beach, dragged himself off the stretcher and into a shallow hole. He nearly passed out from the pain of moving his shattered leg.

When the sirens stopped, Jockel couldn't get out of the hole. He began yelling for help. A soldier came close, looked down, and said, "You got yourself in, get yourself out."

Jockel was helpless, but the soldier finally yanked him out and put him back on the stretcher. Eventually Jockel made it to a hospital ship for treatment.

LANDINGS

Major General Matt Ridgway, the commander of the Eighty-second Airborne Division, made the crossing from Africa on the *Monrovia*, Patton's command ship, and came across the beach around seven-thirty on the morning of D-day. (Although criticized by some for not jumping, Ridgway was merely letting Gavin do his job without interference.) Ridgway and his aide, Don Faith, made their way to Major General Terry Allen's First Division command post, which was just a couple of hundred yards off the beach, east of Gela.

Ridgway still had no word from any of his men. There were no messages waiting for him in Allen's headquarters. No runners had been dispatched from the paratroopers' objective area just inland from Gela; the radio waves were silent. As far as he could tell, the thirty-four-hundred-man combat team had flown off into the darkness and had disappeared. He set off from Allen's CP, accompanied by a few GIs for security, to find his soldiers. Once he and his security escort pushed past the forwardmost outposts of the First Division, he was just like the other paratroopers on Sicily, wandering around in enemy territory with little idea of where he was going.

Finally, he found I Company's command post, with Bill Follmer sitting under an olive tree, his broken ankle stretched out in front of him. Ridgway offered help, but Follmer said he'd wait for a medic. Then Ridgway asked the company commander if Follmer knew were the regiment might be, where any of the troopers might be. Follmer didn't know.[1]

As Ridgway and his small band pushed inland, they came across individual troopers and small knots of men, who eagerly shared stories of the jump and told the general about bumping into enemy patrols or stumbling across pillboxes with alerted sentries. But they weren't sure where their companies were, and none of them had any idea where Gavin was.

At about this time on July 10, Gavin was some sixteen or seventeen miles to the east, making his fitful way cross-country with his small band of men, on the hills southwest of Vittoria. Gavin had reluctantly decided that he was going to have to wait for nightfall if he was going to have any chance of reaching his objective alive. As he scouted the hillsides for a likely place to hole up, Gavin was no doubt thinking of Ridgway, waiting for word and looking for some sign of progress down near the distant beachhead.

Both men were conscious that there was more on the line than just this one battle. Ridgway and Gavin had staked their professional reputations on this bet that a large body of airborne troops could arrive on a battlefield with enough concentrated power to make a difference. As Matt Ridgway climbed the gentle rise of the plain that lay inland from Gela, and as Jim Gavin scoured hillsides above the sea for a place to hold out until dusk, these two men of action had to be content with waiting to see what unfolded in the coming hours.

Jim Gavin settled down amid the dry vegetation of the spot he had chosen. He kept one eye out for enemy patrols, and with the other, watched the slow progress of the sun across the sky. Matt Ridgway pointed the straggling paratroopers he found toward the First Division lines and, discouraged, returned to Allen's CP, hoping word had come in about his missing regiment. There was still no news.

*   *   *

Shortly after dawn on D-day, July 10, Lieutenant Bob Piper watched from a concealed position as a squad of German soldiers approached. Piper had spent most of his time in the regiment with G Company, but had been moved up to headquarters to help the adjutant, Major Al Ireland, dig out from the mountains of paperwork necessary to get the troopers ready for overseas movement. He jumped with the headquarters element, and during the night he'd gathered eight other troopers as they made their way cross-country toward the drop zone and the objective area. Because his band was so small, Piper was very concerned that they'd run into a larger enemy patrol, so he'd been extremely cautious in his move. The men stuck to the low ground, used whatever concealment the thin vegetation offered, and were careful about the noise they made.

He couldn't say the same about the enemy soldiers approaching. The Germans were speaking loudly, almost as if they had no idea there had been an invasion and that the island was now covered with roaming bands of Allied troops. They were on foot, naked to the waist, obviously headed out to do their morning physical training. Although the Germans were unarmed, there was no telling how far away their garrison was, or for that matter, how far away their weapons might be. Piper decided that he could not take a group of prisoners numbering as many men as he had, nor could he let them just walk away. The Americans waited until the Germans had passed; then they ambushed the group, killing all of them. Piper and his group moved out quickly.

On the afternoon of Saturday, July 10, Piper and his men finally encountered some troops of the Forty-fifth Division, who had come across the beach near Scoglitti that morning. With their help, he figured out where he was: close to Vittoria, but nearly forty miles from his DZ. The Forty-fifth Division troops had heard that there were paratroopers not too far away along the Vittoria–Gela road, and they let Piper take a jeep to link up with his unit. Piper and his crew piled on the sturdy four-wheel-drive vehicle, and headed out in the direction of Gela. The road took them right to the main body of the Third Battalion of the 505th, and Piper wound up rejoining G Company just east of a dusty brown hill that seemed to be a gathering place for all the paratroopers in the area.

Lieutenant Gerald Johnson, a platoon leader in D Company, was alone until daylight on D-day. As the landscape sorted itself out into distinguishable forms, Johnson found some other troopers. Oddly, there were many more officers than enlisted soldiers in the group. They were huddled together, discussing what they should do, when Johnson heard someone yelling. He looked up a nearby hill and saw a paratrooper—with no equipment or weapon—heading their way as fast as he could run. As he drew closer, Johnson recognized Mike Scambelluri, a soldier from his platoon who'd been loaned out as an interpreter to the battalion intelligence section.

As Scambelluri drew close, Johnson and the others saw that he was bleeding and badly wounded. Scambelluri collapsed, and his comrades tried to stop the bleeding from what looked like multiple gunshot and knife wounds. Johnson was amazed that Scambelluri could move, much less run, down the hillside.

The wounded man managed to get out his story. Upon landing, he'd been captured by an Italian patrol just up the hill from where Johnson had fallen into the deep ditch. They stripped him of his weapon and equipment, and then the GI made a mistake: he said something in Italian. The officer in charge flew into a rage, calling Scambelluri a traitor to all Italians. He had his men tie the American's arms; then the officer emptied his pistol at almost point-blank range into the helpless trooper. When this didn't kill him, his captors threw

Scambelluri's own grenades at him. Somehow, the paratrooper survived and even managed to escape.

Scambelluri was one of the most popular men in the platoon, handsome and hardworking, with a wife back in the States. What had happened was worse than being hit by enemy fire; he had been a prisoner and the enemy tried to execute him. The GIs were furious, but could at least console themselves that Scambelluri, now safe among his own and with medical treatment available, would survive. The medics moved Scambelluri toward the beach, where he was turned over to a British aid station. The troopers who carried him came back with a good report: Scambelluri seemed stable, and they fully expected him to recover. (The danger wasn't over for Scambelluri, who was evacuated across the beach to a British hospital ship lying off Siracusa. When the hospital ship was sunk by German bombers, Scambelluri, in another close call, was one of those rescued. He eventually made it to a hospital in Tripoli, but he died there of his wounds.)[2]

Much farther to the west, light machine gunner Joe Basel and two other men waited for dawn, when they hoped to spot some other troopers. The men had found the bundled, air-cooled .30-caliber weapon, which had been dropped in a wing bundle, and Basel was eager to deliver the important weapon to his unit, the headquarters company of Art Gorham's First Battalion. The men took turns resting and keeping watch, and the night was uneventful until just after dawn.

Basel and the others were shocked awake by terrible screaming close by. They could see nothing from their position, but it was clear that someone was being terribly hurt. Although the tiny group was in enemy territory and moving around posed a great risk, Basel couldn't sit still and do nothing. He turned to his assistant gunner and said, "I'm going to find out what's going on. You stay here, and don't you dare leave that gun."

The Brooklyn-born soldier hefted his M1 and set out across the open, hilly terrain, which was becoming increasingly visible in the growing light. The screams drew him on, until he saw a group of figures struggling. The screams came from the center of the tight frieze. Basel was fifty yards away when he realized what he was seeing. Four Italian soldiers were stabbing a GI, who lay on the ground, stripped of his equipment and uniform, naked to the waist and slathered in his own blood. The Italians were taking turns, their blades flashing in quick hands, torturing the man by holding back any fatal blows.

Basel yelled and shouldered his rifle in one swift movement. The Italians, who were standing over the GI, froze for a second. Basel fired. One, two, three, went down. The fourth reached for something on the ground, presumably his weapon, but Basel's fourth shot hit him and he crumpled. Basel sprinted to the paratrooper, whose chest and stomach were covered in stab wounds. He was bleeding from dozens of deep cuts, and was too far gone for Basel to do anything but kneel beside him and cradle his head. He murmured something Basel couldn't make out; then he died.

The only thing Basel could do for the man was to make sure that his body was recovered later for proper burial, so he looked around and made note of the spot. He checked the men he'd killed, wondering what had prompted such savagery; but there were no answers, nothing more to do. Basel hurried back to his comrades.

Later that morning, Basel and his men noticed another GI moving nearby. After watching for a while, Basel recognized his company commander and went out to meet the officer.

"I've got a couple of other guys over here, sir," he said. "What should we do?"

The captain didn't answer, but just stared at Basel. He didn't look injured, just dazed.

"You have any instructions for us?"

The young officer didn't respond. Basel couldn't figure out what was wrong, so he took the man gently by the arm and led him back to where he and his team had set up their machine gun. He had just returned when he heard the distinctive sound of British hobnailed boots on pavement. Looking up, he spotted some British soldiers advancing in battle formation; they were just as surprised to see the GIs.

"What are you doing here?" one of the Tommies asked.

"I was just about to ask you the same thing," Basel said.

The British had come across the beach. They weren't lost, they pointed out; Basel was. A quick look at their map and Basel realized that he had been dropped some ninety miles from his intended drop zone, down in the far southeastern corner of Sicily where the British were coming ashore on the Allied right flank.

"How am I going to get back to my unit?" he asked.

After conferring a bit, the men decided Basel should take his men back across the British beach, to a ship headed for Africa. There, the GIs could move to the rear headquarters of the Eighty-second Airborne Division, and from there back to their unit at the front. By the evening of D-day, Basel and his troopers, including the still-silent commander, were on board a British landing ship that had just unloaded supplies and taken on prisoners. The prisoners were sent below decks.

A British sailor told Basel, "If this ship gets bombed, just get yourself overboard and leave the prisoners."

Basel was a little shocked, but he figured the Royal Navy was making the rules here. Fortunately, he and his men made it back to Africa without incident.

Anthony Antoniou, a nineteen-year-old bazooka man from B Company, had two immediate concerns when he landed. One was the searing pain in his ankle, which he feared might be broken, and the other was the fact that he was utterly alone. All around him was darkness and complete silence, which was more frightening than he would have guessed. He had expected to land near his comrades, so this wasn't one of the possibilities he had considered during the long months of training for this night. For the moment, he concentrated on his ankle.

Antoniou, who had immigrated from Cyprus as a teen in 1939, was assigned to the combat engineers when he enlisted in the Army. But when he arrived at Fort Belvoir, in Virginia, he found that the men in his unit were, on average, ten years older than he was. All their talk was of wives and babies, things the teenager considered boring. One day, a recruiting team from Fort Benning paid a visit, all shiny jump boots and silver jump wings and swagger, and Antoniou was hooked.

Things had gone well for him until he was issued a bazooka in North Africa. The men were afraid of the weapon, as many of the rounds were defective and had a nasty habit of blowing up shortly after leaving the front end of the tube. Even when they worked, the hot propulsion gases often burned the face of the soldier firing the weapon. Antoniou had taken to wearing his gas mask when he fired the bazooka in training. Although they had spent most of their time practicing on wooden targets and shooting at big rocks in the desert, they had been assured that the bazooka would stop whatever armor they were likely to encounter. Antoniou didn't like the bazooka, but he knew it would be critical if they encountered enemy tanks, so he was determined to find the right bundle just as soon as he could walk.

He shucked his parachute, sat on the ground, pulled off his boot, and, since it was dark, examined his ankle with his hands. There were no bones sticking out anywhere—by this time, every paratrooper had seen his share of compound fractures—so he pulled out the bandage he'd been given and wrapped the ankle tightly, then worked his boot over the fast-swelling ankle. He laced it as tightly as he could, then stood up gingerly.

Antoniou had elected to carry an M1 rifle, even though the bazooka men were issued .45-caliber pistols. He told his comrades that heading into battle carrying only a pistol would be a little like going naked into Times Square. The lightweight carbines, with their tendency to jam, were no better. Antoniou chose the reliable M1, and now that he'd been separated from his stick and couldn't find his equipment, he was glad he'd carried the rifle. He fixed his bayonet to the weapon: Gavin had told the men to use their knives and bayonets at night. Antoniou set out to find some other Americans, and he soon hobbled onto a paved road.

Sticking to the side of the road, Antoniou retraced the flight path of the aircraft, thinking this would lead him to the other troopers, and the rest of his company. Suddenly he saw something move. There was a man close by him, a lone figure standing next to what looked, against the barely lighter sky, like a guardhouse of some sort. The man had seen him, too, and had reacted by turning toward Antoniou. In the darkness, the trooper had walked to within a few feet of what he took to be an Italian soldier. He thought about shooting, but Gavin had told them to use the bayonet. If he fired, other enemy soldiers in the area would immediately know he was there, and the muzzle flashes would tell them exactly where he stood.

For a long, agonizing second or two, the armed men stood facing one another in the darkness: someone had to act. Antoniou, who had learned some Italian as a boy on Cyprus, called out.

"*Paisan,*" he said.

It wasn't much of a plan, but the GI hoped he could fool the guard into thinking a German was coming up the road. The ruse bought the paratrooper the second or two he needed to get within striking distance. He shoved his rifle at the figure, bayoneting the guard before the man could make a noise. The Italian went down, and Antoniou frantically tried to pull his bayonet free. It was stuck. Finally, he put his foot on the body and yanked hard on his weapon until the blade came free. He could not see the man clearly, but there was no movement from the dark form on the ground. A frightened Antoniou limped away as fast as his bad leg would allow him.

He had not gone much farther when he saw another figure, but this one called out, "George!"

Antoniou answered, "Marshall." He was so relieved that he grabbed the man in a rough embrace. Now there were two of them.

The GIs compared notes on which direction would take them to the drop zone; then they headed out. Gradually, an eastern sky lightened just enough for them to see details in the landscape and an amazing sight: twelve men, young Italians, all in civilian clothes and, as far as they could see, unarmed. The men were walking on the road, and Antoniou's first thought was that they were soldiers heading off to surrender.

"Let's shoot them," his comrade suggested.

"No," Antoniou said. They weren't armed, and he didn't have the stomach to murder twelve men. Instead, he called out to them in Italian. The men stopped, and Antoniou questioned them. They were Italian soldiers who'd had enough of the war, and happily pointed the two troopers to a town where they could find other Americans. The two groups left each other peacefully.

After Mike Scambelluri was evacuated across the British beach, Lieutenant Gerald Johnson and a handful of other officers joined a group now totaling some twenty-five paratroopers. The ranking man was Lieutenant Sammon, the Second Battalion intelligence officer. The group of lieutenants, who were without platoons, formed a rifle squad and decided to attack the small town of Avola, which lay across their path to the sea.

The men had trained together for so long that even officers from different companies understood things in the same way: they had come to fight. They all had the same tough training, and expected the same high standards. Johnson felt he could rely on these other lieutenants as much as he could rely on his own platoon.

Avola was a small town of one- and two-story buildings on the southeastern corner of Sicily, south of Siracusa. Italian soldiers had barricaded themselves in and found sniper positions in the upper floors and on the roofs of the houses. Snipers moved easily from one rooftop position to another as the Americans advanced.

Combat in a built-up area is completely different from combat in open country. The ranges are much shorter, and an advancing soldier's field of vision is narrow and limited to the next wall, the next building, the next alley. There are lots of hiding places for the defenders, including the roofs and upper stories.

The paratroopers advanced, catching only fleeting glimpses of the enemy. They fired into open windows, tossed hand grenades into doorways to clear buildings. They could only hope that the civilians had gotten out before the fighting started, or were holed up in deep basements.

The man behind Johnson, a sergeant named Grover Reeves, was hit in the upper arm by something that tore a big chunk of flesh away. Johnson kept firing and advancing in short rushes, scanning the windows and rooftops for targets. About fifteen minutes into the fight, Johnson was leaning against a wall near an intersection, looking for targets, when he heard an engine. A British major driving an American jeep came roaring up the road to tell the paratroopers that his unit was advancing on the town from the opposite side, and he was afraid that the allies were shooting at each other. The troopers quickly passed the word to cease fire until the major could sort things out.

The British, with a larger force, cleared the town while the paratroopers regrouped, sorted themselves out, and treated their wounded. The British confirmed what the Americans had feared: they'd been dropped some sixty miles from their drop zones. The paratroopers commandeered whatever transport they could find: donkey carts and pack animals, to which they began strapping the heavy weapons and ammunition for the long walk. The street was crowded with GIs and this motley collection of transport equipment when Johnson heard a loud noise behind them.

Field Marshal Montgomery was standing in a jeep, yelling at the paratroopers to get out of his way. It was, Johnson learned later, the beginning of his race with Patton to reach the key Sicilian cities and grab the biggest headlines. The tired troopers pushed and shoved their carts and animals out of the way to let the general pass.

The British offered to send the GIs back to Africa by ship, and from there the troopers could link up with their headquarters and eventually the rest of the 505th. Some of the men went that route and others, including Johnson, stayed behind to take the overland trip. Later, when the unorthodox column of donkeys and carts began to roll westward toward their drop zone, the American passed the hasty graves of some of the Italians they'd been fighting. The British had buried about fifteen of them in an empty lot. From each corpse, they'd left one arm sticking up, elbow to hand, and had placed the dead man's helmet on the hand. The sight was bizarre, like a formation of headgear that, on closer inspection, revealed something more grisly. The British, someone explained, didn't do this to mock the dead or mistreat the bodies, but simply to get them out of the hot sun and still make it easy for the graves registration people to find them.

Anthony Antoniou and his comrade closed in on Avola before the shooting stopped and joined the B Company men who were exchanging fire with an Italian garrison. The Americans worked their way through the streets, but soon heard heavy fire coming from the opposite side. At first, the troopers thought the Germans had sent reinforcements, but they soon caught glimpses of the distinctive helmets of British Tommies. The Americans began calling out to their allies, yelling as loudly as they could, but the firing drowned out their calls and the British kept shooting, pinning down the paratroopers closest to them. The Tommies' blood was up, and they weren't expecting to run across any GIs. Finally, a couple of men found some white cloth and fixed it to their weapons, which they waved overhead.

"You tea-drinking limey bastards," one of the troopers yelled as the British finally ceased fire. "We're on your side!"

Like Lieutenant Johnson, Antoniou elected to travel overland to rejoin the rest of the unit. He recovered a bazooka and joined a platoon-sized patrol of about thirty-five men. They had left Avola when they encountered a tank that came up on them suddenly in fairly open ground. The paratroopers dove for cover and called for the bazooka teams. Antoniou and the other bazooka men rushed into position to get a shot at the tank. Although the rounds would not penetrate the armor, Antoniou managed to hit the track, knocking it off and making it impossible for the vehicle to move.

Now the paratroopers and the tank crew were in a standoff. The bazookas couldn't hurt the tank, but for nearly six hours the GIs kept the crew trapped inside with small-arms fire, and the tankers kept the GIs from moving with their machine guns. Inside the tank, the crew could only hope for relief in the form of another tank, or some other German unit that would come along and chase the paratroopers away.

The Germans faced an excruciating dilemma. They could not be certain whether or not they had killed any of the paratroopers. If they had, the angry paratroopers might simply shoot them when they climbed out to surrender. But if they didn't surrender, at nightfall the Americans could move up without being seen and pile explosives around the tank, or get behind it and fire multiple rockets into the lightly armored rear. Trapped inside the big machine, with the Americans moving around outside like circling wolves, the German crew must have sweated through the interminable afternoon. At dusk it would all be out of their hands.

Just before sunset, on what must have seemed the longest day, the crew began calling out.

"Nicht schisen! Kamerad!"

The Germans came out; the paratroopers held their fire and took them prisoners. It had been a long, frustrating, and at times terrifying day for the patrol, but remarkably, they had suffered no casualties. They destroyed the empty tank with explosives and sent another handful of prisoners to the swelling prisoner cages on the beaches.

(Antoniou faced a similar situation in Normandy a year later, where an immobilized tank kept some paratroopers pinned down until dusk. But the tankers had killed several GIs while they were holding out and refusing to surrender. When they finally did come out, the paratroopers killed them.)

Mark Alexander had no way of knowing it, but his battalion was the only one to land in a relatively tight drop zone, albeit the wrong one. By late morning on D-day, July 10, the battalion adjutant, Lieutenant Clyde R. Russell, reported that the battalion had 536 men assembled, including 21 men from the 456th Field Artillery, with one 75 mm howitzer and about thirty rounds of ammunition. The airborne artillerymen had liberated a two-wheeled cart from one of the nearby farms, and they'd piled the ammunition on it. They had nothing to pull the howitzer, though, and so were prepared to drag it by hand.[3]

On the morning of D-day, the Second Battalion was the only airborne fighting force of any appreciable size assembled on Sicily. The rest of the 505th Regimental Combat Team was spread out over nearly a thousand square miles of the island. A map showing the 505th's actual landing would, roughly speaking, reveal a large oval close to the coast between Gela and Santa Croce Camerina. Within this zone, the action was shaping up in three distinct areas. First Battalion commander Arthur Gorham and his A Company under Ed Sayre were on the western edge of the paratroopers' area of operations, closest to the original drop zone at the Y road junction. Jim Gavin and much of the Third Battalion, under Ed Krause, were gathering in the center, near Vittoria, and Mark Alexander and Second Battalion were at the eastern end of the area, close to the Forty-fifth Division sector.

All along the coast, the paratroopers were gathering men and equipment, and, as Gavin had taught them, attacking the enemy wherever they found him.

In full daylight, the men of E Company, including the former lumberjack and boxer Otis Sampson, could see that elements of the entire Second Battalion were gathering on the hillside. Sampson was happy for the company, but still frustrated that he had not found all his own men and equipment. For his second patrol of the area, he gathered a larger group. In addition to Corporal Neil Curtis, he took Harry Pickels, Roy Watts, and William Judah, all from his section. Sampson took point, heading south again toward the building where he had landed the night before. Because the terrain was so open, Sampson insisted that the men keep a good distance between them; if they stumbled across an enemy position, he didn't want everyone going down in a single burst of fire. Sampson put the walled lane on his right and headed directly for the big house. They encountered a lone trooper, a man from another company, coming up the hill toward E Company.

"There's a sniper in those buildings," the GI warned them. "You'll have to be careful."

Snipers are effective in two ways: first, they target leaders. An experienced, well-trained sniper will watch how a group of enemy soldiers moves, and will target the one giving the orders or talking on the radio. Obviously, an insignia of rank makes a man a likely target. In combat, officers often removed rank insignia from their helmets and collars. Snipers also have a psychological effect: because they can strike at any moment, kill, then melt away into the battlefield, they're hard to hit back. Men advancing into an area known to have snipers are overly cautious and unsure of themselves.

Sampson's strategy: be aggressive and careful.

As they got close to the building, Sampson saw it was a two-story house. He decided to go around the east, the left side, as he approached from the north. He was so focused on what was in front of him that he didn't notice when the men behind him veered off. As he neared the building, he turned and saw the last man disappear around the far side. The whole patrol was gone. Once again, Sampson was alone. He had no idea why they hadn't followed, but since they were now on the other side of the building, he had to be careful not to shoot—or be shot by—his own men.

I hope to hell they know what they're doing, Sampson thought.

Sampson circled the eastern edge of what looked to be a walled orchard. Just downhill from the house, he passed the haystack where he had issued a challenge the night before. A little farther down the slope, he spotted a parachute and an attached equipment bundle. It was one of his, but the bundle had been opened, and the sight for the mortar removed. The enemy probably thought this would make the weapon unusable.

A machine gun opened fire behind him, and he spun around. Curtis came running around the southwest corner of the building. He had lost his helmet and his rifle, and there was a wild-eyed look about him as he yelled to Sampson, "They got Watts! They got Watts!"

When he drew close, Curtis explained. "The sniper is in the building on the other side," he said.

Now Sampson was angry. He headed back up the hill, moving quickly and carelessly, thinking only about the loss of one of his men. Sampson thought that if the sniper was on the opposite side of the building—the north or west—he could get at him from the rear. He rushed up to the southern wall, climbed to the top, sprayed the inside of the courtyard with automatic fire, then looked around. There was a parachute inside the enclosure, and a weapons carrier leaning against the wall near a cactus. This was the courtyard Sampson had landed in the night before. He was angry with himself for firing into the courtyard without checking to see if any of his own men were inside. But the mistake cleared his mind. Past his anger, he considered more carefully what he should do next.

Curtis had come around the southwest corner of the building; Sampson would circle around that way. The sergeant put his shoulder to the wall and started moving slowly. At his feet he saw the rocks that had been pushed off the wall by the figure he'd followed in the dark. At the corner of the building, he turned right, into a narrow lane that led north up the hill. The lane was bordered on both sides by a chest-high stone wall. Sampson was sure the sniper was somewhere up ahead, and he hoped the enemy was looking the other way. He checked his weapon, looked around him again, and stepped into the lane, every sense fully alert for the first movement or sound.

He had gone only a few yards when he saw the barrel of a machine gun pointing out from what looked like a haystack, about seventy feet up the lane. The gun was pointing west, to Sampson's left. Now that he was between the walls, he had only two choices: forward or backward. If he advanced and the gunner spotted him, he'd be trapped.

Sampson stepped back, thinking he had to somehow get behind the pillbox. It was almost painful to look away from the grim muzzle of the machine gun, but he had to turn to watch where he was going: it wasn't the time to trip and make noise. With every step, he expected to feel bullets in his back.

Wouldn't that be a great end? he thought.

He suddenly didn't like the idea of turning his back on the enemy. He faced front, trained his tommy gun on the opening and looked to see what the machine gunner might be watching. Out in the field to his left he could see two paratroopers moving down the hill, crossing in front of the enemy's line of fire, as if in a shooting gallery. The gunner was only waiting for them to get closer.

Holding himself against the wall, Sampson raised his arm to signal to the troopers, who spotted the movement right away. When they saw him, he pointed to the haystack in front of him and motioned for them to get down. The two men didn't hesitate.

Then Sampson rushed the pillbox, crouching so that he was below the firing port on his hands and knees. The machine gun, just above his head, fired into the field. Lying on his left side, Sampson couldn't see whether the two troopers had taken cover fast enough.

He heard voices from the firing port, which was about three feet high and just above where he lay, and pulled a grenade from the cargo pocket of his trousers. He had wrapped his grenades with tape to keep the spoon in place, so they couldn't go off unexpectedly (as when he came down through the branches of the tree). He had even slipped a tiny piece of paper under the end of the tape, like a pull tab. But the heat made the tape stick, and he picked at it, fighting to stay calm and focused. If the gunners discovered him, they could kill him with a grenade dropped out the window.

Finally, the tape came off. Samson was so excited that he forgot to let the grenade cook off. (The paratroopers had been taught that when they used grenades in extremely close quarters, they must let the grenade "cook off," that is, let the spoon fly while counting "one thousand, two thousand." This used up two or three seconds of the grenade's five-second fuse, so that an alert enemy didn't have time to throw the grenade back.) As soon as he threw the grenade, the voices stopped, and Sampson remembered that the fuse was too long. There was another agonizing few seconds as he waited for the enemy to toss the grenade back outside.

When the grenade exploded, Sampson stood, thrust the muzzle of his tommy gun into the opening, and raked the inside with fire. Then he noticed an open door in the building beside the pillbox. He'd been right below the loft door when he first spotted the paratroopers. If a sniper had been inside, Sampson would have been dead. He drew another grenade from his pocket, and pulled the tape and the pin. The open door was closer than similar openings they'd practiced on at the grenade range back in the States, so Sampson was sure he'd hit the mark on the first try. He took up a classic throwing stance: feet apart, left foot pointed at the target, left arm extended, grenade in his right hand over his shoulder, just like in a training film. His toss had perfect elevation, but hit the left side of the door, sending the armed grenade, its fuse hissing, back to the stones at Sampson's feet.

He tried to run, but couldn't get any purchase. Then he shot forward for the corner of the building; as he turned, his tommy gun flew out of his hand. He threw himself against the wall, making himself as flat as possible and hoping the grenade wouldn't roll toward him. The noise and smoke from the blast were still in the air as he darted back into the lane to retrieve his weapon. He had a new understanding of why Curtis had come running around the corner without his rifle.

The commotion brought other GIs into the open around the house. Sampson had to go inside the pillbox to make sure the soldiers there were no longer a threat. Figuring his tommy gun was too big for the tight space, he handed his weapon to a trooper named Jay Rand, and took Rand's pistol.

Holding the pistol in front of him, Sampson entered the pillbox through a low door in the rear. A passageway, lined with concrete, led to a wall. A young Italian soldier lay on his back, his shirt front blown open, his chest flayed by shrapnel from the grenade, white dust from the concrete settling on him in a dusty coat. Sampson nudged the man to make sure he wasn't just playing dead. He stepped over the body and peered into the main part of the pillbox, which was a small, dark room. The machine gun rested on planks laid just below the firing aperture. Another Italian was on his knees behind the gun, hands clenched to the sides of his head, as he mumbled to himself. The grenade had shattered the man's eardrums, and landed in the narrow hall, where it had killed the other defender near the door.

Sampson pushed the machine gun aside, grabbed the wounded soldier by his collar, yanked him up, and pushed him out the door, shouting the whole way. When the frightened soldier didn't answer, Sampson grabbed the man's face in his hands in a murderous rage.

Another mortar section trooper, Andrew Piacentino, put his hand on Sampson's arm and gently pulled him away from the prisoner, speaking softly to cool the sergeant's temper.

"Don't hurt him. Let me talk to him."

In the same tone, Piacentino addressed the prisoner in Italian.

Sampson wanted to know about the two troopers he'd tried to warn.

"He says he missed," Piacentino translated.

"Missed which one?" Sampson asked. He had seen the gunner fire at the two paratroopers in the field and had heard that his own man, Watts, had been killed. Before Piacentino could figure it out, Watts appeared at the corner of the building. The prisoner reached into his pocket and pulled out a few scraps of paper, which he handed to Sampson, who shoved them in his own pocket without looking at them.

Now more troopers began to appear. A lieutenant and a couple of men who'd been pinned down by the machine gun walked over to watch the little scene. Two troopers came up to Sampson and thanked him for warning them; they were the men Sampson and the Italian gunner had spotted in the adjacent field. Sampson's signal had saved their lives. One of the soldiers said Sampson should get a Silver Star (a medal for valor) for knocking out the pillbox. He took out a small notebook, wrote his name and home address on a piece of lined paper, tore the page out, and handed it to Sampson, in case the sergeant needed his testimony.

Later, Sampson fished the papers out of his pocket. The prisoner had given him a couple of one- and two-lire notes, worth about three American cents. Sampson wondered if the man had offered the pittance to keep Sampson from killing him. The sergeant found the gesture very sad.

Somewhat calmed by the appearance of Watts, Sampson looked around the little complex to see who else might be hiding there. He tried the handle of a large gate situated between the back of the pillbox and the building with the loft; it was locked. His first impulse was to toss a grenade over the top of the gate, so that there wouldn't be any surprises for him when he forced it open. But with so many GIs around, there was a chance he'd kill one of his own men. He raised his tommy gun and shot the lock, then pushed the gate open gingerly.

There was a small courtyard inside, with a covered veranda running the length of the two-story house. Standing on the veranda, as if lined up for inspection, were a man, a woman, and a young girl between eight and ten years old. They seemed unnaturally calm, considering that armed invaders were tossing hand grenades and shooting up their home.

Sampson approached the man, and through hand gestures, indicated that he wanted to search the man's house. Then he called a couple of his men into the courtyard and told them to check the building with the loft. He followed the man inside the house, which was neat and well kept, and still untouched, at least on the inside, by the fighting going on all around. Sampson noticed a staircase leading to the second floor, and he signaled to the man to lead the way upstairs.

The Italian led Sampson into a large room dominated by a beautiful cabinet, with stacks of wine bottles inside. Sampson pantomimed a drinking gesture. The homeowner ran his hands over several of the bottles, selected one, opened it, and poured a drink. Sampson indicated that the man should drink first. His host tipped the glass toward his mouth, just tasting the wine. That was enough to convince Sampson, who took a couple of small sips. He thanked the man, handed back the partly filled glass, and went back outside.

By now it was a little after 10:00 A.M., the sun high in a cloudless sky, the day quickly heating up. Sampson took comfort in being surrounded by men from his own company, even if they were sightseeing, nosing around the courtyard and outbuildings, climbing to look down the long slope toward the sea.

Watts didn't offer much information on his close call. Ben Popilsky told Sampson that he had been sent from the company command post with his bazooka to take out the pillbox. Sampson was glad Popilsky hadn't taken a shot while he was creeping up the narrow lane: a bazooka round might have killed Sampson, too.

Most of the company was engaged searching for men and equipment. Sampson went back inside the pillbox and picked up the Italian light machine gun and some ammunition, then walked down the hill toward the spot where he'd found his mortar bundle. The mortar was just as he had left it, the bundle open, the sight missing. Sampson set the machine gun down and, motivated by the same curiosity that had other troopers searching for souvenirs, examined the gun. It was a simple design, fed from the top by crescent-shaped magazines. Looking around for a target, Sampson aimed at a pillbox farther down the slope that had not yet been captured by the troopers. Behind him, two of the 75 mm pack howitzers located near the E Company command post opened fire on the pillbox, too, but their rounds went high and they overshot the target.

Samson fired two magazines of ammunition at the pillbox, but figured if the fortification was anything like the one he had just cleared, the machine gun wasn't going to harm the occupants. The only way he could reach them would be to fire through the gunports, and from this distance, he couldn't see where his rounds were striking. He was wasting his time, so he thought he'd try the mortar.

He was proud of his reputation with this weapon. One officer said that if you needed a mortar round dropped into someone's pocket at a thousand yards, Sampson was the man to do it.

The mortar is an indirect-fire weapon that lobs a three-pound projectile in a high arc that can reach over obstacles and defensive works, even into trenches and foxholes. The small 60 mm mortars assigned to the rifle companies (each battalion had a section of 81 mm tubes) had a range of two thousand yards, and gave the troopers a way to hit targets they couldn't engage with direct-fire weapons.

Sampson pulled the square baseplate from the bundle, set the mortar in its hole, then attached the bipod legs. Since the sight was missing, Sampson merely lined up the sight's dovetail holder with his target, the pillbox downslope. He pulled a mortar round from the bundle, set the charge for the close range, and dropped the round down the tube.

He actually saw the projectile in flight. The first round landed just to the right and a little beyond the target. Sampson adjusted the barrel and dropped in another round. Still to the right, but closer. Yanking the barrel slightly left, he put his third round in front of the pillbox's firing port. The small explosive wasn't going to punch through the concrete, but the shrapnel might go through the opening. At the very least, the men inside would be forced away from the firing slits. If Sampson had been firing in support of a ground attack, this would have allowed the troopers to get within hand grenade range.

At the same time that Sampson was dropping mortar rounds in front of the pillbox, the battery of guns on the hill behind him had also found the range. Shells exploded against the front of the enemy position.

Glancing down the hill, Sampson saw a white flag, but it was outside the pillbox. Incredibly, the defenders had left the shelter of their position in order to surrender. The next round would kill them. Sampson turned and faced uphill, trying to get the attention of the gunners on the firing battery.

"Cease fire, cease fire!" he shouted. He ran to a wall nearby and climbed to make himself more visible. From this spot, he saw two troopers moving on the pillbox's flank. The guns stopped firing, and the troopers took their prisoners. Sampson, looking over the scene, realized he had exposed himself to save the lives of enemy soldiers he'd been trying to kill just moments before.

By 10:00 A.M. on D-day, Alexander's Second Battalion troops had knocked out five pillboxes in the area of the olive orchard. He had gathered nearly four hundred men, and his companies were patrolling continuously, looking for more men and equipment.

Jack Norton, the battalion exec, made sure that the staff officers gathered information from the companies so that Alexander would have an up-to-the-minute picture of the unit's assets. The adjutant kept track of unit strength, including numbers of wounded and their condition. The intelligence section plotted known enemy positions on their maps and collected reports from the patrols the companies sent out. The supply section tracked ammunition, including who had found what bundles, and how best to distribute the ammo. And since Paul Woolslayer, the operations officer, had had some sort of breakdown—he looked almost catatonic to Norton—the exec had to run the operations section, which meant issuing orders, coordinating patrols and the perimeter defense, and planning for the next move.

Besides bringing in ammunition and weapons recovered from bundles, the troopers came in with all sorts of booty they had liberated for their own use: wine bottles and even small casks, grapes and tomatoes, and donkey carts for hauling the heavy equipment. More than one cart came in, trailed by their unhappy owners, poor Italian farmers who could not afford to lose their carts or animals. They were determined to follow the Americans and get their belongings back just as soon as the invaders were finished with them.

Using his field glasses, Alexander spotted two German tanks about a mile north of his position, in the direction of Santa Croce Camerina. Startled, Alexander checked again. There were not supposed to be German tanks in Sicily. Suddenly the equation had changed. The lightly armed paratroopers had almost no weapons to take on the armor, so Alexander had to think faster than the tankers. Fortunately, there was no indication that the tanks were about to attack him, and he could see no supporting infantry moving in his direction. He had two choices: dig in and prepare to fight them, or move. Alexander chose to move toward his drop zone and try to link up with the rest of the regiment.

A quick map study showed Alexander that taking a direct route for the objective would slow him down, as the road network in the area ran from between the beaches and the inland towns, perpendicular to where he wanted to go. The hilly terrain was cut by deep ravines that also led to the sea: any move northwest would be across these compartments, and the men would have to climb successive ridges.

Alexander turned his battalion south, toward the sea. The patrols he sent ahead reported that the town of Marina di Ragusa had a coastal artillery battery, its guns aimed at the Mediterranean. Coming from the north, the paratroopers would be attacking the garrison's rear. Lieutenant Colonel Harrison Harden, the artillery commander, and several of his men hauled their two 75 mm guns by attaching a "dog harness" to each trace (the long leg that runs back from the breach and sits on the ground), strapping themselves in like a team of sled dogs. They sat one man on the short barrel to lower it and lift the trace up off the ground. Once the weapon was balanced on two wheels, the six or eight men could pull the gun, which weighed just over twelve hundred pounds.

As they drew within range of Marina di Ragusa, Alexander asked Harden to put a couple of rounds into the fort. Supported by the single gun, the paratroopers pushed into the town and overcame the defenders in a short firefight. Like garrisons all over the island, this one decided their war was over. They could see a British cruiser lying just offshore, with its guns trained inland, and 'that helped influence their decision, as the ship had better range and would be a moving target for the land-based guns. The Italian commander saw no reason to die when the outcome of the battle was already determined. Once they cleared the prisoners, the paratroopers removed the breach blocks from the fort's guns and tossed them into the ocean.

As E Company made its way as part of the battalion move toward the sea, they scooped up more prisoners. Some Italians were so eager for their war to be over that they willingly, even happily surrendered to a unit that was lost, out of contact with its support, perhaps even outnumbered. But many fought the invaders, and in close combat the paratroopers had shown that they would take any objective they fixed on. The Italians who stayed inside their pillboxes, unwilling to surrender and unable to move, revealed the problem with static warfare. Concrete walls were fine for protection, but maneuver was better.

Piacentino, the Italian-American from Sampson's section, wound up guarding one of these prisoners, and the two men were soon having a conversation in Italian, as if they were reunited friends. Sampson noticed that the prisoner was carrying most of Piacentino's heavy load of equipment.

Since Alexander didn't know what they might encounter on the way, he wanted to be ready to maneuver, so he kept the formation spread out. For the individual GIs, this meant that they had to get over the many stone walls wherever they encountered them. Sampson's men, carrying the heavy baseplates, mortar tubes, and ammunition, found the best technique was to lie on the top of the wall and roll over, staying relaxed for the landing.

At one point, the troopers took fire from a house alongside a dirt lane. Every trooper within range opened fire on the house, smashing windows and door jambs and chipping the stone. Those who were closer even lobbed hand grenades. The response was all out of proportion to the threat, and perhaps even showed a lack of discipline. Sampson was concerned that the men were trying to lighten their loads by firing off ammunition.

The company moved farther down the slope toward the sea, and eventually took fire from a long stone building. Lieutenant Long called for his mortars, and Sampson and his squad responded quickly, setting up in some trees with a clear view of the target. But the lead troops swarmed over the building before the mortar could get off a shot.

By the time Sampson and his men got down among the buildings, the garrison had been cleared out. Sampson came upon an Italian officer, lying dead in front of the long building where the first fire had come from. "Hey, Ambrose," a trooper called to the man who'd shot the officer, "you just killed your own brother. He looks just like you." Sampson saw the weird resemblance, and he noticed that Ambrose was spooked by the incident. The men were not yet inured to their gruesome work.

Another trooper, Porter Fay, went into the building to clear the rooms. The men had been taught to throw a grenade in before stepping into a room. Fay threw a grenade through one doorway, then motioned for one of the Italian prisoners to go in first. The man refused, and stuck to his refusal even when Fay threatened him with a bayonet.

Finally, Fay went inside and found piles of stored ammunition. It was a miracle that the grenade didn't set it off, but at least Fay knew why the prisoner balked.

LeRoy Leslie, the F Company radioman who had been wounded by a grenade upon landing, was near a group of prisoners when he heard a hand grenade explode in their midst. Thinking that one of the Italians had turned on the guards, he and several other troopers in the area turned their weapons on the frightened prisoners and were about to open fire when they saw what had happened.

A trooper by the name of Arthur Hendrix, who had been guarding the prisoners, was on the ground, with the lower part of his leg sheared off. Another soldier, Gordon Berry, was lying next to him, bleeding from the stomach. Hendrix had been carrying a hand grenade in the cargo pocket of his trousers, as most of the paratroopers did. As was also the custom, Hendrix had wrapped the grenade in friction tape, which held the spoon down. But Hendrix had removed the pin, trusting that the tape would hold the spoon. In the heat, the tape had given way, and the grenade had gone off in his pocket.[4] Berry and Hendrix both died.

By the time the Second Battalion cleared the prisoners out of the coastal batteries, it was late in the day on July 10, and Alexander decided that his troops would spend the night on the slopes above the town of Marina di Ragusa. As night fell, however, they began receiving machine gun and sniper fire from the hills farther north. Alexander didn't think the firing was a prelude to an attack, but he certainly did not want any of his men killed by harassing fire.

The British cruiser that had helped intimidate the coastal battery was still offshore opposite the town. Alexander had his signals officer, Lieutenant Frank Szymkowicz,[5] signal the cruiser. Using Morse Code and a flashlight, Szymkowicz asked for a few rounds. The Royal Navy obliged, sending a volley crashing onto the hillside above the paratroopers. To Alexander, it sounded as if the big shells were only a few feet overhead. Szymkowicz adjusted the fire with more light signals, and after a few more shells, the hills above them fell silent.

As night closed in, Alexander directed the companies to set up a defensive perimeter. Some of the men would stay awake and on guard while others slept, and they'd switch during the night. Alexander told Paul Woolslayer and another officer to take the first shift in the command post. He and Norton would sleep first; then Woolslayer would wake them at three in the morning. Alexander wanted to be fully alert if an attack came at dawn, which was the most likely time for a counterattack.

Sometime before 3:00 A.M., Alexander heard shots. There had been sniper fire from high up on the slope again, and a few of the men on the perimeter had fired back. He and Norton scrambled out of their slit trenches and made their way along the line, checking reports and calming everyone down. Then Alexander noticed that Woolslayer was not at his post, nor was he moving around, checking the line. Alexander found the captain and the junior officer asleep in the basement of a building near the coastal battery.

There was no need for a scene. Both Alexander and Woolslayer knew what this meant: Woolslayer was finished as a paratrooper and a combat officer. Jack Norton, already pulling the load as both operations officer and executive officer, would keep those roles. (When the 505th returned to Africa, Alexander wrote a scathing efficiency report, rating Woolslayer unsatisfactory. Woolslayer was shipped back to the States.)[6]

By the morning of D + 1, the men of the Second Battalion had assembled a ragtag collection of transport to carry the heavy ammunition and weapons. There were troopers leading heavily loaded donkeys. Others had attached their animals to brightly painted two-wheel wooden carts, in which they piled their gear. Others pushed wheelbarrows, and a few of the prisoners were enlisted as porters. One of the troopers from the battalion headquarters offered the limping Alexander a beautiful saddle horse that had belonged to the commander of the coastal battery. Although Alexander's leg was still sore, he decided he'd make too tempting a target for snipers riding up and down the column on horseback. He declined the offer.

Since Lieutenant Klee had been killed on landing, the battalion was down to one surgeon. Lieutenant Lester Stein told Jack Norton that he'd stay behind with some thirty-two casualties who were too badly injured to move; the battalion exec thought it one of the bravest acts he'd seen. Stein and his medics made the injured and wounded as comfortable as they could, erecting a cargo-parachute tent to shade the men from the sun. Later in the morning of July 11, Stein looked up to see some men approaching. They didn't look like paratroopers, and they took their time. It soon became obvious to the doctor that he'd been found by the Germans. As the patrol took up positions, covering the Americans with their weapons, the patrol leader approached. Stein stood up, exposing himself to the enemy's guns. He let the patrol leader know he was a medical officer, treating wounded, and that he posed no threat. The Germans withdrew.

From the coastal town of Marina di Ragusa, Alexander turned northwest toward Gela and the rest of the regiment. But his lead elements soon ran across a patrol from the Forty-fifth Division, which was pushing inland from their beachhead. The route Alexander hoped to take would have him crossing right in front of an advancing U.S. division. Rather than risk becoming casualties to friendly fire, or interfering with the Forty-fifth Division mission, Alexander once again turned his troops southwest toward the beaches and the coastal roads.

The battalion pressed north and west through the night of July 11–12. The terrain was difficult: rough rocky ground cut by ditches and crisscrossed by rock walls, some of them five and six feet high. These walls had the effect of making the march column bunch up in places and break apart in others. Alexander and the other leaders spent much of the night moving up and down the line, constantly adjusting the intervals.

Several times during the movement, the battalion took incoming fire from what the point men thought was an American unit. Based on where he thought they were, Alexander figured he was encountering more elements of the Forty-fifth Division. He limped to the head of the column to try to sort things out, and soon came under fire himself. Alexander threw himself into a ditch and began hollering that he and his men were U.S. paratroopers. An American voice answered him, but the GI, a captain with the Forty-fifth Division, refused to believe Alexander. Alternately arguing with and cursing the captain, Alexander finally persuaded the scouts that he was telling the truth.

As more Americans poured ashore, and as bands of paratroopers disrupted communications and overran enemy outposts, resistance near Scoglitti began to collapse. Berge Avadanian saw several enemy outposts surrender, even when they outnumbered the approaching Americans. He was surprised to see one garrison come out in dress uniforms, with packed luggage and hands in the air, calling out in their best English, "New York! Detroit!" Apparently they had heard from other prisoners that conditions in the stateside internment camps were good. The prisoners were so eager to escape being killed in a futile fight for a regime they didn't support, that many of the GIs thought guarding them was a waste of time. The elated prisoners, who happily showed wallet photographs of girlfriends, wives, and babies to their American captors, could almost be trusted to get themselves to the prisoner-collection points.

At one point during the move toward Gela, Avadanian was sent to check out a farmhouse. As he approached, some enemy soldiers inside took a couple of shots at him, then ran out the back. When Avadanian finally got inside the small enclosed yard, he found that the house had not been completely abandoned: there were several turkeys. Avadanian shot a couple and brought them back to the battalion area, and later the men fried them in open mess kits.

During rest breaks on this move, troopers who had not had fresh produce in months went into the fields and picked tomatoes, grapes, and melons, collecting helmets full of fresh fruit. Others liberated local wine. A soldier from B Battery of the 456th Field Artillery got so loaded at a rest break that he became belligerent with the battery commander. The officer hauled off and belted the man, then told two other troopers to disarm him and keep an eye on him until he sobered up. The soldier was later transferred out of the paratroops.[7]

Sometimes the paratroopers would come across a dead comrade, a man who had landed by himself or who, wandering alone, had encountered some enemy patrol. Often, they discovered that the GI's boots had been removed by local civilians, who were dirt poor and desperate for shoes. It wasn't unusual to see civilians wearing German and Italian army boots, and even the occasional boots from a British soldier, but a civilian found wearing paratrooper boots was soon relieved of his find.

Through the Forty-fifth Division channels, Alexander was able to get in contact with Ridgway's headquarters. The general was pleased to hear that most of Second Battalion was intact, though some distance from the DZ. Alexander's soldiers and the men of the 456th Field Artillery who landed with them managed to knock out every enemy strongpoint they came in contact with, which helped secure the right flank of the Forty-fifth Division.

MISSION FIRST

When July 10 dawned at the western end of the paratroopers' area, the men of A Company were busily occupying their first objective. As the day grew warm, Ed Sayre's men had to step over the mangled corpses of German and Italian soldiers who, a few hours earlier, had been young men like themselves. The paratroopers, some of them just out of their teens, got through it by doing exactly what their commander did: concentrating on the task at hand.

Within a few minutes, A Company's outposts saw other paratroopers coming up the road toward the winery. As the group drew near, Sayre could see his boss, First Battalion commander Art Gorham. Gorham, whose nickname was "Hardnose," led a group of some thirty troopers, including the two battalion surgeons and some GIs wounded during the night.

Sayre briefed Gorham: A Company was astride the road between Niscemi—where the enemy might have tanks—and the invasion beaches, and positioned to stop a German counterattack.

"Good show," Gorham told Sayre, patting him on the back. "But let's not forget what our original objective is."

Holding his map, Gorham pointed at the Y road junction that was the objective of the entire thirty-four-hundred-man regiment. As far as

Gorham knew, A Company was the only organized fighting unit in the immediate area, which meant Sayre and his men would have to capture the objective alone. Sayre began preparing his men for a move south toward the original drop zone, and from there to the objective at the Y road junction.

Sayre called over Lieutenant Oscar L. Gordon, who had just been assigned to the company in the week before D-day as a supernumerary, an extra lieutenant available to fill a platoon leader slot in the event that one of the other lieutenants was killed or wounded. Gordon needed some experience, so Sayre told him to take five men and head south toward the original drop zone, which was about a half mile away. His mission was to learn what the enemy was up to around the DZ and the objective.

The rest of A Company prepared their defensive position, checking to ensure that the machine guns covered every angle of the road leading from Niscemi. Then Sayre got word from a lookout he'd sent to a nearby hilltop: there was a German armored column approaching, with a scout element in the lead. The Texan felt a sinking feeling in his stomach as he raised his binoculars. There, about two thousand meters away, several tanks appeared on the road. Leading them was a small advanced guard with a motorcycle and a staff car.

Sayre sent word around the perimeter as to what was happening: he believed that keeping the men informed kept rumors—and panic—down, and was the best way to ensure that A Company fought as a team. They all knew their commander intended to stay and fight from here, and they all knew why. The invading troops of the First Division at Gela and the Forty-fifth Division at Scoglitti were most vulnerable while coming across the beach; once Patton's men, with their tanks and artillery, had a foothold in Gela, they would come to the aid of the lightly armed paratroopers. But for now, Sayre's small band was on its own.

It was now straight-up 7:00 A.M. The sky was clear, promising a hot day. The men were in their positions, grenades handy, ammo boxes open for fast access, guns trained on the road as the enemy column wormed its way southward. From the second story of the winery, Sayre could see perhaps half a dozen tanks. About a thousand yards in front of the main body was the advance guard, two motorcycles and a Volkswagen staff car, whose job was to keep the tanks from stumbling into an ambush. Sayre ordered his men to hold their fire until the advance guard was close.

Lieutenant Anthony Pappas, the A Company executive officer, was also watching the road.

"Captain," he said to Sayre, "don't you think you ought to give them a chance to surrender?"

"No," Sayre answered. To be on the safe side, he had to assume that the advance guard was in radio contact with the panzers. "The tanks would be on us too fast."

I didn't go through all that training to get killed on the first day, Sayre thought.

Then he passed the word to the company. "I don't want anybody firing until I fire. When I open up, I want everyone shooting."

The advance guard never saw the ambush. When they were two hundred yards away, Sayre pulled the trigger. A split second later the entire American position erupted, catching the Germans in a firestorm. It was over in seconds, the motorcycle and staff car riddled with bullets, the occupants lying crumpled on the dusty road. Through his field glasses, Sayre saw the tank column halt, alerted by the firing.

He knew what would happen next. Tankers, especially experienced fighters like the Germans, did not drive blindly down the road; they'd send their infantry out ahead to root out the ambushers. It took thirty minutes for the German infantry, called panzergrenadiers, to deploy into battle formation. The open ground, with its sparse vegetation, offered little to hide the advance. Meanwhile, A Company brought all twenty captured machine guns to the north side of the perimeter.

Sayre was surprised to see the panzergrenadiers advancing over the open ground, and he wondered what the enemy commander was thinking. He estimated their strength at about two companies, more than twice as many men as A Company could muster. Once again, Sayre let them get close, then opened fire with his twenty machine guns. Caught in the open, the grenadiers who weren't killed or wounded were pinned down, unable to move.

Now the German commander knew that the garrison at the road junction had been taken by the Americans. Sayre watched as the enemy moved an 88 mm gun, one of the most accurate and deadly artillery pieces used by either side, to a hillside that was just out of range of the American weapons. It would only be a matter of minutes before the longer-range German gun was firing directly into the American position. Sayre had to move his men, and he had to do it quickly.

While all this was going on, the patrol he had sent to scout the drop zone came back. The DZ was not heavily defended, but Lieutenant Gordon had been hit by a burst of machine gun fire from an unseen enemy position. None of the soldiers had been close enough to Gordon to check on him, so no one knew for sure whether he was dead or alive. Sayre was concerned that perhaps his new lieutenant was out on the drop zone, wounded and bleeding. He would check himself, but first he had to get his company moving.

The first shell from the 88 landed close to the American position. The German gunners had used a smoke round, so that they could observe where their fire was landing and adjust. In all their training, the paratroopers had used smoke to signal the end of a field problem and the return to the bivouac. One NCO, seeing the smoke burst from the German shell, yelled out, "Problem's over! Everybody on the road!" The troopers managed to laugh as they hustled to get out of the way of the high-explosive shells sure to come next.

Sayre told his translators to have the prisoners carry the makeshift stretchers with the wounded. One German snapped his heels together, came to attention, and said, very clearly, "*Nein!*"

Sayre didn't need a translator for that. With the enemy pressing down, with accurate incoming fire due at any moment, he was not about to debate the point. He turned to one of his sergeants and said, "Can you make him understand that he and his men will carry the stretchers?"

The sergeant nodded, then poked the German in the buttocks with the point of his bayonet. All of the prisoners got the message, and in a moment, they hoisted the wounded and were ready to go. Sayre left his best platoon leader, Lieutenant Michael Chester, and a squad of GIs to hold the garrison until the company could withdraw. When the main body reached the sheltered side of the first large hill to their rear, Sayre called for the rear guard to withdraw.

The tanks, of course, could move faster than the soldiers on foot, especially since Sayre's men were carrying wounded. But the tanks were not pressing them, and as he moved, Sayre felt that if they could just cover the two thousand or so yards to the drop zone, they'd be safe. The DZ was a critical point: he expected to find the rest of the 505th there, as well as the lead elements from First Division. Sayre needed the artillery and tank support of the invasion force.

As the men hustled along with their heavy loads, they could hear the engines of the German tanks. The panzers were trying to come around their flank.

About the time that Sayre's men opened up with their captured machine guns on the advancing German infantry, A Company platoon sergeant Tim Dyas, the former New York high school track star, was just regaining consciousness. He had jumped at less than three hundred feet, which barely gave his chute time to open before he

slammed into the cement-hard Sicilian soil. He was knocked completely unconscious by the impact, and his head was still ringing when
he finally came to. As his senses slowly returned, he could hear what
he thought were his men around him, some of them groaning in pain.
The sun was already up on D-day, July 10, and Dyas had been unconscious for several hours. He worried about the injured men, and he
worried that he had been out of action for so long. What had he
missed?

Dyas shucked his parachute, checked his weapon, and gathered
his men. They could hear firing to their north, and Dyas assumed this
was Ed Sayre and the rest of A Company (he was correct). He found
Pat Sheridan and John Wroblewski, two of the bazooka men in his platoon, who had located their weapons and rockets. Dyas also found
John Dixon and seven other men from his platoon. Like many of the
paratroopers who landed with no idea of where they were, the platoon
sergeant determined that he should move his little band toward the
fighting.

Dyas could make out a hill in front of him, though the distance
was hard to judge. He put the uninjured men, including the two
bazooka teams, in the lead. Dyas positioned himself at the midpoint of
his battered little column, trying to keep the healthy men from moving
too far ahead of the injured as they moved out. Up ahead, Dyas saw
the bazooka men and their loaders climb a small hill, skirting to the
right so as not to be outlined against the sky. One moment they were
moving well across empty conutryside, and the next moment they
pulled up short.

There were German tanks on the road.

The bazooka men dove for the cover of a roadside ditch as the lead
tank, a smaller vehicle scouting ahead of the column, moved from
right to left across their front. The GIs were just a few yards from the
tank, but the snout of the main gun stayed pointed forward, and the
machine guns were silent. The tank commander sat with his upper

body sticking out of the hatch on top of the turret, oblivious to the GIs who pressed themselves into the dust, hoping their luck held. The soldiers were close enough to see the sweat stains on his uniform.

The paratroopers loaded their rocket launchers as quickly and as quietly as possible. Seconds seemed like hours. Incredibly, the German commander stayed focused on something in the distance. (This was probably the column sent to flank the A Company paratroopers who had been forced to move from the captured winery.)[1]

The bazooka teams fired from close range, hitting the two closest tanks on the flanks, one of the few places where the armor was thin enough for the small charge to penetrate. The explosion blew the commander out of the turret and set both tanks on fire.

When he heard the bazookas, Dyas and the rest of his small band were just reaching the hill. Knowing that he had men on the other side—and it sounded like there were Germans on the other side, too—Dyas hurried up and over the hill, and right into the middle of a hot firefight at close range. Dyas and his men rushed forward and jumped into the ditch alongside the road, the only cover in the otherwise bald terrain.

The paratroopers had gotten in the first deadly shots, but the tankers reacted quickly. The Americans were in a line in the ditch, their backs to the bald hill, with panzergrenadiers on their right side laying down a base of fire. Other Germans moved along the far side of the road, trying to get around the Americans' left flank. The GIs held the lowest ground, and soon there was a rain of potato masher grenades falling in and alongside the ditch. The third tank in the column could not depress its gun far enough to shoot the Americans, but the grenadiers kept up their heavy fire. The outnumbered Americans couldn't raise their heads to shoot back, so they threw grenades—including the sputtering German grenades—onto and across the road.

With the bazooka teams pinned down, another German tank rushed up the road, straddling the ditch to the right of the outgunned troopers. It had perfect enfilading fire along the entire length of the American position. Even if the Americans could have gotten off a bazooka round, the only target was the tank's front glacis plate, its thickest armor.

Dyas was sprawled in the shallow ditch, trying to get some aimed shots at the grenadiers. On either side, men held their weapons up over the edge of the depression and fired blindly. When German grenades tumbled in, the paratroopers scrambled to throw them back before they exploded. Bullets snapped just above their heads. They couldn't move forward, and they couldn't move back, and in a moment, the tank straddling the ditch to their right would simply drive forward, crushing them one by one.

In a matter of minutes, Tim Dyas went from being a highly trained noncom, leading a squad into combat, to a small unit commander looking at almost certain death for his men, if not from German fire, then beneath the treads of a tank. They were trapped, outnumbered, and vastly outgunned, and Dyas had to make a critical decision in a matter of seconds: he was in charge, and the men would fight—and die—on his orders. Or he could try to save them.

Dyas called for his men to cease fire, then laid his weapon down and raised his hands. Incredibly the Germans stopped firing and started yelling at the paratroopers. When the GIs stood up, they saw a grisly sight: the bodies of German soldiers, men they'd just killed, lying in the road. The grenadiers about to take them prisoner—frightened, shouting, flush with adrenaline and in the heat of the killing moment— had to step over the corpses of their own comrades to reach the paratroopers. As Dyas watched the enemy advance, fingers on triggers, he expected to be shot. He heard the Germans shouting about the *"Oberst,"* and he figured that the officer who had died in the turret of his tank was their colonel. Dyas could see that some of the grenadiers were eager to gun down the prisoners—one twitch and the paratroopers were all dead—but the Germans stayed under the control of their noncoms, who defused the situation by immediately moving the prisoners to the rear.

The sounds of the fighting that had drawn them faded as the prisoners were moved away from the beaches and north toward Niscemi. They were, quite suddenly, completely powerless, with no control over where they went or even if they lived, and the transformation left them stunned.[2] Their captors brought them to a collection point, where they met other paratroopers who had been scooped up by German patrols. Dyas recognized another A Company trooper, an American Indian named Fred Bradley, who was badly wounded. Lacking morphine, the German medics gave Bradley wine. Dyas watched an orderly hold a bottle to the GI's lips. When Bradley spotted Dyas and the others, he said aloud, "Helluva way to fight a war, huh?"

A German officer said to Dyas, in English, "You were about an hour late to your drop zone."

If he hadn't been knocked out, if he'd come to and set out earlier, Dyas and the others might have linked up with the rest of A Company. Instead, they spent most of D-day walking north and west, away from the invasion beaches. The men were hungry and thirsty, worried about what would happen to them and where they'd end up. Dyas replayed the events of those short, sharp minutes along the road. Could he have done something different? Did he make a mistake that put his men in the hands of the enemy? Had there been another choice? There were no answers, only the questions, coming over and over as he put one foot in front of the other along the dusty road that would lead Dyas, eventually, to a prisoner of war camp in Germany. (One of the men in Dyas's patrol managed to escape, so the families of the other men eventually learned they had been captured alive.)

Sayre and his men, now numbering approximately eighty troopers and forty prisoners, moved south along the ridge that paralleled the

Gela-Niscemi road to the high ground that had been their original planned drop zone. To the north and west, they could see the long open plain and the airfield near the Ponte Olivo, the bridge over the Gela River. Somewhere behind them were the panzers of the Hermann Goering Division, and somewhere in front of them, they hoped, were the GIs of the U.S. First Infantry Division, which came ashore at Gela at dawn that morning. The best protection against the German tanks to their rear was the American armor somewhere to their front.

Sayre moved along the column of paratroopers, trying to keep the small band from becoming too strung out. The men could move only as fast as the stretcher bearers carrying the wounded. Although the tanks did not appear to be right on their heels, the paratroopers were eager to get to a defensible position. They had already stopped the enemy once; they were sure they could do it again, as long as they could pick the ground. Sayre, who had seen the German tanks through his binoculars, was convinced they'd have a fighting chance once they stopped, but if the enemy tanks caught the troopers on the move, things would not go well for the Americans.

Sayre's band reached the drop zone around nine-thirty in the morning, and the lieutenants and noncoms immediately started putting the men into a defensive position. There were advantages to the hilly terrain: since the armored vehicles couldn't climb the steepest hills, the enemy tanks were channeled to a few predictable routes. The GIs knew how the enemy would approach. The thin vegetation and almost total lack of trees also gave the defenders long views; they would spot approaching columns at a distance.

There were disadvantages, too. The soil was baked hard by the Sicilian sun, meaning it was difficult for the exhausted men to dig fighting positions deep enough to protect them from tanks. (In North Africa, they had practiced digging holes they could hide in even as a tank rolled over the top. It wasn't foolproof, and a tank could simply pivot over the same spot until the sides of a position caved in, but it gave the defender a chance.) While the steep hills and gullies kept the tanks channeled to certain routes, it also hid them from view. Clever attackers would use the hills to mask their movements.

There were no other paratroopers on the DZ, no sign of the missing A Company platoon or the other companies. From the drop zone, Sayre could see the regimental objective, the Y road junction on the Gela-Niscemi road. Several large pillboxes covered every possible approach, and the whole thing was surrounded by wire and, no doubt, minefields. Navy ships off the coast were shelling the area, and Sayre's men could feel the rolling concussions from the big explosions. Overhead, the troops could see a small U.S. Navy spotter plane, which, they reasoned, was probably in radio contact with the ships, adjusting the fire onto the target. As they watched, a German fighter rushed in over the brown hills and shot down the slow-moving, unarmed Navy plane.

The shelling continued, but Sayre could see that it was not going to be effective. The large-caliber shells would have been enough to destroy the pillboxes or at least stun the defenders, if they could score hits, but that wasn't going to happen. The enemy positions had been built in low ground protected by surrounding hills, where the Navy guns, with their low trajectory, couldn't reach them. Instead, the rounds exploded harmlessly a hundred yards or more to the north, along the road to Niscemi.

Thus the fire support he had been counting on was useless, and Sayre doubted that the Navy was going to send another unarmed spotter plane while there were German fighters around. Ed Sayre and eighty-some men of his company had managed to get to the right spot, but it looked to Sayre as if they were the only ones.

Sayre turned his attention back to the fortifications at the road junction. Gorham's order had been a model of simplicity: "Let's not forget what the objective is." Now the objective was right below him. Never mind that, instead of being part of a regimental attack, Sayre had less than a rifle company. Never mind that they had just learned that they faced German armor. Never mind that his men had been chased from their first position by accurate enemy fire. His duty was as simple as Gavin's admonition to "find the nearest enemy and attack him."

The objective was to take control of the pillboxes, but that did not mean Sayre had to launch a bloody assault, not if he could get the defenders to come out. As he watched the white bursts of high explosive from the Navy shells, he figured the men inside were probably terrified that the Americans would soon find the range. Sayre, of course, knew the defenders were actually safe from the fire.

But the enemy didn't know what he knew.

Sayre called Calandrino, his interpreter, and told him to pick one of the Italian prisoners to carry a message down to the pillboxes.

"You tell those people, if they don't come out with their hands up in ten minutes, that we're going to bring all that fire down from the guns out there and just blow them to hell."[3]

Calandrino translated, but the prisoner didn't move. When Sayre asked what was wrong, Calandrino said the man was afraid he'd get shot if he tried to approach the fortifications. Sayre showed him that he might get shot if he didn't go. The frightened prisoner moved out and managed to get close enough to shout at the defenders as Sayre and his men watched from the hill above.

Evidently, the Italian made a good case, because a few minutes later, the defenders abandoned their positions and walked out, their hands in the air. The A Company men moved quickly down the hill and took forty more prisoners. Sayre was elated. His ruse had accomplished the regiment's objective, without the loss of a single man. Of course, there was still the matter of those tanks nosing around somewhere to the north.

It was 10:45 A.M. now, the sun high and hot and the troops sweating, but Sayre kept them moving. Once again, he put his men into an enemy position to watch the road from Niscemi for the tanks that had chased A Company from their first blocking position just hours before. The GIs were still directly in the avenue of advance that the enemy would use to attack.

Sayre's men moved the enemy guns so that they faced Niscemi, and prepared to defend a road junction. They opened boxes of machine gun ammunition; they sent men forward as lookouts; they moved the prisoners back toward the beach. Sayre was immensely proud of his men, who worked fast and without a trace of panic. As he checked his new position, Sayre kept glancing to the road from Gela, hoping to see American tanks approaching from the First Division's landing beaches. He didn't get his wish.

The A Company men had been in place for only a few minutes when they heard tanks coming from the north. Sayre was in the center of the position when he saw the first panzer nosing around a bend on the dusty road. With no antitank weapons, all the Americans could do was open up with small arms and hope for the best. Machine guns would not penetrate the tanks, of course, but they might make the German commander think there was another ambush waiting for him.

A Company fired on the tanks, which stopped. Sayre could guess that, inside the second or third vehicle, the German commander was trying to assess his chances of blowing through the stronghold. The Navy shells were still landing intermittently on the road to Niscemi, between the panzer column and the strongpoint. The German commander probably assumed (incorrectly) that the Americans now in charge of the road junction controlled and could adjust that fire. But Sayre knew that if the panzers decided to roll down on the Americans, there was little to stop them, and with open ground all around, no chance the GIs could withdraw.

There was something else the German commander had to consider, something Sayre knew nothing about at that moment.

A Company's antitank squad, led by Tim Dyas, had killed the

commander of the *Kampfgruppen*. The new commander, having seen his boss incinerated by a handful of paratroopers on foot, did not press this attack. Sayre watched the lead panzer idle in the road, machine gun bullets *spanging* harmlessly off its armor. Then, amazingly, the tank began to back up. The Germans withdrew.

Sayre's men whooped and hollered their relief, but kept a watchful eye on the road and the surrounding hills for panzergrenadiers or another appearance of one of the deadly accurate 88s that had driven them back earlier that morning.

A Company had captured two major enemy strongpoints. The mistake that the defenders made in each case was giving up their ability to maneuver. When the Germans and Italians holed up in their pillboxes, they let the GIs have the run of the hills around them, and they gave up any advance warning about what was coming. Sayre wasn't about to make the same mistake: he needed to know what was going on in the area, especially since he was unsure of the enemy strength and intentions. He formed a patrol, picking five soldiers to help him make contact with the GIs of the First Division. He needed their support in case the Germans came barreling down the road from Niscemi, and he wanted to evacuate his wounded and turn over his prisoners, who now nearly outnumbered the paratroopers.

By this point, Sayre had been awake for more than thirty hours, had made his first combat jump, led several attacks on enemy strongholds, moved his men through enemy territory under fire, and had managed to reduce significant defenses without heavy losses. But there was more to be done.

He briefed his platoon leaders and first sergeant, and left Lieutenant Pappas, the executive officer, in charge. Then he and his men headed south to find the First Division. They hadn't gone far when they spotted GIs heading toward them from the direction of Gela. In broad daylight, recognition was easy. The men were scouts from the 16th Infantry Regiment, part of the First Division. They took Sayre to their battalion command post, where communication teams had already laid a telephone line to the beach. Sayre was patched through to First Division headquarters, where Matt Ridgway, the Eighty-second Airborne Division commander, had just returned from his own frustrating search for the missing 505th. After Sayre had identified himself and given his location, Ridgway asked, "What about the regimental objective?"

"It's in our hands," Sayre said.

There was an audible sigh of relief on the other end of the line. A Company's actions in securing the junction meant that Major General Terry Allen's First Division was safe, for the moment at least, from an armored attack along the Gela-Niscemi road. Now it was up to Allen to get enough firepower up to Sayre's position so that the road junction didn't change hands again.

Ed Sayre, the former Texas National Guard sergeant, who had not had a single day of training at the Infantry School before joining the 505th, led the scouts back to his A Company troopers.

13

SEVENTY-TWO HOURS

Just before noon on July 10, troops from the First Division relieved Ed Sayre's A Company at the Y road junction. Sayre's two platoons, as well as some troopers from the battalion headquarters, were now placed under the command of the Second Battalion, Sixteenth Infantry, one of the regiments of the First Division. Until the 505th consolidated and was under the tight control of its own leaders, Sayre and his men would fight with the First Division, known as the Big Red One (its shoulder patch was an olive green shield with a red numeral one). Sayre told the commander of the Second Battalion, Lieutenant Colonel Crawford, about the German armor that had pursued them and had probed the Y road junction just before 11:00 A.M. Crawford had only one 57 mm gun that could take on the German tanks; it wouldn't take much of an effort to overrun the GIs. But their mission, as George Patton had made abundantly clear, was not to defend; it was to attack. In the early afternoon, Crawford and the attached paratroopers moved north from the road junction, picking their way cautiously over the hills.

Their objective was the German force that American intelligence believed to be near the inland town of Niscemi, which sits amid steep hills some nine miles northeast of the landing beaches at Gela. Patton's staff figured—and initial reports from the battlefield confirmed—that the Germans had pulled their tanks and troops inland, away from the deadly concentrations of naval gunfire. Counterattacks from the hills beyond Niscemi would have to pass through or near the little town. The Second Battalion, Sixteenth Infantry, with the attached paratroopers of Sayre's A Company, were headed inland to find the enemy and attack.

The road to Niscemi climbs slowly from the Y road junction, with plenty of open space on either side. Some of the fields stretched for a few thousand yards, with plenty of shallow gullies and gentle slopes where a tank could hide and wait for the approaching Americans. Crawford pushed his infantry out to the sides as the GIs advanced, so that the main body couldn't be surprised by an ambush. Since he didn't know exactly where the enemy was, his goal was to make contact with only a small part of his unit. (The Germans operated under this same principle when they sent a motorcycle and staff car ahead of the tanks earlier in the day. They learned where the Americans were and didn't lose any tanks.)

The First Division had many veterans of the fighting in North Africa. The division was one of the units Eisenhower had taken ashore in Operation Torch in November 1942, and was also among the first to face German ground troops. Many of the men Sayre saw were veterans, but nearly half of the soldiers in the Second Battalion had joined the unit only weeks before, and so were about as green as they could be.

Like the paratroopers, they were seeing action for the first time, but Sayre had two distinct advantages over his counterparts from the Sixteenth Infantry. Most of Sayre's men had been training together for a long stretch, some for more than a year, and the tough training solidified the bonds among the men. Men fought, took risks, endured hardships, and made sacrifices because of those bonds.

Sayre's men also believed they were elite soldiers, better than the average. Many of them had volunteered for the difficult parachute training specifically because they bought into the notion of the paratrooper as a special soldier. For all the bravado surrounding how they arrived on the battlefield, once they were on the ground, the paratroopers were really just lightly armed infantrymen. Part of what gave them an edge was that they believed they were better fighters than the average GI.

The A Company paratroopers and the men of the Second Battalion spent the last few hours of daylight on July 10 preparing a defensive position. They had advanced about one mile along the Niscemi road and so far had encountered only light resistance. Thankfully, there was no sign of the tanks Sayre's men had driven off before noon.

Sayre had now been awake for thirty-six hours, but he couldn't stop to rest yet. He asked permission to take a patrol to look for lost and wounded paratroopers, including his own Lieutenant Oscar Gordon. He hadn't received confirmation that Gordon was dead, and he was concerned that the young, inexperienced officer might be lying wounded and in need of medical attention. Sayre picked seven men to go with him, including Corporal Jim Ricci, an expert marksman who had honed his skills hunting squirrel in southern Illinois. The patrol headed to the spot on the drop zone where, according to the report he'd received earlier, he might find Gordon's body. Sayre took his time approaching the open area. The drop zone looked abandoned, but he supposed it had looked that way to Gordon as well.

Just before sunset, he found the body on a piece of flat, open ground. Gordon was lying facedown, arms spread, legs twisted beneath him. Sayre, moving in a crouch, turned him over. A machine gun had stitched dark holes across the young man's chest. The lieutenant never even had a chance to draw his weapon. Sayre unbuckled the flap on Gordon's holster; just as he pulled the weapon free, he heard the crack of incoming rounds and saw the dust fly where bullets tore into the soil beside him. He jumped to his feet and sprinted for the nearest cover, a long fifty yards away. There was a cactus fence between him and the low spot he was heading for. Sayre ran right through the thorny plants as the machine gunner tracked him, then slid into the covered position. He lay there, catching his breath, watching the sky darken, and figuring that only the failing light had kept the enemy gunner from hitting him.

Around 9:00 P.M., when it was fully dark, the patrol moved out again under moonlight, heading north away from the DZ. Sayre spread his men out in a wedge, positioning himself just behind the point man. He was close enough so that everyone could hear his voice. The land was almost treeless, and Sayre knew that he and his men were visible to anyone in front of them, but the hilly ground meant they were never exposed for too long.

The patrol had gone only about a half mile when they came under fire. The men immediately went to ground and started crawling for cover. They moved backward to a dry streambed they had just come through. All of Sayre's men made it to the streambed. They were winded from the exertion of crawling several hundred yards, and shaken up by the close call, so he gave them a moment to recover while he considered what was next.

Sayre sat on the ground at the bottom of the gully, which was some four or five feet deep, wiping the dust off his pistols with a rag. Suddenly, other figures appeared on the edge of the streambed and, before Sayre knew what was going on, they jumped into the ditch. It was an enemy patrol, nine Italian soldiers who were just as surprised as the Americans they landed on.

Within seconds, the tight confines of the streambed became a tangle of legs and arms, grunts and curses, as the mingled patrols struggled in a vicious hand-to-hand fight. Sayre pulled his own pistol and the one he had taken from Gordon and began shooting, gunfighter style, with both hands. The muzzle flashes from the pistols lit up the tiny space and the confused frieze of tumbling bodies. An Italian soldier dove at him, hitting Sayre at his waist. The captain swung the butt of his pistol at the man's head, knocking him off.

The fight lasted only a moment, and the paratroopers soon had the upper hand. They had killed three men, including the one Sayre had pistol-whipped. The troopers guessed that six more had clambered out of the ditch and run off into the darkness. This was clearly no place to spend time, as Sayre had no idea if the escaped enemy would come back with reinforcements. The troopers hustled back to the Second Battalion position.

When he checked in at the battalion command post, Sayre was told to prepare for a dawn attack on a prominent hill, marked "Hill 41" on the U.S. maps, which was about a half mile farther north, toward Niscemi. Hill 41 dominated the Gela-Niscemi road, and for that reason, the Americans expected it to be defended.

Sayre made the rounds of the platoons, talking to his junior leaders and checking on his men, who were exhausted but in remarkably good spirits. He ensured they had water, rations, and ammunition (they were now being supplied over the beach by the First Division); he also gauged their morale. The men knew they had accomplished something important at the road junction, and they were confident they could handle whatever came next.

An impatient Jim Gavin watched the sun move slowly toward the western horizon on July 10. His first full day in Sicily had been mostly frustrating. In his first hours on the ground, he had managed to collect a sizable band of troopers, only to lose them in the darkness. The smaller group he'd been left with had run into an enemy patrol that cost the life of one man. He had spent most of D-day—arguably the most important day of his life as a soldier thus far—pinned down in a hillside gully somewhere south and west of Vittoria and nowhere near his objective. When darkness finally came on the evening of July 10, Gavin and his men climbed out of the ditch, glad to have escaped detection during the day and even happier to be moving again.

"Sitting and worrying had been the hardest of all," Gavin said later. "And I had done a lot of it."[1]

Gavin's band had been moving for about an hour when they were challenged by an American voice. They found a small group of wounded and injured paratroopers under the command of Lieutenant Al Kronheim of the regimental headquarters. Gavin's men traded their morphine styrettes for M1 rifles and ammunition, then continued west.

At 2:30 A.M. on July 11, D-plus-one, Gavin was pushing toward Gela when the paratroopers heard another challenge come out of the darkness. They answered with the countersign and found a machine gun crew from the Forty-fifth "Thunderbird" Division, a National Guard unit originally made up of soldiers from four western states. (The division's original shoulder patch used a Native American symbol—the swastika—which was replaced by a stylized bird after the Nazis adopted the bent cross.) The Forty-fifth had come ashore at Scoglitti, some eleven miles from the 505th's objective near Gela. The Thunderbird soldiers helped Gavin pinpoint his position, which was about five miles southwest of Vittoria. There was no way they would reach the objective area on foot, moving cross-country at night, so Gavin struck out for a road. After covering another mile, they found the paved Gela-Vittoria highway, as well as roadside foxholes and the bodies of dead Italian soldiers.

The commander's group now consisted of nine men, and the small patrol cleared off the road when they heard armored vehicles approaching. Gavin called to his men to hold their fire, as there was a good chance these were American tanks. But one of the jumpy troopers opened up when the lead tank appeared, which unleashed a hail of bullets. The tank was American. Fortunately, the crew was buttoned up inside, and no one was hurt.

Near the edge of Vittoria, Gavin borrowed a jeep and went to check out rumors of paratroopers on Highway 115, the road to Gela. He had been on the island for nearly thirty hours. He knew where he was, and he knew where his objective was, but he still could not account for his men. There was no reason to believe his plane was the only one blown off course, and it was obvious that the mission hadn't worked out exactly as planned. But Gavin had trained his men to act in the absence of instructions. He had made clear to every last man in the regiment that their job was to disrupt enemy counterattacks on the beachheads, to make operations as difficult and as costly as possible for the island's defenders. If the assault didn't go exactly as planned, he had confidence that the men would still fight. Even his message to the troops, handed out on mimeographed sheets at the departure airfields, had been a model of simplicity. No matter what happened, every soldier knew what was required. *Attack him wherever found,* Gavin had said of the enemy.

Now, as he hurried to find the main body of his regiment, Gavin would see how the long training had paid off.

Dean McCandless, the First Battalion communications officer, was still alone with Ott Carpenter when night fell on July 10. Like Jim Gavin, they'd spent D-day pinned down, waiting for darkness to make it safe to move again. Although the invasion force had clearly landed, there was plenty of enemy activity in the area, so the two troopers moved cautiously from their hiding place. The last thing they wanted was to run into an enemy patrol or, worse, another column of tanks. They took turns, one man moving while the other man watched, and in this way they leapfrogged slowly off the big hill and toward the valley that lay between them and the objective area. They moved like that, tediously, slowly, all through the night of July 10–11. Near dawn, McCandless nearly tripped over something sticking out from some low shrubs. When he saw that it was the dark barrel of a weapon, he leaped past the muzzle and shoved his own carbine into the bush, right into the chest of a sleeping soldier who shouted, in a heavy southern accent, "God Almighty, don't shoot!"

McCandless nearly laughed aloud as he felt the tension of the two long nights he'd spent lost outside of friendly lines slide off him. The soldier, who was from the First Division, directed the two troopers toward his command post, where they learned that there were other paratroopers nearby. Energized at the prospect of being with their own, the two men moved quickly. They found Arthur Gorham and a collection of men from the First Battalion. McCandless thought Gorham might be angry that it had taken him a full day to find the right spot, but the twenty-eight-year-old lieutenant colonel greeted the two men warmly.

Gorham had positioned himself and the few dozen stragglers he'd found on the high ground near Comiso airfield. The terrain here was relatively flat, making it a likely avenue for a German counterattack against the Gela beachhead. Gorham put himself and his men directly in the path he expected the enemy to use.

McCandless and Carpenter went to work digging foxholes and had only managed to scrape shallow holes when several German tanks rammed the American line, spitting fire from their big guns. McCandless lay flat in his hole, heart pounding, knowing that if a tank rolled over him, he'd be crushed. He couldn't see anything, but he heard plenty of small arms and machine gun fire, as well as some bazookas. He felt helpless.

Arthur Gorham was on his feet, dodging incoming fire and moving around the position, bucking up his outnumbered men. He was a clear target—hardly anyone was moving above ground—but the tankers somehow missed him. When one of his bazooka teams was killed, Gorham sprang for the weapon, loaded it himself, and went after one of the tanks, a lone infantryman on foot attacking a panzer bristling with guns. He hit the tank's vulnerable side, which set the monster on fire. Gorham's example worked, and other GIs left their holes to attack, knocking the wind out of the panzer assault and leaving the paratroopers in possession of the hill.

By the time the first pink slivers of light appeared in the eastern sky on July 11, Ed Sayre and his men were ready to lead the day's advance toward Niscemi. The move was uneventful, and the within an hour the GIs were occupying abandoned enemy trenches on Hill 41, a steep and rocky outcrop that loomed above the Gela-Niscemi road. The Americans set up their crew-served weapons to cover the ground on the north side of the hill, and peered over the ramparts, watching for the next enemy move. They opened the boxed ammunition, unwrapped their grenades, and removed the bazooka rounds from their canisters. Then they waited.

Soon, Sayre heard a buzz pass among his troops. From the vantage point of the high ground, the GIs identified a German Tiger tank in the distance. It wasn't yet headed for them, but there was little to stop it if it did. Then the GIs saw something that gave them hope. On a brown hill some thousand meters to the south, they saw the first evidence that the First Division's heavy weapons were getting ashore: an antitank platoon, four armored half-tracks with 105 mm guns. The U.S. gunners had spotted the lone Tiger, and they opened fire.

The Germans responded immediately. The first shot from the Tiger hit one of the half-tracks, and Sayre's men saw the crew thrown into the air like rag dolls. Incredibly, the antitank platoon stayed put to slug it out with its much heavier opponent. The Tiger quickly got off three more shots, scoring a hit each time. Inside of two minutes, this single German tank had destroyed the entire American platoon. It was a sobering sight for the paratroopers, who had put themselves directly in the path of this massive and seemingly unstoppable weapon.

Soon afterward, six German tanks broke cover north of Hill 41, then leapfrogged south, moving and stopping to shoot. Once again the tank fire was accurate, but here the GIs were sheltered by stout earthworks. Risking a look over the parapet, Sayre saw panzergrenadiers moving alongside the tanks. Their mission, he knew, would be to get into the trench works and clear them of GIs. And, as in the fights on July 10, Sayre's men had no weapons capable of stopping a tank without scoring a flank shot, so the panzers could drive up to the trenches, collapsing them and burying the GIs.

The Germans had apparently corrected the mistakes they'd made on D-day. They were not attacking piecemeal; the assault headed toward Sayre's position was part of a coordinated attack by at least ten German tanks. The sight of this massive steel wave was too much for the green troops of the Sixteenth Infantry. One man climbed over the rear lip of the trench, crawled clear, and ran away. Then another man did the same, then another.

Sayre heard the Sixteenth Infantry noncoms shouting encouragement to the men who stayed. He didn't warn his own men against running, but kept talking to them, just as he had been doing all along.

"Steady. Pick your targets. Aim at the infantry. Steady."

His paratroopers didn't waver. Sayre had told his men that the quickest way to get killed was to run. "The enemy can shoot you in the back without worrying about dodging your bullets."

When the Germans were in range, the troopers opened fire with machine guns and rifles, trying to separate the grenadiers from the tanks. The small-arms fire also made the tankers button up, which limited what they could see. But the tank gunners kept shooting, and the big guns spit fire and steel at the Americans. Some of the tank rounds buried themselves into the hard soil in front of the trenches. Others hit the berm and bounced up, screaming like banshees. Still others pierced the lip of the trench and exploded, spraying hot shrapnel inside the dugout. The hill was enveloped in violent crushing noise as Sayre's men heaved everything they had at the attackers: rifle fire, rifle grenades, rockets, and machine-gun fire. Farther down the line, Sayre saw two junior officers from the Sixteenth Infantry wrestle a 57 mm gun, which had been abandoned by its crew, into firing position. Braving machine-gun fire and the exploding tank rounds, the men zeroed in on the closest tank. They scored a direct hit, and the panzer caught fire.

The panzergrenadiers stalled on the hillside, unable to close on the steep-sided American position in the face of heavy fire. The German commander knew his tanks risked exposing their thinly armored bellies as they climbed the incline, so he pushed harder on the American left. There, the tanks were forced into the open, where U.S. Navy gunnery officers called for devastating fire from the ships offshore. As the shooting died down, the paratroopers and men of the Sixteenth Infantry were still in command of Hill 41, and more than half a dozen German tanks burned on the hillside.

Once the wounded were evacuated, there were fewer than two hundred GIs on Hill 41. The panzers had pulled back for the moment, but if they returned, if they concentrated their attack, they could breach the line. Lieutenant Colonel Crawford, commanding the Second Battalion of the Sixteenth Infantry, ordered a withdrawal to another hill some five hundred yards to the rear, where the rocky slopes would make it impossible for tanks to reach the Americans. The maneuver—pulling back from a position while in contact with the enemy—was one of the riskiest options a unit had in combat. The men had to move in one direction while keeping their attention, and plenty of firepower, focused in the other. For the second time in thirty-six hours, A Company was about to move with German tanks at their backs.

The A Company noncoms kept tight control of the men, and the paratroopers withdrew in good order. During the move, Sayre's paratroopers picked up half a dozen Browning Automatic Rifles, called BARs, which had been abandoned by the First Division troops who ran. Once the company was in its new position, Sayre distributed ammunition and food that had been brought across the beach by the First Infantry Division. He and his men could hear the rumble of American artillery and naval gunfire, background noise they found reassuring as they prepared for their next showdown with the panzers. When dusk came at the end of their second full day on the island, the paratroopers took turns standing watch and finally getting some much-needed sleep.

As darkness fell on the evening of July 11, Arthur Gorham worked frantically to secure his position near the Comiso airfield. The paratroopers had not yet been heavily reinforced, and Gorham knew, just as the German commander must, that the window of opportunity for a successful counterattack was shrinking. If the enemy was going to make something happen, it would be soon. An exhausted Gorham dragged himself around the perimeter again, making sure there were no gaps in the coverage. He put listening posts—a couple of GIs whose job was early warning—in front of his lines so that the enemy couldn't sneak up on them. Gorham asked McCandless to establish one of the outposts, and the young communications officer, pleased to be entrusted with the mission, told Gorham that he'd spent more time training as an infantryman than as a communications officer. Gorham gave the lieutenant a bazooka team, a machine-gun squad, and a direction. McCandless led this group out about a hundred yards from the main line of defense, on the right flank of the battalion position. He found a 57 mm gun from the First Division out there and, after setting up his men, checked in with the crew. The sergeant in charge greeted the paratroopers as if they were long-lost friends; he was happy to have the extra measure of protection the additional men brought.

McCandless and the sergeant took turns keeping watch during the night. During the long hours the men, who had never met before, talked about their homes and the families they missed. The sergeant mentioned that he was married, and McCandless complimented him on his wedding ring, an extra-wide gold band which, the sergeant said, had belonged to his grandmother. There was something comforting in this communion of the mundane. At dawn on July 12, Gorham recalled the outpost, and McCandless and his men moved back to the main position.

Gorham was still concerned with putting together as much of his battalion as he could. Like any good infantry commander, he also wanted to keep an eye on what was going on around his position, and that meant patrolling. Now that it was daylight, Gorham wanted to see for himself what was out there. He called McCandless, as well as Lieutenant Carl Comstock, the assistant battalion surgeon; Corporal Thomas Higgins; and a Private Williams to join his little scouting party. Gorham was not only acting in the role of a noncom, he was armed like one, carrying the bazooka he'd used the day before.

The men were moving to the right of the battalion position, climbing a low hill, when they heard the crackling of small arms in front of them. Moving forward a few paces to see over the crest of the hill, they spotted what the men were firing at: a German tank had moved up to the battalion position, and every GI who could see it was shooting at it. The tank was in some low ground, only about two hundred yards away.

McCandless dove to the ground, but not before noticing that the tank had stopped. Gorham motioned to his small patrol to keep down, then turned and moved forward over the crest of the hill and toward the enemy, the lightweight bazooka in his hand. His long legs carried him quickly across the open, deadly ground. Like most of the hills in the area, this one was bald and offered little concealment; in order to get a shot at the tank, Gorham had to get close, well within range of all of the panzer's weapons.

Other bazooka teams were doing the same thing; the GIs were attacking like a pack of wolves, worrying the target from multiple angles. The tank was a Mark IV, which, unlike the Tiger, was vulnerable to the bazooka.

Gorham had managed to kill a tank the day before, and he pressed his luck again, racing to get into position before the tank crew could react. He knelt and raised the bazooka, but before he could get off a shot, the tank fired its main gun. There was a tremendous flash where Gorham had been kneeling, and when it cleared, the men saw that their commander was down. Comstock, the doctor, leapt to his feet and scrambled over the crest of the hill to reach Gorham. Seconds later the tank fired again, putting another round on the same target and flattening Comstock, too.

Now McCandless was on his feet, running to his stricken comrades. Amazingly, the tank did not fire at him. When he reached the two men, he lay down beside them, trying to keep a low profile. Gorham had a large triangular hole in the center of his forehead, probably caused by shrapnel from the tank round. There was no pulse, no breath, no sign of life. McCandless checked the doctor, Comstock, who had gone forward to help. The shrapnel and force of the explosion had torn a long gash across his face, laying it open on an oblique angle; his nose and lips lay on one side of his face. Comstock was still alive, though obviously in great distress. McCandless yelled for Corporal Higgins to find a jeep to evacuate the wounded man.

The paratroopers didn't have their own jeeps, but McCandless made it clear that he wanted a vehicle, even if Higgins had to steal one from a friendly unit. Then McCandless dug into his musette bag, pulled out a morphine styrette, and pushed it into Comstock's arm. The doctor tried to protest, making pitiful noises through his shattered face.

As he lay beside the wounded lieutenant, McCandless looked up in time to see a man running from the panzer. He quickly raised his carbine and fired, and the man went down. Later he would find out that he'd wounded a paratrooper who had closed in on the tank for a kill shot.

Higgins quickly found a jeep, and he and Williams came roaring over the crest of the hill and skidded to a dusty stop. Aware that they were under the guns of the tank, the three men fumbled to get the wounded doctor into the front passenger seat. McCandless jumped in the back, reached over and held Comstock by the shoulders to keep him from falling out as Higgins gunned the engine to get away from the enemy tank. It was a two- or three-mile ride to the beach, and all the while the doctor moaned softly. McCandless tried his best to comfort Comstock, repeating over and over that everything would be all right, that they'd get him to the hospital, that he'd be okay. McCandless knew that if the doctor lived, he'd be terribly scarred. Soon they spotted the crowded invasion beach, and drove up yelling that they needed an evac hospital. They found one, set up in the open, with medics running back and forth while wounded men waited attention from the doctors, and others waited evacuation to hospital ships offshore.

McCandless was in shock, and he began yelling at the medics, screaming that they had to help Comstock. The distraught para-trooper, still holding his weapon, grenades hanging from his gear, caused some concern on the beach, and at least one of the medics tried to calm him down. When they took Comstock away from him, a medic gently suggested that McCandless stay put. He had been mov-ing almost continuously, with little rest or food, since leaving North Africa. He had spent one of those nights in a ditch with only one other man, isolated and believing that they would be captured or killed. When he stopped moving, he lay down on the ground and immediately went to sleep.

In the morning, McCandless watched the amphibious trucks, known as "ducks," shuttling supplies ashore and wounded back out to the hospital ships. The medics, still concerned about his stability, encouraged him to ride out to the ship, where the sight of a grimy paratrooper, in jump boots and baggy pants, was unusual. The ship's crew fed him a breakfast of bacon, eggs, and toast, which seemed incredibly delicious after three days of no sleep and no hot food. Armed with his first night's sleep and first hot meal in three days, McCandless was in better shape to be of some use to his unit. He caught a ride ashore and headed back into the hills above Gela.

As he made his way toward the battalion, McCandless passed the location of the earlier fighting, and the outpost he had manned with the talkative sergeant the night before Gorham was killed. There he saw a hand sticking out of a shallow grave. On the hand was the thick gold wedding band he had admired just two nights earlier.

At 2:00 A.M. on July 12, Ed Sayre and the company commanders from the Second Battalion, Sixteenth Infantry, got word that they were going to retake Hill 41, before it got light. Sayre quickly roused his men, who had been catching what rest they could on the hard ground. They sipped water from their canteens, munched on K ration bars, checked their ammunition and grenades. In less than an hour, the troopers were ready to move again. The attack jumped off at 3:00 A.M., in the pitch dark after moonset. Sayre's paratroopers took the lead, with the First Infantry Division companies following.

Crawford told Sayre to follow a German telephone wire that led directly to Hill 41. Sayre held the wire in his hand, and put one platoon to his right and one to his left. Crawford was directly behind

Sayre's A Company, as was the Heavy Weapons Company of the Second Battalion. Sayre, centered among his men, set out down the steep side of one hill, across some gently rolling terrain, and up the slopes of Hill 41, where they had been the day before. There were plenty of rock walls to slow and scatter the tired troopers, but A Company made the move in good order.

The night was quiet, except for the sounds of men bumping into and climbing over the ubiquitous fences, and the constant jingling of weapons and equipment as they felt their way forward. Sayre, with the wire in his hand, felt the ground rise and knew they were climbing Hill 41. It loomed in front of them, a black mass that was somehow blacker than the sky. The silence was eerie, an unsettling prelude, and each step forward in the darkness added to the tension, as the paratroopers braced themselves for a sudden explosion of fire, the muzzle flash of incoming rounds, and white burst of hand grenades. The Germans had been unsuccessful in their attacks on the American positions the previous afternoon, but they were still out there; it was just a matter of moving far enough to run into them. As A Company started up the slope, Sayre strained to see that his men didn't spread out too far or bunch up too close.

Then they found the enemy.

Machine guns near the top of the hill opened up on the advancing Americans. The gunners were firing high, so the rounds passed over the paratroopers, who were in the front, but hit the First Division troops behind A Company. Sayre could hear men behind him screaming in pain, yelling for medics.

A Company kept moving forward, determined to get into the trenches and clear out the enemy. The machine gunners fled when the troopers closed in, and Sayre got busy organizing his line. He got word that Lieutenant Colonel Crawford, commander of the Second Battalion, Sixteenth Infantry, had been wounded and had to be evacuated.

Command now passed to a captain, one of the Second/Sixteenth company commanders.

Once again, the GIs made the trenches and gun emplacements their own, sighting their weapons to make sure all approaches were covered by fire, tying in the company flanks, checking and rechecking.

Down below them, the enemy was also busy analyzing the situation. The Americans' aggressiveness had worked against them: they had pushed forward in only one spot, creating a bulge in their lines. By morning, the Germans had maneuvered around the back side of Hill 41, cutting off the GIs' withdrawal route, surrounding the men inside the bulge. For the first time since he'd landed, Sayre thought he and his men were in a bad position; but when his worried exec, Lieutenant Pappas, asked, "Do you think we'll get out of this alive?" Sayre answered firmly, "Yes."

The German assault began with fire from big 120 mm mortars hammering the American lines. One round landed inside the trench, within a few yards of where Sayre crouched at the forward lip of the position. He actually saw it hit and bounce, spinning on the floor of the trench. All time stopped, and Sayre waited for the explosion that would kill him.

It never came. The round was a dud. It came to rest just a few feet away, in plain sight.

The German attack on July 12 looked like a replay of the previous day's assault, this time with several Mark IV medium tanks and a single Mark VI Tiger, a behemoth that created its own dust storm as its massive treads churned up the hill. Standing in their trenches, with their tiny rifle grenades and rocket launchers, the troopers of Sayre's A Company wondered if their luck would hold.

But during the twenty-four hours that had elapsed since the last fight here, the invasion force had pushed ashore a continuous stream of men and metal, a parade of fighting power that spilled over the beachheads into the area surrounding Gela. With every hour, American combat power grew dramatically. The men on Hill 41 were now backed by a battalion of 155 mm howitzers, twelve big guns that could put heavy fire on the enemy.

Sayre had the forward observer, a lieutenant from the artillery, with him. The FO had laid out his fire plan and relayed his targets to the artillery battalion. Back at the fire direction center, the targets were plotted on the maps, and the aiming information sent to the gun crews, who had already adjusted their tubes and were waiting for the call.

The first rounds came in short, landing among the Second Battalion soldiers, killing three men. Others were temporarily blinded by the flash, or found themselves stumbling in the dust, trying to focus on the enemy. By this time, the lead tank had closed to within a hundred meters of the trenches, and still it was barreling in, its commander no doubt thinking that the best way to escape the American artillery would be to get in among the Americans.

The artillery observer had just killed some of his own, but there was no time to mourn, no time to hesitate. Making his adjustments, he called for another salvo. He had to get the rounds away from the trenches, but not too far, as the Tiger tank had clawed its way to within seventy-five yards. The noise was deafening: the paratroopers' line was a storm of fire, and the panzer's heavy machine guns and big 88s were hammering the GIs as fast as they could load. All around was smoke and fire, flying steel, and the screams of the wounded. The tank was so close that it couldn't depress its main gun far enough to fire at the Americans, but it was clear that the panzer commander had no intention of stopping until he was collapsing the trenches and crushing the infantrymen.

Now the Tiger was close enough for the paratroopers to see the dark slits where the driver and commander peered out. They fired their rifles and machine guns at the openings, but the tank didn't slow down. It was only fifty yards away when the next artillery salvo came crashing down, landing so close that the troopers pressed themselves into the trench floor to escape the shrapnel buzzing overhead. When one of the big rounds hit the lead German tank, there was a bright flash and a hollow steel clang. The explosion jammed the tank's turret; then, just a few yards shy of the American position, the tank caught fire and stopped. The on-board ammunition "cooked off," detonated by the intense heat. Sayre could hear the screams of the men trapped inside. Mercifully, it lasted only a few seconds (though Ed Sayre would hear those screams in his nightmares for decades). The forward observer adjusted fire again, walking the impact back toward the other approaching tanks, which withdrew.

Behind Hill 41, the GIs saw Sherman tanks of the U.S. Second Armored Division take on the Germans in the valley. The U.S. tanks were outgunned and outweighed by their German counterparts, as would be the case all through the war in Europe. The fifty-six-ton Tiger mounted an 88 mm gun; the thirty-one-ton Sherman mounted a 75 mm gun that could not pierce the Tiger's front armor from any range. In contrast, the highly effective 88 could penetrate the Sherman's armor from a thousand yards away. The Americans often had the advantage of numbers, and frequently struck in packs. Since they were built for speed and mobility, their preferred maneuver was to flank the panzers, looking for kill shots on the less heavily armored sides of the German tanks.

The troops on Hill 41 had grandstand seats for the fight in the valley below, and they watched and cheered as the lighter American tanks maneuvered against the fearsome panzers. While the Germans engaged the tanks to their front, another section of Shermans did an end run, popped up on the German flank, and fired. Several panzers caught fire, and the remaining tanks withdrew.

*   *   *

The Germans tried Hill 41 two more times on July 12. Each time, the rain of steel delivered by the artillery forced them back. Between attacks, the men of A Company rested, cleaned their weapons, wolfed down K rations, and kept a sharp eye on the open ground to the north.

During one of these lulls, Sayre asked Vincent Calandrino, his interpreter, if he'd brought along the company barber kit. Calandrino, who had been a barber in New York City before the war, had his clippers, so Ed Sayre sat down on an ammunition box for a haircut. He wanted to send a message to his men that everything was going to be fine, that the old man was still making long-range plans.

Around 5:00 P.M. on the afternoon of July 12, Sayre received a warning order: the Second Battalion, with the attached paratroopers, would attack a ridge some three thousand yards to their front. The attack was to be supported by a platoon of Sherman tanks, and would kick off as soon as the tanks were in position. The infantry moved forward to a line of departure some three hundred yards forward of their trenches and waited for the tanks.

Sayre had managed only a few catnaps since leaving North Africa three days earlier, and he was afraid that his judgment and reactions might be hampered by exhaustion. He rifled through his musette bag and found the bottle of Benzedrine tablets he had been issued to keep him awake, and he popped one of the small white pills. It wasn't as good as sleeping, but it would have to do for now.

When the platoon of Shermans moved out to the jump-off point for the attack, the German 88 mm guns on a far ridge opened up with a deadly accurate barrage, destroying all but one of the five tanks before the infantry attack began. With the supporting tanks out of the picture, headquarters delayed the attack until morning.

Sayre and A Company were pulled out of the line and sent back to the Second Battalion command post where they could get some rest.

It was the first time they had been out of enemy contact since landing on Sicily. Sayre and his men found a grove of olive trees, dug shallow trenches, and lay down just before dusk on July 12. The artillery duels around them continued through the night, with the big 155 mm U.S. guns throwing shells directly over their heads in a preparatory bombardment of the next objective, and the Germans responding with mortar fire to keep the GIs off balance. The paratroopers were not fazed in the least. Even Sayre, who had just taken a Benzedrine pill designed to keep him awake, fell asleep as soon as he lay on the ground. He had stopped moving and his troops were in a relatively safe spot. Sayre slept as if he'd checked into a hotel.

14

A NEW MISSION

In the early-morning hours of D-day, July 10, Major Ed Krause had established a command post about two miles southeast of Scoglitti and sent out patrols to find his troopers. They were about sixteen miles from their objective, and Krause decided that his first task was to consolidate his unit. Throughout the night and into the morning of July 10, when he was supposed to be securing the high ground and road intersections near Gela, Krause gathered stragglers and equipment bundles, and pulled his battalion into something like a fighting force. By early evening on D-day, he had gathered some 180 men[1] and made contact with elements of the Forty-fifth Division, in whose sector the battalion had landed.

Krause's operations officer, Lieutenant William J. Harris, gathered some sixty paratroopers and three guns of the 456th Field Artillery after landing, then attacked the Italian garrison in Vittoria. In a short fight, the GIs nabbed eight prisoners and several vehicles, but Harris was captured. Although unarmed and in a precarious position, the quick-thinking Harris persuaded the Italian commander that further resistance would only bring more American firepower, more paratroopers, and more Italian casualties, and that the final outcome was not in question. The garrison commander surrendered the remainder of his force, some eighty men, to his American prisoner.

When Harris and his men joined the main body of the battalion, Krause headed for the Vittoria–Gela highway and the regimental objective. Along the way they ran into Lieutenant Colonel Herbert Batcheller, the regimental executive officer, who told Krause to dig in across the highway about five miles northwest of Vittoria and stay there for the night of July 10–11. Krause did as he was told and was in this position, still some ten miles from the objective, when Gavin found him around 0600 on July 11.

Since landing almost eighteen hours earlier, Gavin had been pushing hard to get to his objectives, and he wasn't pleased to discover the troopers of the Third Battalion just waking up in foxholes dug in a tomato field. He found Krause sitting on the edge of a foxhole, his feet dangling inside. Gavin asked what he was doing. Krause said that he had been reorganizing the battalion and had about 250 troopers present.[2] Gavin pressed his battalion commander.

"What are you doing about your objective?"

Krause said he had done nothing yet. Gavin told him to get his men ready to move at once.[3]

Gavin left the Third Battalion and pressed toward the objective. About two miles west of Krause, Gavin encountered a platoon from the 307th Engineers under Lieutenant Ben L. Weschler. The engineers told Gavin that there was a German force astride the highway to the west of them, but could give no further details. That put the Germans between the paratroopers and Gela.

The situation was far from clear, but there were a few things Gavin could tell from a quick map study.

The Americans had come across the beach in two places, separated by about fifteen miles, the First Division at Gela, the Forty-fifth Division at Scoglitti. Biazza Ridge lay like a long finger pointing at the sea between the American beachheads. (Though the ridge entered American military history as Biazza—there is even a street at Fort Bragg named after the battle—the estate on the hill is named Biazzo.) A German force on the ridge could launch an attack against the flank of the Forty-fifth Division, which was reaching inland behind Gavin. The ridge would give them a commanding piece of terrain right in between two American positions that, as far as Gavin knew at this time, were not strongly held. The Germans could keep the Americans from linking up and could attack the divisions one at a time.

Gavin deployed his twenty engineers as infantry, then moved out on the road to Gela. The small group had just started forward when a German motorcycle came around a bend in the road, with an officer in the sidecar. Amazingly, the motorcycle drove right into the midst of the paratroopers. Even more amazing, the troopers didn't immediately open fire, but instead took the men prisoner.

The German officer protested, pointing to his insignia and claiming that he was a medical officer and should be released. But he had grenades in the sidecar, which the paratroopers thought trumped his claim to be a noncombatant. Besides, he was the first live German the paratroopers had seen in combat, and they were not about to let him go. Gavin questioned the officer, trying to get an idea of what the Germans were up to. The officer told Gavin that he had traveled from Biscari (modern-day Acate), which lay farther inland to the north.

The American commander figured the Germans had moved their men and equipment inland to avoid the big guns of the U.S. Navy lying offshore. But what were their intentions? Would they stay inland and meet the U.S. forces outside the range of naval gunfire? Would they attack?

By this time it was full daylight, around 8:30 A.M. on July 11. Gavin could hear firing to his front, somewhere on the other side of the long, low ridge that lay directly across his path. From the southeast, where Gavin stood, the slope was broad and nearly flat and climbed gently to the horizon, about five kilometers away. On either side of the road were olive orchards, lines of short trees with shiny leaves and twisted trunks, interspersed with fields of sunburned grass. For the moment, there was no enemy in sight.

He signaled to the engineers. *Move out.*

The men could see a good distance, although the folds in the terrain gave an enemy plenty of places to wait in ambush. They'd gone another mile when Gavin and his engineers found where the railroad that connected Vittoria to Gela crossed the highway. There was a simple gate, a striped pole that could be lowered to stop the donkey-cart traffic when the train passed by, and a stone gatekeeper's house on the north side of the road. The ridge in front of them wasn't all that impressive, climbing only a hundred feet or so across a half mile, a gentle slope covered with more olive trees and very little else. On the other side of the ridge, and running parallel to the crest, lay the road from Biscari, where the Germans might or might not be massing for an attack.

Gavin now saw the ridge for what it was—a key piece of terrain in the unfolding battle, perhaps even critical to the entire invasion.

The Germans' best chance of defeating the two-pronged U.S. invasion was to keep the troops on one beachhead from linking up with the troops on the other. A counterattacking force might then be able to defeat the Americans in detail—one at a time—before they could gain a secure foothold on the island. If the Germans came roaring out of Biscari and seized this ridge, they could use the high ground to hit the Forty-fifth Division's flank, perhaps even force the abandonment of the southern beachhead.

At that point the 505th—or at least that part of it under Gavin— took on a new mission: they would seize this high ground to protect the flank of the Forty-fifth Division.

Gavin was not in contact with any higher headquarters, so he could not ask for guidance. Everything he knew about the Germans had been inferred from what the captured medical officer had told him. Yet his map study convinced him that the ridge was critical. In the worst-case scenario, he had to bet that the German commander would see the same opportunity.

But there were many reasons for him not to try the ridge. He had a tiny force—only twenty men at this point—and no idea when help would arrive. He was sending lightly armed troops into a fight with no idea of enemy capabilities (there had been that armored scout car the day before . . . did the Germans have anything heavier?). At stake was not just his own safety and that of his men, but all the work he and others had done to put together the American airborne. Plenty of people had argued against using paratroopers the way Gavin and Matt Ridgway had envisioned it; even Eisenhower had been highly skeptical. As of Sunday morning, July 11, Gavin still didn't know what had happened on D-day at the regimental objective; for all he knew, his mission was a bust. If the paratroopers failed to accomplish the mission, and if he got a good portion of his command slaughtered fighting a more heavily armed enemy, the doubters would claim to have seen it coming all along: they'd say paratroopers were too lightly armed and couldn't concentrate in numbers big enough to make a difference on the modern battlefield.

He could have withdrawn, waited for his own Third Battalion, waited for help from the Forty-fifth Division—this was their sector, after all. He could have argued that his first priority was to get to his own objective near Gela, but Gavin saw his responsibility in bigger terms: he was here to make sure the invasion succeeded. Circumstances had conspired to put him in this particular time and place, so this is where he'd do his work.

Gavin told Lieutenant Weschler to deploy his platoon on the right of the road, to get ready to move on the ridge. He also sent a runner back to Krause with orders to bring up Third Battalion as fast as possible. With twenty men and more than his share of audacity, Gavin moved forward.

As the engineers pushed uphill, the firing picked up, and bullets tore through the branches of the olive trees, making a sound, Gavin thought, like bees buzzing. Clearly there were enemy soldiers on the ridge in front of them, and they'd spotted the Americans. Judging by the amount of incoming fire, the ridge was only lightly held, maybe by a small outpost, a patrol, a few skirmishers. The only way to find out for sure was to press ahead.

Gavin was near Weschler when the lieutenant was hit and fell, badly wounded. Other troopers went down, grunting and cursing in pain as the bullets found them, but the platoon pushed forward, finally crawling under the incoming fire. The enemy skirmishers withdrew, allowing the GIs to reach the crest. Chancing a look down the western slope of the ridge, Gavin saw that they had arrived just in time: a large body of German troops on the other side was crawling toward him. They'd won the race; now all they had to do was stay.

H Company platoon scout Cloid Wigle, who had knocked Gavin down playing football back at Benning, found Major Éd Krause just behind Biazza Ridge on the morning of July 11. Wigle and thirty other H Company men he'd found moved quickly up onto the hill above the gatekeeper's cottage.

The men were well trained and used to working together, so they didn't need their noncoms or junior officers to pick positions for them. They moved forward, spread themselves out, figured out how they could support each other, and started hacking away at the hard shale. Later, the leaders would come around and confirm their positions or, if necessary, move them.

Wigle worked hard on his foxhole, which he quickly determined was not going to be very deep. He scraped out enough hard soil to form a trench just long enough to stretch out in. The heat here was nothing like North Africa, but it was hot, and Wigle's uniform was soon soaked in sweat. He managed to get about twenty inches deep before the first German attack came.

Wigle threw himself into the hole and peered over the lip. Off to his right, he could hear heavy firing. There were a few mortars behind him, and they were dropping rounds onto the slope below. Wigle could also hear the rapid firing of German machine guns in the vineyard at the bottom of the slope; the *crack* of the muzzle blast told him the rounds were headed his way. His vision had suddenly been reduced to the few square yards of dry grass and couple of trees he could see from down in his hole. Cut off from his buddies—who were presumably flattened out in their own holes—he was effectively alone in a world that was about to turn very violent.

The first German advance up Biazza Ridge was not a dramatic charge. The big tanks poked their way carefully through the conceal-ment provided by the thin trees, orchards, and vineyards that covered the western side of the slope. Wigle could hear the enemy drawing closer, but could not see what was happening or—and this part was torture—do anything about it.

Suddenly a German tank nosed through the brown and green below him. Even at a distance, Wigle could see the tank was huge, bigger than any American tank he had ever seen. The fact that the paratroopers were not expecting any tanks at all made the panzers' ap-pearance all the more unsettling. Wigle, armed with an M1, was help-less, trapped in his hole that was much too shallow to protect him. He watched in horror as the tank's big 88 mm gun rotated, slowly picking out the positions of individual troopers. With no Allied tanks to shoot at, with no fortified positions to take on, the German tankers were content to use the big main gun on individual GIs.

Wigle was in the path of one tank as it made its way uphill. He hoped that it would veer to one side or the other, but as he watched—horrified, fascinated—the turret turned toward him like the head of some monster, and the black maw of the gun pointed right at him. Wigle forced himself as far down into his hole as he could go. The Tiger fired high, and the big shell splintered a tree immediately behind Wigle's hole. The concussion threw him out of his position, and he landed hard on the ground nearby. One second he was in the hole, and the next he was out, as if plucked by a giant. His first instinct was to seek cover elsewhere, but there was nowhere to go on the open hillside, and no way he could outrun the machine gun. Wigle threw himself back into his hole.

Rather than waste another round, the tank commander decided to crush the paratrooper who had somehow survived the shot. Wigle, stunned by the near miss, clawed at the bottom of his hole as the noise grew louder and the tank—all fifty-three tons of it—rolled closer, its steel treads squealing as the driver pivoted and aimed for the narrow hole. Wigle was trapped, and he prepared to draw his last breath. Now the tank was above him: a huge monster from some child's nightmare, come to stomp him into the earth. The walls of his hole began to collapse as the driver pivoted, turning above the GI, trying to crush him under the awful weight. Dirt filled the hole, filled Wigle's mouth, eyes, and ears. There was nothing but darkness and the measureless noise and the taste of dusty shale.

Then the tank moved on.

Wigle, amazed that he did not seem to be dead, had the presence of mind to lie still. He thought there might be German infantry coming up behind the tank, and he'd rather they think he was dead then lift his head up and surprise a frightened panzergrenadier. He waited, drawing in dusty breaths for which he was grateful. When the tank seemed to have moved off a good distance, he chanced a look. He got to his feet and stumbled out of his hole, semiconscious, wobbling, bleeding from the ears and nose. He looked down at what had almost been his grave. The treads of the Tiger had cleared him by inches. He was aware of some other troopers coming up, grabbing him by the arms and helping him back over the crest of the hill, back toward some semblance of safety.

The fight at Biazza Ridge pulled paratroopers from the entire area west and south of Vittoria. By the time Alex Burns, H Company's supply sergeant, arrived, he'd already had a campaign's worth of fighting.

Burns had landed after moonset, but managed to find four other men in the darkness, and the five decided they'd do best to find a small hilltop where they could defend themselves and wait until dawn. The hilltop they picked was already occupied by a handful of Italian soldiers, and a sharp firefight broke out. The muzzle flashes were unnaturally bright, and the GIs had been told repeatedly that firing in the dark only let the enemy know where you were, but the enemy was too far away to attack with bayonets, and it wouldn't do to throw hand grenades uphill when they might roll back. Once they got into the fight, it didn't occur to the paratroopers that they could pull back. They pressed the attack, and the Italians abandoned both the hilltop and a machine gun.

Unfortunately, all the shooting had attracted another enemy patrol, and in the dim light just before dawn, Burns could make out a large body of enemy soldiers below them in some open ground. The paratroopers, now heavily outnumbered, hid behind a stone wall and fired the Italian machine gun at the advancing patrol. Incoming rounds chipped the rock wall or zipped over the troopers' heads. Burns, who had turned twenty-three years old while the unit was in Africa, thought he'd probably die on this hilltop when the enemy overran their position. But the Italians were pinned down by the heavy fire in the open space of the slope. When the GIs realized that they had the advantage, they poured it on; they had to keep the Italians from regaining the initiative, or else they'd all wind up as prisoners, or worse. Finally, there was some shouting among the men caught below, and they threw down their weapons and surrendered.

Now the paratroopers found themselves holding a body of prisoners that outnumbered them. They disarmed the men and sent them walking, in formation, on a road that seemed to lead to the beach. They were less concerned that the prisoners might make a break for it and rejoin the fight than they were that such a large group would slow them down and make them conspicuous targets.

Burns picked up a few more troopers later in the day, and the small group was moving along a road, spread out at decent intervals, when a German fighter roared in over the hills and strafed them, sending paratroopers flying into the roadside ditches. The big machine gun bullets chunked along the hard dirt, sending rocks and sand flying, but none of Burns's men was hit. They waited to make sure the fighter had left the area, then climbed back onto the road, dusted themselves off, and started moving again. So much for the protection of Allied air forces, "the largest assemblage of air power in the world's history" promised in Gavin's D-day note to the troops.

Burns was following the road toward Gela on the morning of July 11 when he recognized Jim Gavin, who had set up a small command post just behind a the crest of a low ridge.

"Take your men up there to the left," Gavin told Burns. He was patching his lines with the small groups as they came in, rather than trying to reconstitute whole units on the back side of the ridge. Gavin was a picture of calm. Burns had never seen him any other way, and apparently combat was going to be no different for Slim Jim. But there was no mistaking what he wanted: speed. Burns took his handful of men up the low rise and over the crest, through some trees that reached over the top of the slope. The Germans were to the north and west, off the right side of the thin line Gavin was putting together.

Nick Kastrantas, the sergeant from the S2 section who had jumped right behind Gavin, had been with the commander's group until the break in contact during the early morning hours of July 10. Kastrantas spent D-day wandering around with two other men, and they had their first encounter with what lay ahead when they stumbled across two dead paratroopers lying in a hole alongside a nameless road.

On the morning of July 11, Kastrantas found Gavin, and he set to work to help establish the command post. Kastrantas had with him the map boards, thin pieces of plywood on which he'd post situation maps. His job was to keep the maps updated with current information—enemy locations and friendly unit locations—so that Gavin and his staff could oversee the fight. Kastrantas still had the map boards on his back, lashed beneath his musette bag, when the Germans dropped some mortar rounds near the command post. Hot shrapnel punched Kastrantas in the back, penetrating his musette bag but stopping in the thin plywood.

Harold "Pop" Eatman, the North Carolinian who'd had to leave his wife in the hospital on his last weekend pass, was following the Vittoria–Gela road when the sun came up on July 11. The group he'd collected on D-day paused by a stone gatekeeper's cottage where the highway crossed a railroad. Up ahead, they could see a low ridge with thin, burned grass and a few stunted trees, and they could hear gunfire on the opposite side of the hill. The little band moved toward the fight.

The ridge wasn't steep, but the wide open spaces made climbing it risky, as they were completely exposed to fire from any enemy on the crest. Eatman and a companion—a soldier from another company whose name he did not know—made it to the top and looked down into a vineyard on the other side. The grapevines were about waist high, and though they wouldn't protect the men from fire, they provided some concealment. Eatman listened to the machine-gun fire coming from the vineyard. In North Africa they had trained with enemy weapons, and they knew that the German machine guns had a much higher rate of fire than the American weapons.

"That's an American," he said. "I'll bet that's Blubaugh and his tommy gun."

Eatman had seen Elmer Blubaugh, another H Company soldier, move up the ridge ahead of him.

Eatman crossed the crest of the ridge and began crawling downhill, toward the sound of the guns. By the time he got close enough to the firing to realize that he'd been mistaken—it was a German weapon—the enemy had spotted movement in the vineyard.

Eatman and the other soldier were out in front of whatever American line was on the ridge, and had almost reached the Germans. They had to turn around, put their backs to the enemy, and crawl on their bellies up the long slope, veering to their left in the hopes of finding other troopers. As they clawed through the grass and rocks, churning dust into their eyes and mouths, bullets snapped above their heads and showered them with shredded leaves. Eatman did not think the shooter could see them, but he clearly knew the GIs were out there. He was soaked in sweat, his face caked with dust, his throat parched. He had crawled down the slope and was now crawling up it—hundreds of yards on his belly, with the sun beating down on him, with his equipment catching on the rocks, and now with someone shooting at him.

The two men reached a fence made of thick cactus that ran along the edge of a road. On the uphill side of the road was the olive grove, which they'd have to cross before they reached any other GIs. Crawling through the vineyard behind them had been hard, sweaty work; but the olive grove posed another problem: the tree branches did not reach the ground, and there was little in the way of grass; a man running through the grove would be fully exposed.

Eatman and his companion hugged the cactus fence and plotted their next move. The spiny plants were four or five feet thick, and the road on the other side was lower than the surrounding fields. They could not see along the road, but they could see through a gap in the fence to the uphill side. They caught an occasional glimpse of a paratrooper just uphill, and the two sorely wanted the company. Below them, they could hear sporadic fire from the Germans. They did not see anyone pursuing them, but that didn't mean they were safe.

The plan was simple. Eatman's companion would dash across the open road, with Eatman following a few steps behind. They crouched beside the cactus and eyed the open ground on the other side. They had already crawled hundreds of yards on the dusty ground, with bullets zinging just overhead. Now they faced the prospect of crossing an open area—the road—and running up a hill with little to conceal them. At some point they would be running right at whatever Americans were in position up there, and there was always a chance that the other troopers would mistake them for advancing Germans. Eatman pushed that thought out of his mind. One challenge at a time.

The other trooper dashed across the road, his equipment jangling and bouncing against his body. The road was only yards wide, but from behind the fence it looked as wide as a football field. Eatman jumped up when the other man was halfway across the road, and as soon as he stepped clear of the fence, he saw the German tank, just yards off to his right and hidden on the sunken road.

The tank crew had been startled by the first trooper, and they couldn't react fast enough to shoot him. But in the next second or two—about as long as it took Eatman to step out in front of the tank—the gunner had found his weapon and opened fire. Eatman whirled around and leaped for the downhill side of the road. His upper body was concealed by the cactus fence, which had also hidden the tank from the troopers' view, but his legs were exposed.

The machine gun pounded away at him, and Eatman felt something hitting his legs and back. His first thought was, *This is what it feels like to be shot.* Then he realized that the machine gun was pulverizing the cactus, and he was being splattered with big chunks of the plant.

The gun stopped firing. Eatman did not know if the crew could see his legs, but he played dead, hoping that the Germans did not get out to investigate. After a few long seconds, he heard the tank's engine; then the sound seemed to grow fainter—or was it his imagination? Eatman waited, finally deciding that the tank was backing up. He slowly pulled one leg off the road, then the other. When he finally got the nerve to look, the tank was gone. He had been so close, almost directly in front of the tank, that the crew could not depress the machine gun far enough to hit him. Of course, the driver could easily have rolled forward to crush him, but Eatman tried not to think about that.

He worked his way to the left, north and east along the ridge, and finally crossed the road. Now he was in the olive grove: he could see farther, but he could also be seen. He moved up the slope at a dog trot, dodging amid the thin trees for whatever concealment he could find. He had lost sight of the Americans higher up on the ridge. He knew there were Germans behind him, and to the right, and probably to the left. Someone was in front of him. He would either head right into the teeth of whatever American line was on the ridge, or he'd bump into the back of advancing Germans. It was going to be tricky either way.

As he picked his way up the slope, he heard engines again. He hit the ground at the base of a tree and peered off to his left. He was just able to make out the enormous bulks of two more German tanks, much bigger than the one he had encountered at the edge of the vine-yard. These two monsters—he would later learn they were Tigers—seemed uncertain about their advance up the hill. There was no supporting infantry that Eatman could see, which meant that the tanks were vulnerable to any American infantryman with the guts to crawl up with a bazooka. The panzers moved uphill in a slow leapfrog, a very cautious advance.

Then, as Eatman watched, the two tanks started to back down. Perhaps they were uncertain about what lay near the top of the ridge, or they had decided to try another approach, but the two rolled back-ward, covering the same tracks they had left in their advance. When they were far enough behind that he thought they wouldn't see him, Eatman jogged off under the low canopy of olive branches. He had been running and moving almost continually since he'd landed thirty-six hours earlier, but he was desperate to be among his own.

Eatman spotted the head and shoulders of a man in a shallow hole scraped into the stubborn shale. He shouted his unit, hoping that the GIs on the line hadn't been so spooked that they'd just open up on him. He ran to the man and was surprised to find it was Jim Gavin, out in front. Eatman slid to the ground next to him. He was drenched in sweat, and his canteen was empty.

"Is there any water here?" Eatman gasped.

Gavin reached around for his own canteen.

"Here, son, take some of mine."

Eatman, tired and hot and dusty as he was, thought that he shouldn't be drinking the colonel's water. He was a paratrooper, and he was supposed to practice water discipline. He put the canteen to his lips but did not drink. He handed it back and thanked Gavin, then took his place on the line.

Two paratroopers came roaring up in a captured Italian vehicle, a lightly armored personnel carrier. Incredibly, they wanted to attack the

German tanks. Several GIs advised them against it—they'd be easy targets for the tanks—but the two men, armed only with rifles, insisted that they could take care of themselves.

"We want to scare the Krauts into thinking we have armor, too," the driver told Gavin.

They drove up the slope and had just cleared the crest when a German 88, probably a main gun round from one of the Tigers, hit them, incinerating the two men. Their smoking remains stayed at the top of the ridge throughout the fighting.[4]

The regimental medical officer, Captain Daniel B. McIlvoy, drove up the back of the slope in an Italian truck he intended to use as an ambulance. With him were Privates First Class Murray Goldman and Marvin L. Crossley. McIlvoy's zeal to get close to his wounded men pushed him right into the line of sight of a German tank, which fired on the truck. The three men managed to dive clear of the vehicle, which was riddled with shrapnel.[5]

McIlvoy was not one to give up easily. He found his way to Gavin's command post, looking for some guidance on how to best remove the wounded, and arrived just as German 88s laid down a barrage that made the area sing with flying shrapnel. McIlvoy dove for the nearest hole, landing in Gavin's already too-small trench. Gavin, McIlvoy would remember later, invited the doctor to dig his own hole.

Engineer Sam Ellis saw a soldier, armed only with a carbine, move close to the German tanks, only to be cut down by machine-gun fire. An engineer named Johnson went down when the Germans fired a main gun round at him. Ellis just had time to think that he had seen the last of his comrade when Johnson jumped up and ran to another position. Ellis's battle was cut short when a German mortar round landed close to his shallow position and peppered him with hot steel.

When he thought it was quiet enough, he made his way back over the ridge, seeking medical help. There, in a makeshift aid station, the eighteen-year-old paratrooper saw a German soldier also being tended by the American medics. The German had been shot between the eyes—a neat hole just above his eyebrows. The man was fully conscious, and also clearly doomed. There was nothing the medics could do for him with their tiny aid packs, and they could not move him quickly to any of the hospital ships lying offshore. The German merely asked for some American cigarettes, and he sat smoking calmly until he died.[6]

Gavin put troops on the line as soon as they arrived, but he was still looking for Krause and the bulk of Third Battalion. He hurried back to the railroad crossing, just behind the ridge, and was joined there by Major William Hagan, the executive officer of Third Battalion. Hagan had hurried out ahead of his troops, and he assured the regimental commander that help was on the way. Gavin asked where Krause was, and was surprised to hear that the battalion commander, instead of leading his troops into the fight, had gone back to retrieve the men and equipment left at his original command post. Gavin was incredulous. Krause, for all his warrior posturing, was giving up a chance to take his unit into the toughest fight around. But Gavin didn't have time to worry about it then.[7]

Gavin told Hagan to have his troops drop their heavy packs and, carrying only their weapons, ammunition, and water, hurry forward to hit the Germans coming up the other side of the ridge. At about 10:00 A.M. Hagan and some two hundred men advanced rapidly along the Gela road, sweeping over the top of the ridge, saving the embattled engineers and pushing down the far slope of the hill. They took fire, and some of the paratroopers went down, but they killed or scattered the German scouts who were closest to the top of the ridge.

* * *

At the same time Gavin was pushing his paratroopers to grab the ridge, more German infantry was coming up the west side. With the exception of Hagan's assault, the Americans came up piecemeal, as they arrived. On the German side, the advances were somewhat tentative. Some enemy infantry arrived at the crest only seconds before Alex Burns, the H Company supply sergeant, and his men. The Germans did not even have time to pick firing positions, but they opened up as soon as they saw the paratroopers.

Machine gun rounds tore into a lieutenant from Third Battalion who was no more than twenty yards away from Burns. The sergeant was thrown backward as something slammed into his shin with the force of a mule kick. He rolled onto his back and looked down at his leg, where a bullet had broken the skin but not the bone. He shook out his combat dressing and wrapped the knee, keeping one eye out for the enemy infantry who had fired on him. His men were returning fire, and he could see fleeting images of the Germans as they ran down the west side of the slope, apparently headed for a stone building set amid a vineyard farther down the enemy side.

Burns and his men spread out as best they could. The ground here, like everywhere on the ridge, was too hard for digging, so they'd have to keep pushing. Burns sent a man down to check out the stone building, to see what the Germans had done there and if they would need rooting out. Burns couldn't stay on the slope, which had concealment but no real cover, if the Germans had a strongpoint with a machine gun right in front of him.

The trees here were thicker than at any other point along the west side of the ridge, as far as Burns could see, and though they were small trees, there were enough of them, he hoped, to keep the Germans from pushing tanks through. He would have to deal only with infantry, which was as close to a fair fight as any that took place on Biazza Ridge.

The trooper sent to check the barn came upon the German patrol that had pulled off the crest. They hadn't set up their machine gun, so the GI started shooting. The Germans were stunned: a lone American with a rifle was chasing them. Who were these men?

It may have been the shock of being pursued, or their surprise at being chased off the hill when they thought the ridge was empty. It may have been the rumors spreading on the German side—that the island had been invaded by thousands of paratroopers. It may have been their command's disorganized response to the Forty-fifth Division landings. Or it may just have been that these Germans soldiers, who had already been at war for nearly four years, were tired. Many had survived the Russian front only to be stuck on this remote island among a hostile people and alongside an unwilling ally. Whatever it was, for this small segment of the mighty Wehrmacht, the war was over. The machine gun team surrendered to the lone paratrooper, who hustled them back up the slope and over the top, on past the tiny command post and down to a collection point near the railroad crossing.

No doubt the prisoners were surprised to see, on the opposite side of the hill, no sign of a strong defensive line. One tall, thin man was sending his troops into battle as fast as he could collect them. Small knots of paratroopers were collecting by the gatekeeper's cottage, organizing themselves for a consolidated push. But there were no masses of men here, no tanks, no artillery, no vehicles, just a bunch of lean and grimy footsoldiers, in uniforms festooned with hand grenades and bandoleers of ammunition. Some of them had their faces painted black, and they all wore the flag of the United States on their sleeves. The Americans had come to stay.

On the morning of July 11, Third Battalion communications officer Lieutenant Bob Fielder and the small band of troopers he'd collected on D-day moved parallel to a road as they made their way west toward the objective area. The vegetation on this southern shore of Sicily was sparse, which meant long views from the hilltops, but the constant zigzagging of the road also meant that any bend might lead to a surprise. Fielder spread the men out. If they were going to walk into an ambush, he wanted as few men as possible in the line of fire. Early that morning, the point man rounded a bend and saw another band of paratroopers, this one led by Jim Gavin.

None of the men with Fielder was from his communications section, so he told them to find their own units amid the GIs gathering at the ridge, which had become a magnet for troopers in the vicinity. There was a general milling about as the paratroopers reorganized and got ready to move up.

Fielder saw Gavin near the stone gatekeeper's cottage where the railroad crosses the Vittoria-Gela road. The regimental commander was talking with Beaver Thompson, the *Chicago Tribune* reporter who had jumped with the regiment. The reporter was dressed in the same combat gear the other paratroopers wore, minus a weapon, but was instantly recognizable for the bushy beard he wore. Thompson had jumped last from Gavin's plane, and had spent D-day wandering around and looking for the regiment.

Fielder made his way to the crest and found a likely position near Gavin's tiny command post, figuring that he could best do his job as a communications officer from there, and that any of his radio operators or wiremen who came in would be sent to the command post. Gavin came up and began scraping his own shallow foxhole about fifteen feet away from Fielder. No one was making much progress in the rocky soil.

Slim Jim was a picture of confidence. Like the other men who saw Gavin that day, Fielder drew courage from his commander's example, and the lieutenant felt compelled to say something, something momentous perhaps, fitting the drama of the moment, something that would let the commander know that his men appreciated the example he was setting.

When Gavin drew close, Fielder said, "We won't take off, sir."

Gavin, who knew he had problems but didn't assume that this was one of them, looked at Fielder and said, "So what?"

Gavin pushed units that arrived intact over to the right, where he expected the German attack. Working under their own officers and noncoms, these men formed the strongest building blocks for the defense. Small groups and individuals got sent to the left of the line, toward the sea. Fielder and the men around him were ordered over the crest, toward the vineyard at the bottom of the slope on the northwest side.

A rush of images and impressions hit Fielder as he moved downhill. Down the slope was a grim sight: a dead paratrooper hanging in a tree, suspended from his parachute harness. The firing grew heavier. Fielder was amazed at the rate of fire of the enemy machine guns, and the comparatively slow rate of the American guns. (The German light machine gun could send nearly twelve hundred rounds per minute downrange. The light machine gun the paratroopers carried could spit out only half that.) German fire dominated the hillside. Even more unnerving was the sound of heavy diesel engines and the squeaking of tank treads. The GIs could not see the tanks, but they could hear them, and they didn't sound far away.

Fielder heard someone shouting that they were to move farther down the slope, toward the enemy. Fielder and the others ran downhill and to the left side of the American position. There were no foxholes here, and no time to dig. The troopers immediately went to ground; they were all riflemen now. It was clear that Gavin had been right in his estimation, that the Germans were preparing another counterattack.

Fielder was on the far left of the American line, with no one to his left: he was the American flank. When he heard someone coming up behind him, he turned to see Lieutenant William Harris, the Third Battalion operations officer (who had captured Vittoria), who had come to check on him. Was Fielder okay? Did he have ammunition? Did he know where the next man over was located?

While Harris crouched by Fielder, a German machine gunner spotted him and sent a burst of fire into the grass around the two men. Harris cut short his visit, wished Fielder good luck, and took off to bolster up some other part of the line.

At first Fielder lay on top of the ground, as there had been no time to scrape out a hole before the Germans started shooting. The thin grass beneath the trees gave him some concealment, but there was nothing that would stop a bullet. The Germans fired a couple of phosphorous shells at the American line to set fire to the grass and burn out the troopers, but the fires didn't spread. Fielder also saw a German shell, fired in his direction, bounce along the ground, and pass him without exploding. Still another shell buried itself in the ground right in front of Fielder's position without exploding.

At one point, Fielder, lying flat on the grass, heard a German Tiger pull up close. With his face pressed to the ground, Fielder couldn't see the enemy, but they saw him. The tank opened fire with its machine gun, stitching the dirt just beside him. Fielder lay there, helpless. Amazingly, even over the roar of shooting around him, over the straining of the tank's engine, Fielder heard metallic clicking as the gunner traversed the turret a few degrees to adjust the fire. Fielder thought this might be the last sound he heard on earth, but the next burst of fire hit on Fielder's other side. They had missed both times.

There was nothing for Fielder to do but stay put. His personal weapon was of no use against the tank, and he couldn't move to another position. He was frightened, and all of his senses were fully engaged, but he had not reached the point of panic. In fact, as he ran through his limited options, the only one that did not occur to him was to run.

The Tiger finally left him alone. Either the gunner thought the paratrooper was dead, or the tank commander wanted to move on to other things.

Throughout the morning, the German armor continued to probe the American position. Fielder, like most of the men crouched on the forward slope, could see very little of the bigger fight. In the midst of all this confusion Major Krause appeared, armed with a bazooka. He had another trooper with him, who acted as loader, and they moved to a point less than twenty feet away from Fielder. From there Krause could see German tanks below him on the slope, but that meant that the tankers could also see him. The loader hurried though his drill, eager to get out of the open. When he was finished, he slapped Krause on the shoulder, the signal that the rocket was ready. Krause, kneeling, fired at a tank, but the round bounced harmlessly off the German armor. Kraus managed to get out of the way before the tankers spotted him.

Krause had been lucky, Fielder thought. He had already seen the bodies of men who'd been crushed by onrushing tanks, their ineffective bazookas ground up amid the bloody pulp.

Around noon the Germans made a determined push against the Third Battalion, on the center and right of Gavin's line. Much of the ridge was covered in vineyards, and the low-hanging vines, with their wide, shiny leaves, gave good concealment to the GIs when they dug in, even in shallow foxholes. From those positions, the Americans were able to fend off the German infantry, but the attack was also supported by at least a dozen of the monstrous fifty-six-ton Tiger tanks.[8]

Bob Piper, the lieutenant from the regimental headquarters who had been so happy to see his G Company buddies, witnessed the lopsided fight between German tanks and U.S. infantry. The tanks came and went as they wanted, rolling through the American positions, while the GIs fought back with their tiny bazookas. While the occasional flank shot might disable a tank, the panzers clearly had the upper hand.

Piper saw a G Company sergeant named Gerald Ludlam climb onto the six-foot-high back deck of one of the huge Tigers, apparently hoping to shove hand grenades into the crew hatches. But the Germans were buttoned up tight, the hatches locked from the inside. Ludlam was knocked off the tank and crushed beneath its treads in full view of his horrified comrades.

Another G Company man, Boston native Phillip Foley, moved around the forward slope of the ridge, finding targets for the G Company bazooka teams. Foley was famous for being a screwup in base camp, but some of the noncoms in G Company had noticed that he came into his own on the field problems. His fellow troopers, who had seen him drunk and fighting and under company punishment, were amazed to see him scrambling over the hillside, seemingly without fear. And he was charmed that day: although wounded, he survived the battle and won a Silver Star.[9]

Some artillerymen from D Battery also made it to the fight on the ridge. The men had been unable to find the bundled .50-caliber machine gun they were supposed to use to defend the firing batteries from air attack, so Private Gene Fallon and other men of D Battery fought as infantry. A lieutenant told Fallon to take a bazooka and move forward on the right side of Gavin's line. The lieutenant pointed to a rock wall the men could see from the top of the ridge, and he told Fallon he should dig in there.

Fallon had just turned eighteen in May, shortly after the unit arrived in North Africa. Desperate for work before the war, he had lied about his age to join the Civilian Conservation Corps. With that paperwork and its false birth date, he had been able to enlist in the Army.

Fallon picked up the bazooka and headed downhill, convinced that the lieutenant was going to get him killed. For one thing, it took two men to fire the bazooka: one held the tube on his shoulder while the other loaded the rocket from the back. It was possible that Fallon could operate the weapon himself, but that meant fumbling with the rocket, then hoisting it onto his shoulder, all the while hoping that the enemy did nothing except sit and wait to be shot.

Fallon made it to the wall without incident. He had dumped his folding-stock carbine and traded it for an M1 he found, and he had the bazooka and two rockets. He was a quarter mile from the main line that was growing near the crest of the ridge; if the Germans attacked, he probably wouldn't make it back. Fallon took out his entrenching tool and hacked away at the tough soil. Soon he was sweating heavily, so he removed his helmet and web gear and set it beside his weapon, which was leaning against the wall.

Then Fallon heard a bullet hit the wall just a few feet from his head. He leaped over the rock wall and crouched as low as he could, hoping that there was only one sniper, and that the wall hid him. It took him only a second to realize his mistake: he left his weapons and gear on the opposite side.

He lay there, out in front of his own lines, counting seconds that passed like hours. There was no sound of anyone approaching, though there was sporadic firing all across the ridge. Finally, he got up the nerve to scramble back over the wall. He kept close to the ground as he retrieved his weapons, helmet, and other gear; then he went back up the slope to find the lieutenant who'd sent him forward.

The young officer listened to Fallon's story and went off to investigate. When the men heard more shooting, they crawled forward and found the lieutenant had been hit. The bullet had bounced around inside the rim of his helmet, peeling the skin and hair away, but not penetrating the skull. The artillerymen helped the officer back over the crest to the aid station.

DESPERATE HOURS

By midmorning on July 11, the noise of the fight on Biazza Ridge was pulling troops from the entire area west of Vittoria, and the paratroopers on the ridge were happy to welcome anyone who could carry a weapon. Besides his own men, Gavin scooped up a platoon from the 180th Infantry, a Forty-fifth Division unit that wandered into the area; and he even grabbed a couple of sailors who had come ashore with the infantry. A few men from regimental headquarters came trickling in, including a twenty-one-year-old radioman from Maine named George Huston, and his friend Bill Blake.[1] Blake had turned eighteen on July 9, the day of the jump. The headquarters men set up a command post, a central place to collect incoming messages for Gavin. They had no radios, so Huston and the other communications men acted as runners, carrying messages for the commander.

Huston was armed only with a folding-stock carbine. The infantrymen called it a "peashooter," and it didn't give him a lot of confidence. Although he'd had no infantry training, he was willing to do whatever Gavin asked. Perhaps because he was a communications man, or perhaps because he was armed only with a carbine, Huston wasn't picked by Gavin to move forward to reinforce the line. Huston was told to stay at the command post; his friend, the teenage soldier Bill Blake, went forward.

Now mortar and artillery fire began to fall on the ridge, and soldiers scrambled to find cover. In the open spaces beneath the trees, the bright yellow and orange flashes were clearly visible, and the bursts sent sharp rocks flying like shrapnel. Huston dove for one of the shallow holes they had managed to scrape, but a lieutenant beat him by a second or two, and Huston landed on top of the man.

With mortar shells bursting all around him, Gavin tried to scrape out a shallow foxhole to provide some cover from the hot shrapnel ripping the air. He pulled his entrenching tool—a folding shovel—from its carrier, but it proved too flimsy to dig in the hard shale. He tried using his helmet to scrape at the ground, but that wasn't much better. Still, he needed whatever protection he could get, so he kept digging.

The paratroopers were holding their ground, but casualties began to stream back from the ridge, walking wounded and men half carried by their buddies, uniforms torn and bloody. Gavin moved among them, and they told him stories about firing their bazookas at the German tanks, only to watch the shells bounce off harmlessly. Worse, when a bazooka fired, there was a telltale plume of smoke, which gave away the team's location. Alert tankers fired at this signature with machine guns and even the big 88 main gun.

Major Hagan, the Third Battalion exec, was one of the wounded who came back, his thigh badly torn by enemy fire. Major Krause had come up the back side of the slope and immediately gone into the fight. Along with the wounded GIs came some German prisoners, being hustled to the rear by paratroopers. Gavin questioned them and found they were with the Hermann Goering Parachute Panzer Division. The name was misleading, as the title "Parachute" was honorary, and the unit did not have enough tanks to constitute a full-strength panzer division.[2] Nevertheless, many of the individual soldiers were combat veterans, and even if they only had one tank, that was one more than the paratroopers had.

Gavin moved along the ridge, trying to get an accurate picture of the enemy's strength. He could hear the tanks, and though the smoke and dust hid them from view, it was clear he'd run into a sizable force. This was no German platoon scouting the enemy position, but the lead element of a deliberate push for the ridge.

Gavin worried about his flanks. On his left, down toward the landing beaches, there would be units of the Forty-fifth Division. While he wasn't tied in with those troops yet, their mere presence made a German end run on the beach side unlikely. The enemy was on his right flank, on the inland side, and he had to get someone or something over there to shore it up. He had held some of his intrepid engineers back as a reserve, as well as two 81 mm mortars commanded by Lieutenant Robert May. (May had been the first sergeant of C Company, 503rd Parachute Infantry, when Gavin commanded that unit.) May sent a couple of troopers off to the right to keep an eye on things over there and give warning if the Germans attacked the flank.

Gavin, ostensibly in command of thirty-four hundred men, was dealing in ones and twos, sending individual soldiers on missions that called for a company.

Sergeant James Ross of C Battery, 456th Field Artillery, heard the firing on the low ridge and headed that way with five other artillerymen. They'd managed to assemble a pack howitzer from the bundles, and now he and his men were dragging the gun by hand, using a long canvas sling called a "dog harness." One man sat on the short barrel of the piece to keep the heavy trail, where the ammunition was fastened, off the ground.

Ross was the motor sergeant for C Battery, but of course they had no motor transport with them on Sicily, at least until the troopers could figure out how to steal some from the Italians, from the Germans, or even from American units that didn't keep a close eye on their equipment. Ross had celebrated his twenty-first birthday on July 9, and on the flight to Sicily, he had looked out of the door at the darkened sea and thought, *At least I made it to twenty-one*.

As they crossed the railroad track behind the ridge, they saw troopers moving forward on the gentle slope ahead of them. The artillerymen quickened their pace, churning up dust on the hard soil, sweating as they manhandled their gun. Instead of sending a reconnaissance element ahead, they just bulled forward, dragging their piece.

They crested the ridge and immediately saw what looked like a hedge just a hundred yards below them. Alongside the hedge was a German tank, and another one sitting not too far away. The tanks were close, and huge. The troopers immediately turned around, yanking the gun off the crest of the hill, where they were silhouetted against the sky. Then the eight men—armed with the wrong weapon for the job and only yards away from two of the most fearsome tanks on this or any other battlefield—attacked.

Since the howitzer was designed as an indirect-fire weapon (it threw its shell in a high arc), its sights were no good for firing directly at a target. Instead, the gunner opened the breach and looked through the empty barrel for the target, or sighted along the top of the barrel. The crew inched the gun forward until it just cleared the top of the ridge and the gunner, on his hands and knees, found the target. Then the crew slammed in a round and fired.

The round didn't penetrate the heavy armor, but the explosion knocked a track off one tank. The Germans, unable to move and expecting another shot at any moment, abandoned the vehicle, and the artillerymen opened fire with their rifles as the tankers tried to run. Around the gun crew, infantrymen moved forward to give chase as the second tank pivoted, belched exhaust and took off for a more covered position.

Not long afterward, Lieutenant Ray Grossman arrived at the foot of Biazza Ridge with the other three guns of C Battery. The troopers had quickly tired of dragging the heavy pieces, and so had enlisted two small Italian personnel carriers and a couple of donkeys to help pull the equipment. Rather than silhouetting themselves on the top of the ridge, they stopped short of the crest. Incoming mortar fire, set to burst above ground (called "tree burst"), wounded a couple of soldiers.

Grossman had the gunners spread out on the back side of the slope. When they learned that Tiger tanks were playing havoc with the lightly armed infantry, the men pushed forward, with Sergeant Thomas's section in the lead. Battery commander Captain Ray Crossman helped drag the gun into place, while Grossman swept the forward slope with his binoculars. The valley below them was smoky, with just the tops of the small trees poking through. Grossman called out that he had a tank in sight. Sergeant Thomas and his crew went into their practiced loading drill, and sent a round downrange. But they had set up in such a hurry that they hadn't anchored the trail of the gun, the long metal brace that rests on the ground behind the barrel. Amid all the shouting and excitement, no one had jumped onto the trail to weigh it down. The whole weapon jumped with the recoil and one of the tires hit the gunner in the chest, knocking him backward but not inflicting too much damage. The gunner scrambled forward to his post, another man stood on the trail, and they fired again.

With all the dust, Grossman couldn't see if they had damaged the tank, but he did see smoke that might be from a fire. Then the panzer crew got the range, and put an 88 mm round just to the left and behind the howitzer. The near miss convinced Captain Crossman that he should pull his guns back off the ridge and find another firing position.

Gavin checked on his two mortars and found that Lieutenant May was among the wounded. The mortar crews had limited ammunition and were in danger from the incoming German fire, but Gavin needed them. He talked to the crews and reassured them that they were all going to stay on this ridge.

Then Gavin visited Captain Crossman and his artillerymen. The howitzers were turning out to be important antitank weapons, and Gavin was concerned about losing them. The gunners were exposed to German tank, artillery, and mortar fire, which had already killed C Battery's Lieutenant Charles G. Derby, but they had stood their ground.

Gavin told the artillerymen to remain concealed as best they could. Any tank that came over the crest would expose its underside, which was not heavily armored. If the gun crews were careful and patient, they could put a killing shot right into the belly of a tank. This was a dangerous tactic, of course, requiring the gunners to hold their fire while the tanks advanced. Gavin told the men from C Battery that if the tanks overran the guns, the troopers should fight on the ridge as infantrymen.

By midafternoon, the troopers had been running up and down the ridge, fighting, digging, and dodging tanks for hours. They'd had no re-supply of rations, though many of them had found tomatoes on vines alongside the farmhouses, the first fresh food they'd had since landing in North Africa. More important, there was no way to get water to the men on the line, who were baking under the Sicilian sun and breathing dust and burned powder.

Gavin turned to Lieutenant Bob Piper, who had delivered eight men with a borrowed jeep. Gavin told him to climb back into the jeep and head down to the beach where the Forty-fifth Division was unloading supplies. Get water. Get food. Get ammunition.

Piper was apprehensive about trying to pass through the Forty-fifth Division lines; the advancing front line troops would have jumpy trigger fingers. Piper knew there was a chance the GIs he'd encounter would mistake him, in his paratrooper garb, for a German. With their slash pockets and high collars, the troopers' uniforms looked nothing like what the rest of the U.S. Army wore. On a battlefield populated by frightened men carrying weapons and thinking that everyone is out to kill them, different is bad.

So it was a nervous Lieutenant Piper who climbed behind the wheel and raced off down the road toward Vittoria, past the railroad crossing and the caretaker's cottage where they had staged for the assault on the ridge. As he left his fellow paratroopers behind and before he saw any other GIs, he began singing "The Star-Spangled Banner" as loudly as he could. It was a bit ludicrous, but it was the best idea his could come up with on short notice.

Before long, he spotted some GIs in the low hills along the side of the road. In spite of the fact that he was in an American jeep and wearing an American helmet, in spite of his accent and his singing "The Star-Spangled Banner," a few of the jumpy soldiers were convinced that, coming from the direction he did, he was a German.

Piper distinctly heard, "He's a Kraut, shoot him!"

Piper began yelling, "I'm an American! I'm an American!" expecting at any second to hear gunfire. He jammed the brakes, stopping the jeep in the road, and held his hands up high where everyone could see them.

"I'm coming down to get water and food," he said.

It took a long few moments for the scouts to come into the open, where they could see for themselves that Piper was telling the truth.

Gavin stole a few minutes here and there to return to his command post and scrape away at his foxhole. He had given up on ever making one deep enough to hide him, especially if a tank came rolling over the spot, so he decided to dig the front end deeper than the back, reasoning that he could sit and double over, squeezing himself just below ground.

At some point on that hot afternoon, German fighter planes

popped up over the hills to the north. They were low enough for the men to see the black-and-white Luftwaffe crosses on the wings as the planes lined up for a gun run. With so little concealment on the ridge, the troops were exposed to strafing, and they ducked into their shallow holes. To Gavin's surprise, the fighters concentrated on the gate-keeper's house, which was a good distance back from Gavin's command post. Evidently the fighter pilots thought that the American command would set up in a place that afforded some cover and was well back of the line, rather than in an eighteen-inch-deep foxhole right in the midst of the shelling.

As German mortar rounds fell around them, Captain Al Ireland, the regimental S1, suggested to Gavin that the Forty-fifth Division might have enough troops ashore that they could lend a hand to the paratroopers. Someone should go back for help. Gavin had been so busy with the tactical situation, moving men and weapons from place to place, constantly checking and bolstering the line, that he hadn't even thought of going for help. He sent Ireland running back in the direction of Vittoria.

Gavin got up again to check his fragile right end and was caught in another mortar barrage. He hit the ground, but bounced into the air with each concussion. He put his palms flat on the ground and raised his body slightly, as if he was about to do a push-up, which helped absorb some of the jarring.[3]

With the mortar barrage, and with tree-burst artillery going off, showering the men in their foxholes with deadly hot shrapnel, Ben Vandervoort, the operations officer, suggested the command group pull back to a concrete culvert just one hundred yards behind the top of the ridge. But there was no way Gavin would move to a safer position while his men lay exposed on the ridge. He looked at his operations officer and said, "Ben, you don't appreciate what's at stake here."[4]

Gavin dodged the mortar fire to go back to the all-important guns at the right end of the line. Just as he arrived, the troopers from

C Battery, 456th Field Artillery spotted a target below. Gavin could see a small group of low-slung, dun-colored buildings beyond the vineyard and about four hundred yards to the right. The gunners called out range and direction as a German tank slowly revealed itself. First the right track of the tank came around the corner of a building, then the muzzle of the big 88 gun came into view. The gunners waited nervously.

As the panzer inched forward, the tank commander's problem became clear to Gavin: he had to get the tank out from behind the building far enough to swing the big gun toward the Americans, but that meant that half the vehicle's hull would be exposed.

The paratroopers—their gun aimed, loaded, and ready to fire—were on their knees or lying flat in the brown grass, eyes fixed on the target, waiting for the tank to reveal itself enough for them to hit it, but not so far that it could use its main gun. The seconds stretched out, and all around them, the small-arms fire continued along the ridge, while the GIs stared, mesmerized by the movement in front of them. It was like being in a slow-motion version of the gunfights that were a staple of American westerns.

The tank fired first.

There was a tremendous explosion right in front of the gun, and the troopers were thrown backward by the blast. Gavin, standing just to the left of the gun, was also knocked to the ground. The artillerists scattered, but within a few seconds they got control of their fear and hustled back to the gun. They fired, and their shot hit the front of the tank, or the corner of the building, or both. In the smoke and dust the tank backed out of sight.

Gavin picked himself up and checked the gun crew. Remarkably, the gun was intact and not one of the men was hurt, though they were a little sheepish about their initial reaction to the incoming tank fire. When he looked down the hill, Gavin couldn't see the tank, meaning it had pulled back, but was not destroyed. He hoped Al Ireland found help fast, and that the help came on tank treads.

*   *   *

Behind the left of the American position, the medics had established
an aid station where they could stabilize wounded paratroopers and
get them ready for evacuation to the Forty-fifth Division field hospital.
All morning long they came back over the smoky crest of the ridge,
men wounded by small-arms fire, by shrapnel, by the heavy machine
guns on the tanks, by mortar fire, by flying rocks from the ground
bursts. The medics gave morphine to those in severe pain, and put the
new drug, sulfa, on the wounds before bandaging the troopers as best
they could. The medics operated in the open, just like everyone else,
and were exposed to the indirect fire coming over the ridge.

Cannonball Krause found Gavin in midafternoon. Lieutenant Bob
Fielder, Krause's communications officer, who had been pulled back to
the CP from his lonely outpost on the left flank, overheard Krause's
bleak assessment. All of his men, Krause said, had been killed or
wounded or were pinned down by German fire. He judged his entire
battalion combat-ineffective.

"I'm not sure we should stay here," Fielder heard Krause say.

"I don't know about you, Ed," Gavin answered, "but I'm staying
right here."

Gavin told Krause that the paratroopers would fight the German
infantry that was sure to come up with the tanks, thus stripping the
panzers of their important protection. Krause was unconvinced, and
said the paratroopers were finished if they stayed. When Krause left,
Gavin thought he was going to the rear again.[5]

On top of everything else he had to worry about, Gavin now had to
wonder if one of his battalion commanders was about to fall apart. He
had relieved Gray, the commander of Second Battalion, weeks before
the invasion, and had watched carefully to make sure the unit didn't

falter as the former exec, Mark Alexander, took over. Krause's executive officer was wounded, so if he fired Krause, he'd have to find someone else to take command. The company commanders were very junior, only first lieutenants. For the rest of the day, at least, he would have to stick with Krause, if for no other reason than he needed every man who could carry a rifle.

In midafternoon, Al Ireland reappeared with help: a liaison party from a 155 mm artillery battalion that had come across the beach with the Forty-fifth Division, as well as with a Navy ensign named G. A. Hulton, who had jumped with the 505th. Hulton, a spotter with the Shore Fire Control Party, was in radio contact with Navy ships that could provide heavy fire support.

Gavin was a little concerned about calling on the big guns for fire support. In order to do it accurately, the caller has to clearly know his position, so that he can avoid bringing the shells down on his own head. Gavin and Ensign Hulton studied the map, using the point at which the railroad crossed the highway to fix their position and outline, on the ensign's map, exactly where the GIs were. If the map was off, even by just a few hundred yards, the result could be big U.S. Navy shells landing on top of the already beleaguered paratroopers.

Hulton called for a single round, which came down exactly where he wanted it. He now knew his position, as well as that of Gavin's men, and his plot was correct. He called for concentrated fire where the enemy tanks seemed to be massing for an attack up the ridge.

It didn't take a direct hit on a tank to knock it out. Private John Foster of H Company saw one of the big Navy shells explode behind a Tiger, sending shrapnel into the engine compartment and setting it on fire. With the Navy's heavy steel pounding the ridge, the Americans finally had a weapon that evened the fight.

The Germans pulled back out of range of the naval fire, but kept up indirect fire on the Americans with their own 120 mm mortars. As the rounds exploded, their steel cases ripped into hot, jagged pieces that could tear through a man. In soft soil, a round might bury itself before exploding, but on Sicily's hard, rocky ground, the explosions made shrapnel out of rock. Since the troopers were unable to dig very deep into the shale, there were quite a few casualties from the mortar fire. The two forces had reached an impasse: the troopers did not have the strength to advance against the Germans, and the Germans were reluctant to advance against the stubborn paratroopers and the murderous fire from the artillery and U.S. Navy. But time worked in favor of the Americans: every hour meant more U.S. troops ashore, more tanks, more artillery, more firepower. The Germans were only getting weaker.

As the tanks tried to hide from the Navy guns, Hulton kept moving closer to the enemy, where he could see the rounds land so that he could radio for adjustments and thus keep the fire on target. He couldn't do that from a foxhole or even from the command post. He was out doing his job—and doing it well—when a friendly round fell short. The concussion killed Hulton.[6]

At 6:00 P.M. Gavin got word that Lieutenant Harold "Swede" Swingler and quite a few troopers from his regimental headquarters company were closing in fast. Swingler, a former intercollegiate boxing champ, was an aggressive soldier, and Gavin was glad to hear he was on his way. Around 7:00 P.M. Gavin looked east and saw Swingler on the road below, with a column of troopers and a half-dozen Sherman tanks from the Forty-fifth Division. The GIs on the back side of the ridge cheered the American tanks, and the yelling swept along the American position. Gavin was sure that the Germans, who were so close by, could hear the cheering, and that they must have wondered what was happening on the American side of the ridge. They were soon to find out.

Dust and smoke from the shelling covered the ridge in an acrid haze. The flow of wounded back to the American aid station had all but stopped, and the artillery and Navy shelling had given the paratroopers a pause that allowed them to reorganize. (Gavin had beaten one of the three counterattacks the German commander, General Paul Conrath, had pushed forward on July 11. The other two, both aimed at Gela, had been turned back by the First Division.)

The action was slowing, and with the Germans as exhausted as the Americans, the two sides seemed to have reached a stalemate. But Gavin knew the respite wouldn't last long. The Germans were sure to attack again, if not in the last light of day, then certainly in the morning. His troopers, with considerable help from the Forty-fifth Division and the U.S. Navy, had held, but the battle wasn't over. Holding the high ground was good, but the best solution would be to destroy or drive off the German force on the northwest side of Biazza Ridge. As he considered his options, Gavin knew that somewhere down past the vineyard, the German commander was probably reorganizing and coiling for a renewed attack on the ridge. The enemy was vulnerable after the failed push for the ridge, and had probably been knocked off balance by the heavy shelling. Now was the time for the paratroopers to attack.

Gavin's exhausted men had done everything he'd asked. They attacked when they didn't know the enemy strength, had stood their ground in the face of panzer assaults that would have unnerved other green troops, had kept their hold on the ridge under heavy fire even though they couldn't dig proper shelter. Gavin was about to ask more of them.

The colonel rounded up everyone who could hold a weapon, including the clerks and drivers from the regimental headquarters company, even a couple of sailors who had come ashore with the Forty-fifth Division and had wandered to the fight. At 8:45 P.M. he pushed over the top of the ridge as the sun's rays began to slant in from the west.

Swede Swingler, whose reinforcements were relatively fresh, was now on the leading edge of the American attack. He came upon a German Tiger tank about two hundred yards down from the top of the ridge, parked in a small road cut. The vehicle was not moving, but it didn't look as if it had been disabled by artillery. Swingler watched and waited, then carefully crept forward, a lone GI stalking a tank.

Soon he heard voices, and through the brown grass he spotted the crew. They had dismounted and were standing in the road talking, looking for all the world as if they were on a training exercise. Swingler pulled the pin from a hand grenade and heaved it at the center of the group. The explosion killed all five men.

When Swingler's men moved up, they examined the scorch marks on the tank's thick front glacis plate, where ineffective bazooka rounds had bounced off. The holes were deep enough for the men to put their little fingers inside, but only penetrated about an inch into the four-and-a-half-inch-thick armor.

Many of the Germans on the back side of the ridge were hardened veterans of years of fighting. As the Americans pushed forward, they did not panic, but increased their fire. Once again the slopes of Biazza Ridge were lit with bright bursts of white-and-yellow fire as mortar and 88 rounds slammed into the hard ground or burst in the treetops. Some of the troopers were cut down by hot shrapnel that tore the air, but others kept coming, scuttling down the long slope in small groups that covered one another as they advanced. Relentless, a tide borne by gravity and aggressiveness, they hammered away at pockets of German resistance, overwhelming small knots of defenders, killing, outflanking, pushing the enemy back. Behind the ridge they captured some armored cars as well as a battery of 120 mm mortars that had been shelling them all day. The mortars had additional ammunition stacked nearby, and Gavin took this as a sign that the enemy had been planning to attack, either that evening or the next morning. The 505th beat them to it.

The unexpected attack by Gavin's ad hoc force finally cleared the

Germans from Biazza Ridge. The enemy left behind some fifty dead, and the GIs took another fifty or so prisoners. Gavin set his men to consolidating their position, closing any gaps and tying in to the left and right, redistributing ammunition, taking care of the wounded. With the threat of German attack now gone, Gavin pulled his command post off the top of the ridge, back about a half mile into another grove of olive trees. The morning would probably bring an attack from his right, along the road leading from Biscari to the beach, and he positioned his command post to control that fight.

While the paratroopers were dueling for control of Biazza Ridge, Bob McGee, the demolition man who had broken his leg on landing, dragged himself to an aid station on the beach, where he was placed among the less seriously wounded men who could wait for evacuation to a ship. By midday on July 11, the beaches near Gela were piled with equipment, supplies, and vehicles waiting to move inland. Beachmasters tried to maintain order, sending the most critical units, such as the artillery, and the most critical supplies, water and ammunition, inland first. Just above the beach, the combat engineers had cleared a path through the belt of German mines. There were still signs visible on the wire on either side of the clearing that said, ACHTUNG: MINEN.

McGee passed through a narrow lane, like a beach access road, that had been cleared by combat engineers. The lane was about fifty feet wide, and in the immediate area it was the only way for the men, weapons, and rapidly growing piles of supplies to get off the beach and join the fight inland. Out on the sea, McGee could see an entire fleet, launching Patton's force in a huge wave of men and steel; the lane through the minefield was a bottleneck.

Much of the material was carried by small landing craft that came to the water's edge to be unloaded by hand. Other supplies were carried on DUKWs, amphibious trucks that drove right out of the water to join the queue heading off the beach. There was just enough Luft-waffe activity to convince McGee to dig a small trench where he could take cover, but he was more worried about speeding trucks than German aircraft. The drivers were in a hurry to get off the crowded beach, where they made inviting targets amid the huge piles of ammunition and fuel. The trucks moving from inland, which had already dropped off a load, also drove too fast. Like the paratroopers who had been so eager to get out of the airplanes, every driver wanted to get to the right pile of equipment, get loaded as quickly as possible, and move out again. The beach was the most crowded, most dangerous, and least popular place to be.

Because the beach climbed from the water's edge, the trucks entering the lane from the beach side could not see what was coming from the inland side, and the vehicles hurrying back after making their runs could not see what was coming off. McGee watched, fascinated, waiting for the inevitable collision and explosion that would close the only exit.

Crouched near his slit trench, McGee watched a lone military policeman direct traffic from the middle of the lane, surrounded by mines and nervous truck drivers. Even more amazing, the MP was decked out as if he were in garrison: he wore suntans, the khaki-colored uniform that was appropriate for the weather but not for the field. His outfit was topped off with a white helmet, a white Sam Browne belt, white puttees, and white gloves. He directed traffic with all the calm demeanor of a policeman on a stateside street corner. When a German fighter made a strafing run over the beach, McGee dove into his shallow hole, but the MP maintained his post and kept the all-important supplies moving to the men who desperately needed them.

Up until that point McGee had shared the paratrooper's view of MPs: they were more cop than soldier, and they had a habit of interfering with anything the paratroopers thought was fun: whoring, drinking, fighting, and gambling. That one MP, standing up and doing his duty under fire, changed McGee's mind.

Sometime after nightfall the medics began sending the less seriously wounded to the evacuation ships. McGee was lashed to a stretcher and carried onto a landing barge. The seas had become rougher at the end of the day, and the barge heaved up and down as it pulled alongside the ship. At the top of a swell, the side of the ship loomed twenty feet above the men on the landing craft; a moment later, the small craft dropped and there were forty feet of steel above them. McGee's stretcher and another were tied together and hooked to cables that came down out of the darkness. Then the barge suddenly dropped away beneath McGee's stretcher, and he was once again airborne. He worried that the landing barge would rise faster than he was being hoisted upward, smashing the stretcher from below, but the crew somewhere above hoisted McGee clear of the rising craft. The big ship was blacked out, and McGee could just make out the lone cable rising into the darkness, connecting him to safety.

In the next an instant, the sky was lit with fire. All of the ships around them became visible, as every gun in the fleet turned upward to throw a vast sheet of flame and steel at aircraft McGee could not see. Even the DUKWs, which were armed with machine guns, joined in. The Navy gunners were out to make the Luftwaffe pay for all the bombing runs they'd endured that day. The fiery lines rose to a point that seemed to be just over McGee's head; the noise threatened to overwhelm his senses.

It is light enough, he thought, *to read.*

Then he realized that he was hanging, not moving; the men manning the crane apparently had gone to their battle stations. McGee wondered where all those rounds would come down.

The crane men returned before the firing was over, and hoisted McGee safely on deck, where he had a ringside seat to the flak show. Above his head, an aircraft was hit. When it burst into flames, McGee saw, to his horror, that it was a C-47. An American plane. A sailor nearby agreed with him, but said that once all those gunners started shooting, there was no way to stop them.

Around 10:00 P.M. on July 11, Gavin and his troopers, exhausted but in command of Biazza Ridge, also saw the streams of antiaircraft fire from the fleet. Then they heard, above the firing, the steady drone of aircraft engines, which seemed to be heading toward them, inland from the Mediterranean. The troopers around Gavin grabbed their weapons and prepared to fire on what they assumed were German bombers headed their way, but Gavin and his leaders passed the word to hold fire until they had a clear idea of what was going on.

Then the men on Biazza Ridge were treated to a sickening sight that was being repeated all over the Gela area, as the easily recognizable silhouettes of C-47 transport planes came in at about six hundred feet. The Navy was shooting at the U.S. paratroopers. Some of the planes were on fire, and Gavin and his horrified troopers watched as their comrades leaped or fell from burning planes.

Later they would learn that their sister regiment, the 504th PIR, had been called in to reinforce the First Division near Gela. German bombing and strafing runs all that afternoon had given antiaircraft gunners, in the fleet and on land, testy trigger fingers.

(Ridgway, who had repeatedly stressed the need for coordination among the services to avoid just such an incident, watched in horror from the beach. Sixty of the 142 planes were hit, and 23 of those were shot down. Six crashed into the sea before the paratroopers inside could jump clear. The 504th paratroopers suffered 229 casualties, including 81 killed. The Fifty-second Troop Carrier Wing also sustained heavy losses: 60 dead and 30 wounded. Both the paratroopers and the pilots were stunned and demoralized by the incident: all the hard work, all the training, the years separated from home and family—only to be killed by what the Army called "friendly fire." Eisenhower was furious, and the incident nearly ended the use of airborne forces.)[7]

After the 504th incident, the battlefield quieted. Gavin scraped another hole and lay down. He had been on his feet and moving almost continuously for sixty hours. He fell into a deep sleep and awoke with the sun shining full in his face. All around him, other troopers were also nearly comatose with exhaustion from the previous days. Gavin climbed out of his hole and found that his left leg was stiff and sore. Looking down, he noticed that his trousers were torn and his shin, below that, was red and swollen, with a small cut. He figured he had been nipped by a mortar fragment during the previous day's fighting, but had been too busy, and too adrenalized, to notice. He went to the aid station where the medics put on some sulfa powder and mentioned that he would get a Purple Heart. Gavin didn't respond.

Although the tanks had withdrawn during the night of July 11–12, Gavin was concerned that the Germans might have left snipers behind to pick off paratroopers as they walked around on the ridge. On Monday, July 12, he sent a small patrol, made up of some of the men from the command post, to sweep for snipers. Radioman George Huston, still armed only with his folding-stock carbine, was one of the men who went over the ridge. They did not encounter any German snipers, but Huston was taken aback by the sight of a dozen or so paratroopers, still lying where they'd fallen, out in the open. Some of the bodies were mangled, run over by tanks. Others were in the trees, where they'd been killed before they could even get out of their harnesses. There were Germans, too, and Huston thought they all looked alike in death. Once the ridge was cleared, a detail came out to remove the bodies. That was when Huston learned that one of the dead was his friend Bill Blake, who had lived two days past his eighteenth birthday.

*   *   *

With the Forty-fifth Division still pouring ashore and pushing inland, Gavin was ready to turn over his mission of protecting that unit's flank and move his own men toward Gela and his original objective. But his first order of business was to evacuate the wounded and bury the dead.

There were about one hundred men wounded seriously enough for evacuation to a medical center in Vittoria, established by Captains Lewis A. Smith, the regimental surgeon, and Daniel B. McIlvoy, the Third Battalion surgeon who had survived being blown off the running board of his ambulance. The two doctors were assisted by Lieutenant Alexander P. Suer, the dental officer, who ran a shuttle service between Biazza Ridge and Vittoria, using an Italian ambulance. From Vittoria, the most seriously wounded were transported by Forty-fifth Division ambulance to the beach and a hospital ship lying offshore.

During the morning of July 12, Bob Fielder watched Chaplain Wood supervise a detail of German prisoners digging shallow graves near the top of Biazza Ridge, a temporary cemetery for the dead paratroopers. The bodies were swelling up in the hot sun, and Wood didn't want them to turn grotesque, out where their buddies could still see them. The troopers were wrapped in blankets, parachutes, whatever shrouds were available. The chaplain fashioned headstones out of wooden ration crates, and he saw to it that each of the thirty-six men[8]—including a Navy man and a soldier from the Forty-fifth Division—got a proper burial.

Fielder was struck by the sight of the men's boots, sticking out from the ends of the sad bundles. Just a short while before, the owners of those boots had tied them on, expecting that they would get to take them off again, performing the small daily task without knowing it would be the last time. Fielder thought it was the saddest thing he had ever seen.

A little while later, a jeep drove up, and Fielder recognized Krause's driver. Krause was going to reconnoiter the road toward Gela, and he wanted his communications officer along, so the lieutenant climbed in. Krause joined them and they drove over the ridge that had been so hotly contested the day before. They had only gone a short distance when they began to see dead paratroopers, on the ground and in the trees, who had been part of the 504th serials shot down the night before.

Second Battalion closed on Biazza Ridge on July 12. Along the way, Berge Avadanian became physically ill when he came across the bodies of an Italian family that had been killed by artillery or aerial bombs. They had been in the sun for several days, and were covered with flies and maggots, but it was the smell that he couldn't escape.

Jack Norton was busy doing two jobs—exec and operations, in place of Paul Woolslayer. Norton was still trying to account for all the battalion's men, who had been scattered all over the island. Some were wounded and evacuated, some were already back in hospitals in Africa, some were in the British sector, and some with other American units. He had to get the supply system working, which also meant taking care of the wounded, and collecting dog tags from those killed; and he had to keep an eye on Woolslayer, who was effectively under arrest. Norton couldn't spare anyone to guard the captain, but he didn't think Woolslayer would run away.

Norton's frantic movements stopped momentarily at Biazza Ridge, at the sight of those new graves. He knew, rationally, that this was the price to be paid, the risk they all ran. With the death of Lieutenant John Sprinkle, with the rows of freshly turned earth on the side of the hill so far from home, Norton came to know—emotionally—the cost of what they'd been asked to do.

July 12 found Ed Sayre's A Company still attached to the First Division's Second Battalion of Sixteenth Infantry on the western end of the American sector. The paratroopers were roused around 4:00 A.M. and Ed

Sayre got word that the attack on the ridge south of Niscemi would jump off at dawn. Sayre went through the procedures they'd practiced hundreds of times on field problems, passing instructions down through the chain of command, checking his own equipment—map, compass, pistols, and ammo—and watching the men do the same. All around him were the familiar rhythms: the men coming up out of a deep sleep, strapping on their helmets and gear. They pissed on the ground, hooked clips of M1 ammo to the webbing of their musette bags, and checked the pins on hand grenades. A few of them unwrapped ration bars they'd been carrying in their trouser pockets and chewed patiently. They wiped the sleep from their eyes with dirty hands, and were ready for the next mission.

A Company advanced on a wide front, with another rifle company to Sayre's left and the heavy weapons company to his right. First Division artillery, firing from near the Gela beachhead, pounded the ridge in front of them as the GIs advanced. There was some desultory machine gun fire from the ridge, but the artillery made short work of that. Enemy snipers took occasional shots at the Americans, but A Company suffered no casualties.

Fred Morgan, the medic who had dodged U.S. Navy shells and direct fire from an Italian tank to carry a dead man to the beach, had by this time rejoined A Company. Like the other medics, he positioned himself in a central spot, close to the center of the company, and walked behind, his heavy aid bag on his shoulder. The events of D-day had already changed the way the infantrymen looked at their medics. In training, the foot soldiers had always been a little suspicious of the medics, who didn't carry the same loads and didn't seem to work quite as hard. Once the bullets started flying, once men began to fall with burning wounds and shattered limbs, the medics became more important. The change was simple, but profound: when a wounded man or his buddies yelled for a medic, a medic came up. It didn't matter that the unit was under fire, moving forward, or retreating, the medic's first concern was to take care of the wounded, and they often did so at great risk to themselves.[9] And for this, the infantrymen loved them.

When the GIs reached the ridge, they found an abandoned mobile 88 mm gun, the kind that had been harassing them since D-day, probably the same gun that had knocked out the Sherman tanks the previous afternoon. Several dead Germans lay around the gun in grotesque poses, their bodies shattered by the artillery barrage. No one had stayed behind to defend the position, which meant the GIs had the enemy on the run.

The commander of the Sixteenth Infantry ordered his Second Battalion, with Sayre's attached paratroopers, to continue toward Niscemi, which was now within a thousand yards. Once again, after only a short breather, the GIs moved out, scanning the terrain in front of them for German tanks. The advance stopped on a hill overlooking the town of a few dozen streets lined with stucco-covered buildings, perched on the edge of a steep-sided plateau overlooking a broad valley to the north. On its north and west sides, the hills fell sharply for hundreds of feet; to the south, the incline was less steep, but still formidable. Only the eastern approach was relatively flat. With the Americans approaching from the south, any German forces inside the town would have their back to the wall, as the cliffs made withdrawal difficult, if not impossible.

When the advancing troops halted on a hilltop just a thousand yards south of the town, the commander of the Second Battalion, 16th Infantry called his company commanders in for a quick conference. He wanted five volunteers from each of the four companies (three from the 2/16th Infantry, part of the First Division, and Sayre's A Company of the 505th) to go forward and check out Niscemi. The circle of men stayed silent, and no one volunteered his men.

Sayre saw what was happening. The new battalion commander, a captain, had been just a company commander when he came ashore: he didn't want to order one of his former peers to take the lead. But

Sayre knew this was wrong. The paratroopers had been taught: when in charge, take charge. Besides, it made no sense to send an ad hoc collection of men, who didn't know one another and had never trained together, into a potential fight. Better to have the soldiers operate under their own leaders. Sayre figured that if he were in the battalion commander's shoes, he'd have the paratroopers take the lead, since they'd had some rest during the night and were the freshest troops available.

When the captain looked at Sayre, the paratrooper nodded. A Company got the mission.

Sayre led his two platoons into the town, moving carefully through the narrow streets. Here the men had to be concerned about who was on the rooftops, who might be aiming at them through an open window. Their fields of vision were much shorter, making this fight more like a brawl in a telephone booth. The men stayed close to the walls, scanning the rooftops and dodging past open alleys. There was some ineffective machine gun fire from the opposite side of town, but whoever was shooting thought better of standing up to the advancing GIs and left after firing a few shots.

When the paratroopers reached the north side of the town, Sayre sent word back to the Sixteenth Infantry. Niscemi appeared to be theirs for the taking. Soon the soldiers from the Sixteenth passed through Sayre's position and pushed their line to the far edges of the hilltop town. The paratroopers once again found themselves in a rear area, and Sayre let the men relax a bit. They plopped down on sidewalks and in doorways, and some of them fell asleep immediately. Others, more enterprising, started looking around for something to eat. Sayre warned his noncoms not to let the men wander. There could be snipers in the town, or even die-hard fascists who would like nothing better than to find a couple of GIs walking around with their guard down.

Sayre and Calandrino, his interpreter, poked around the town a bit. Many of the inhabitants had fled, but many more were shuttered in their homes. The two paratroopers came upon a barber shop, which was open but empty. Calandrino, the former barber, asked Sayre if he wanted a shave. The captain, who had not bathed or been out of his clothes in four days, was delighted. He dropped his gear and sat back in the chair while Calandrino looked around for a razor and shaving brush. Calandrino lathered Sayre's face, then began shaving him with the straight razor. He was halfway through the job when an excited GI ran into the shop.

"Patton's coming!" the man said.

Sayre jumped out of the chair, grabbed a towel and wiped the lather from his face, then palmed his gear and ran outside, where he found Patton and his retinue. Sayre had never seen the general up close, though the Eighty-second Airborne Division had been treated to Patton's pep talks, which were full of crude scatological and sexual references. The corps commander always set out to give a speech the men would remember, and he succeeded. In person, with his trademark ivory-handled revolvers gleaming in their holsters, he looked bigger than life.

Patton wanted to know what was going on. Sayre told the general that his A Company had entered the town first and, finding it nearly empty, had stopped to let the 16th Infantry pass through.

"Good job. Keep it up," Patton said, shaking Sayre's hand.

Then the general climbed back into his jeep and roared off. Sayre went back inside to finish his shave.

"IT WAS A GOOD FIGHT"

Gavin and the men on Biazza Ridge, the majority of them from Ed Krause's Third Battalion, spent Monday, July 12, resting, refitting, taking care of the wounded, and burying the dead. Gavin had orders not to advance west of the Acate River, on the western side of Biazza Ridge, but he took a patrol down toward Ponte Dirillo, the concrete-slab bridge that spanned the bone-dry riverbed. Along the way, the patrol found disabled German tanks and trucks, as well as abandoned mortars and small arms, but no sign of any Germans, living or dead. Everywhere there was evidence of the deadly killing power of the American artillery, which had turned the battle: craters and scorched earth, trees shredded by shrapnel. In places, the jagged steel shards lay on the ground, shiny bright against the brown soil.

Gavin aimed the patrol out onto the flat ground west of Biazza Ridge, then ventured into the valley. They were in the open, so they stayed spread out, moving cautiously, eyeing the pillboxes that dotted the next ridge, but no one fired at them. Another surprise: the riverbed was filled with just-ripened tomatoes. The paratroopers, who had been eating canned rations for months, waded into the patches and helped themselves, biting into the juicy tomatoes, filling their helmets and pockets. Gavin enjoyed a few as he watched the far ridge, which climbed steeply about eight hundred yards in front of him. In the distance, to the right of the road, he could see a pillbox connected to an open firing position that had probably housed a mortar crew. On the left side of the road, another small pillbox crouched against the hill, its black slit of a firing port peering out over the valley. Everything was quiet, and Gavin was eager to move west; he had heard reports that Arthur Gorham's First Battalion had landed closer to the planned drop zone, where they'd had a tough fight.

He let the men gather ripe tomatoes, making sure that the patrol leader never lost control or let the men wander off carelessly. Gavin had lost a lot of men in hard fighting over the past few days—the tally was just coming in—he didn't want to lose any more picking fruit. The wide, flat valley was clear of enemy as far as he could see, so Gavin told the patrol leader to move back. They climbed the steep west side of Biazza Ridge, sweaty and drained but happy to be alive.

Meanwhile, the regiment pushed patrols west and north from the position on Biazza Ridge, to make sure that the Germans had completely pulled out and weren't gathering in some hidden valley for a counterattack.

Ray Kenworthy, the H Company machine gunner who had been one of the men policed up by Gavin on the way to Biazza Ridge, went out on a patrol led by platoon sergeant John Sabo. Although the Germans seemed to have withdrawn, there was no guarantee that they wouldn't run into a rear guard, or some lost tank unit, or even that they wouldn't be fired on by jumpy Americans who had come across the beach and were now crisscrossing the southern shore of Sicily.

The patrol had not gone far past Biazza Ridge when they came across the body of a second lieutenant wearing the shoulder patch of the Forty-fifth Division: the officer had been shot in the face. Kenworthy went over to the body, which was lying all alone, but he did not want to touch it: there was something obscene about the mutilation of such a young face. The patrol moved on without burying the officer.

Later in the day, the men spotted three small Italian tanks moving on a distant hard-surface road. Sabo stopped and checked the area. It looked to him as if the tanks would cross in front of the patrol, on a road below the hill the GIs were on. Sabo ordered Corporal Warren Lyons, whom the troopers all called "Pop" because he was in his thirties, and two other men down to the side of the road with two bazookas and orders to ambush the tanks.

To Ray Kenworthy, the whole deal looked like a bad idea. There was very little cover or concealment alongside the road, and once the men made it to the bottom of the hill, there was no way they could get back to the top—and to the rest of the patrol—without a long run across open ground. The only good thing was that the Italian tanks looked like toys compared to the huge German Tigers. The paratroopers dutifully headed for the side of the road and hid themselves well enough so that the tank crews would not see them.

The first rounds from the bazooka hit the lead tank, punching a hole in its side and setting the vehicle on fire. But the paratroopers had now exposed their position, and the second tank in line immediately opened fire with its heavy machine gun. Corporal Lyons and the other two H Company troopers were killed beside the road.[1]

The rest of the patrol pulled out in a hurry. Ray Kenworthy was shaken by what he had seen, and he wondered if Sabo had failed his men. The platoon sergeant had made a difficult call, and it had turned out badly. As the fighting dragged on, there would be no end of difficult calls to make. It was a lesson junior leaders were learning all over Sicily.

By the next morning, Tuesday, July 13, the First Division area to the west of the Acate River was secure enough for Gavin to go forward in a borrowed jeep. He drove to the Y road junction, passing a still-burning German tank along the way. The strongpoint holding the Y was impressive: every road, every small gully, every angle was covered by the machine guns of one or more of the dozen or so pillboxes he could see.

He had his driver turn right onto the Niscemi road, then up the short, steep hill onto Piano Leggio, the high ground that had been the original objective of the 505th. Here he saw a sight that sickened him, a number of dead paratroopers lying on the ground and stuck in the trees. Many of them were still in their harnesses, and Gavin figured these were the men of the 504th who'd been shot down by the U.S. Navy. The bodies had become bloated in the hot July sun, their open wounds oozing gas, their only shrouds swarms of black flies. The commander made a mental note to get the men interred as quickly as possible, out of a sense of decency, and also to spare his other troopers the grisly sight.

Gavin drove along the coastal road to Gela; to his left was the Mediterranean, crowded with ships, landing craft, and lighters. The journey was deceptively easy: he and his men had fought for Biazza Ridge to keep open this route between the Forty-fifth Division area, behind him, and the Gela beaches to his front. The fragment of Arthur Gorham's First Battalion that had landed near the original drop zone had struggled, first to keep from being overrun, then to keep the panzers bottled up near Niscemi. Men had died to keep the Germans and Italians from blocking this road; now Gavin and his driver made the trip in a borrowed jeep without escort. The drive was almost anticlimactic.

On the high ground outside of town, Gavin spotted a cluster of staff officers, and in their midst the unmistakable figure of George Patton, his ivory-handled pistols slung in hip holsters. Patton surveyed the busy harbor scene and cast glances inland, where the broad valley north of Gela beckoned him to advance. Gavin walked up, caked in the dust of three days' fighting, still carrying the M1 Garand he'd used on Biazza Ridge. Patton whipped out a big silver flask.

"Gavin," he said, "you look like you need a drink—have one."[2]

On July 16, the rest of the Eighty-second Airborne Division was air-lifted to Sicily in a daylight move with fighter escort. Gavin took a moment to write a short note to reassure his daughter that he was okay.

"Dear Babe," he began. "Well, it was a good fight, but the censor will not let me tell you about it.

"I didn't miss a minute of it—believe I got a purple heart [sic]—never felt better in my life—tell you more about it some other time. Love, Pappy."[3]

On July 19 the division became part of a larger attack to clear out the western end of Sicily. With the Germans in a headlong rush to clear the Strait of Messina and escape to the mainland, the only enemy units left defending Sicily were poorly trained and generally disinterested Italian regiments, which surrendered in droves. The move west became "little more than a road march," in the unit's official report. Unfortunately, some Italian garrisons felt the need to open fire on the advancing Americans, launching a few rounds to preserve their "honor," but these actions caused very few real casualties.

As the 505th closed in on Trapani on the northwest coast of the island, they ran into an Italian garrison at Papparelli that blocked their path. Major Walter Winton, recovered from his jump injury and now taking Arthur Gorham's place as First Battalion Commander, prepared to attack. As Ed Sayre prepared the men of A Company, his interpreter, Vincent Calandrino, kept up his chatting with the various prisoners they had taken along the way. He approached Sayre with one of these prisoners in tow.

"This man says the garrison will surrender if we just give them a chance," Calandrino reported.

Sayre, who had seen his share of reluctant Italian soldiers, thought there was some merit in checking out the story. After checking with Winton, Sayre and Calandrino, accompanied by the prisoner, walked forward of the U.S. position. They knew the Italians up ahead were watching them, and soon they saw weapons trained on them, but no one fired. The two paratroopers followed their prisoner into the town, right under the noses of the defenders and into the headquarters of the garrison commander. Sayre stood by, watching the door and hoping that this had been a good idea, while Calandrino and the prisoner spoke to the Italian officer. The entire conversation, of course, was unintelligible to Sayre, but he had great confidence in the Italian-American barber-turned-GI.

Calandrino explained that the entire Eighty-second Airborne Division was prepared to attack the garrison, and that there was really no question of the outcome.

"If you surrender," Private Calandrino explained to the commander, "you can save your soldiers and a lot of civilians."

The Italian responded, and Calandrino translated for Sayre.

"He says that he'll surrender if we treat them like prisoners of war," Calandrino explained. The garrison commander wanted a guarantee that the Americans would abide by the Geneva Convention. Since Sayre had no intention of doing anything else (and since he would most likely not get out of the town alive unless these negotiations worked), Sayre agreed. The enemy commander took his pistol from his holster and presented it to Sayre, who stuck the weapon in his belt. The Italian called his officers, and Sayre soon heard the sounds of the garrison preparing to march out. Calandrino stayed with the Italians while Sayre hurried back to his own lines, arriving just in time to have Winton call off the attack. Shortly afterward, Private

Vincent Calandrino walked out of the garrison at the head of a column of nearly one thousand Italian prisoners.

By July 22 the capital of Palermo was in American hands, and the 505th had moved within striking distance of Trapani, on the northwestern tip of the island. On the twenty-third, the troopers were loaded into trucks for the final leg of the movement. Sicilians lined the roads, hailing the Americans more as liberators than as invaders, tossing fruit and candies to the soldiers. But the convoy was met with artillery fire at a roadblock short of the seaside town.

Matt Ridgway and Gavin brought up some guns of the 456th Airborne Artillery, which had fought so well with Gavin at Biazza Ridge. The Italian artillery zeroed in on the American guns, scattering one gun crew in a burst of fire. Ridgway, seeing this, calmly walked up to the abandoned gun and called for the crew to return, which they did.[4]

When the artillery duel quieted about midafternoon, Al Ireland, who had moved from regimental staff to be Winton's exec in First Battalion, offered to approach the enemy garrison under a white flag. Ireland tied a white cloth to the windshield of the jeep and drove slowly forward, passing machine guns and dug-in troops who seemed surprised but did not fire on him. Ireland brought the Italian admiral in command of the town, along with his staff, to the bottom of the hill and introduced him to Ridgway.

Meanwhile, Ed Krause's Third Battalion had deployed and advanced so quickly that most of the enemy artillery landed behind them. The infantrymen had their bayonets fixed, and when they were told to hold up as negotiations progressed, some of them speared ripe melons they found in roadside patches. When word came that the Italians had given up, the troopers sat down and enjoyed the fresh fruit.[5]

The occupation of Trapani marked the end of the Sicily campaign for Gavin's 505th and the rest of the division. The men enjoyed the four weeks they were bivouacked two kilometers east of the town. There were fresh eggs, a variety of fruit, plenty of local *vino rosso,* and, as with invading armies throughout history, women who practiced the world's oldest profession.

Characteristically, Gavin began training right away, paying special attention to the problem of paratrooper versus tank. The men used captured German vehicles to test their vulnerability to bazooka fire. Since the bazooka had proved so important, and since employing them required tremendous courage, Gavin figured out a way to recognize the bazooka men. He contracted with the nuns at a local convent to embroider special patches for the teams: crossed bazookas with a lightning bolt, in the regimental colors of red and blue. There was no accommodation for such a patch in uniform regulations, but Gavin issued them anyway, and the men were proud of the recognition.

As the paratroopers rested, reorganized, and received drafts of replacements to fill the spots left by the dead and wounded, a fierce debate raged over the future of the airborne. The British had launched two large airborne drops (the second, on July 13, also fell victim to a friendly-fire incident), and consensus in American headquarters was that both British operations had been failures. Gavin's 505th, by virtue of the way it fought, was considered a qualified success, but many senior officers were not convinced that parachute drops of large units, single or even multiple divisions, were a good idea. Even Matt Ridgway thought that a regiment was probably the largest airborne unit that could be used effectively (though he kept his views within the division staff).[6]

One of Eisenhower's observers, John P. Lucas, stated boldly in his report that "the organization of Airborne Troops into [units as large as] divisions is unsound."

The terrible waste of men in the 504th's shootdown contributed to

Eisenhower's view, later expressed to Chief of Staff George Marshall: "I do not believe in the airborne division. I believe that airborne troops should be organized in self-contained units . . . all about the strength of a regimental combat team."

But both George Patton and Omar Bradley, his subordinate, thought that Gavin's 505th had made a great contribution to victory. Bradley wrote that "the scattering of U.S. airborne troops throughout that target corner panicked the enemy and caused him greatly to exaggerate our strength." Patton said that the paratroopers' fight had speeded up his inland advance by as much as two days. German commanders, in their postwar memoirs, speculated that, were it not for the paratroopers, the Hermann Goering Division might have pushed the invaders back into the sea.[7]

Meanwhile Gavin and Reuben Tucker, commander of the 504th, both ardent proponents of larger drops, pushed for improvements to airborne doctrine, including the use of pathfinders: highly trained troopers who would jump ahead of the main body to set up directional signals and beacons. Captain Jack Norton was detailed to experiment with and train U.S. pathfinders, which were used to great effect in Normandy.

For the most part, the young soldiers, noncoms, and company officers resting amid the hills and olive groves outside of Trapani were oblivious to these debates. When they weren't training, they found diversions. Berge Avadanian and his buddies in the intelligence section used captured Italian hand grenades—which were much smaller than the American version—to "fish" in the tidal pools along the coast. Others found a convent that sold *glace,* a fruit-flavored Italian ice that seemed an incredible delicacy after months of privation.

In the evenings, when they weren't out on night maneuvers, they gathered in small groups in the bivouac area. Someone coming upon them, drawn by their laughter, with their uniforms invisible in the darkness, might have mistaken them for schoolboys, or young men on a camping trip. When they talked of friends they'd lost, the stories tended to be about stateside liberty, or some funny incident in pre-invasion training; their mourning was done in private, when all the lights were out, when the soldiers who felt like crying could, when their buddies could pretend not to hear. It was a pattern they'd stick with over the years, and those who survived the war would repeat only the funny stories over six decades of reunions. The nightmares remained intensely personal.

They had five major campaigns ahead of them, and just a long summer short of two years of war. But all of that was, mercifully, hidden from them, and in the manner of young men, they tended not to dwell on their worries. If they no longer thought they were indestructible, they still believed in luck and in the good men around them.

EPILOGUE

While the fighting went on in Italy through the remainder of 1943 and into 1944, Allied planners focused on the coming battle in northwest Europe: the invasion of France and the nearly straight-line drive for the heart of Germany that was the only route to victory. When the time came for the Allies to make the critical leap to the Continent, the airborne led the way. In those first hours of June 6, 1944, 13,400 American and nearly 7,000 British paratroopers were the first to breach the Atlantic Wall in Normandy. They seized critical road junctions, causeways, and bridges, and, as they'd done in Sicily, spread alarm and misinformation through the enemy command.

It very nearly wasn't so.

After Sicily, Eisenhower and key members of his staff were ready to consign the paratroopers to small-unit actions, or to write off their efforts as a daring experiment that had failed. But supporters—among them Chief of Staff General George Marshall—pointed to the success stories: the aggressive small-unit fights—like Ed Sayre's A Company and Lieutenant Peter Eaton's ad hoc platoon—and to the stubborn defense of Biazza Ridge, where a few hundred men protected the vulnerable flanks of the invasion beaches.

Various airborne commanders—Gavin, Ridgway, and Tucker—

fought hard to keep the concept of a large-scale airborne invasion alive. They had help from senior officers, such as Marshall, Patton, and Bradley. But in the final analysis, the airborne survived because of the actions of a few score men, most of them citizen soldiers, over a few hot days in July. Their success, pieced together from small actions and individual decisions, gave Allied commanders a useful tool—the large-scale airborne invasion—that helped shorten the war. For these men, who wanted nothing more than to do their duty and return home, that was a grand objective.

Jim Gavin commanded the 505th through the fighting in Italy and was made assistant division commander of the Eighty-second Airborne Division in December 1943. When Matt Ridgway took command of the XVIII Airborne Corps in August 1944, he recommended Gavin for command of the Eighty-second. Gavin, at thirty-seven, became the youngest two-star general and division commander since the Civil War.

After the war, Gavin and the Eighty-second became the first U.S. unit to enter Berlin, and in 1945, through Gavin's and Ridgway's efforts, the All-Americans marched at the head of the official victory parade in New York City. In 1953, Matt Ridgway, then the Chief of Staff of the Army, brought Gavin back from Europe to be his deputy. At the time, the French were asking for help with their war in Indochina. Called to testify on Capitol Hill, Ridgway and Gavin told congressional leaders that the United States should not become involved in a ground war in Vietnam. Their view held sway until the Johnson years.

Jim Gavin retired from the Army as a lieutenant general and served as ambassador to France under President John F. Kennedy from 1961 to 1962. During Gavin's time in Paris, the irascible Charles de Gaulle decided he no longer needed a U.S. military presence in his country. He summoned Gavin and told him he wanted all the Americans out of France. Gavin, mindful of the American boys resting in cemeteries from Normandy to the German border, replied, "Yes, Mr. President. Does that include our dead?"[1]

James Gavin died in 1990 and is buried at West Point.

For his actions in Sicily, Captain Ed Sayre was awarded the Distinguished Service Cross, the nation's second-highest decoration for valor (after the Medal of Honor). He continued to serve as the commander of A Company and made the jump into Salerno, Italy, on the night of September 14–15, 1943. The 505th Parachute Infantry led the American assault north into Naples, and in October was preparing to cross the Volturno River. Sayre was conducting a reconnaissance of possible crossing sites for his company when the recon element came under enemy mortar fire. Moving his men toward cover, Sayre tripped a small German S mine. It exploded just behind him, and Sayre "felt as if he'd been kicked by a mule." He reached around and was able to put three fingers into the entry wound. Looking down, he saw that whatever had entered from the back had passed through him and come out just to the left of his groin. He lay down and waited for a medic. Sayre was evacuated to an aid station and a hospital, but his wound soon became infected. After being transferred through several hospitals, which included a ride in an ambulance on the trail of a medical unit that had moved, Sayre became very ill. Fortunately, a doctor who had been a leading urologist in civilian life came across the wounded man during rounds, operated immediately, and saved Sayre's life.

Sent back to the States to recover, Sayre later rejoined the 505th in Germany just before the enemy surrender. He stayed in the Army after the war because, unlike running a dairy farm in Texas, "in the Army you get a day off every once in a while." He retired from the Army after thirty years of service, including a tour of duty as commander of the 505th at Fort Bragg in the early 1960s. He lives on Sayre Ranch in Breckenridge, Texas.

In a 2001 interview, Ed Sayre spoke of a visit to Europe, where he paid his respects in the big American and British cemeteries, and also visited many of the small graveyards where his former enemies were buried.

"I never went into a German cemetery without being profoundly affected," he said. "War is a horrible waste."

Richard Knopf, who carefully folded and saved Gavin's D-day message, still had that slip when I interviewed him in May 2001. On D-day, Knopf killed an Italian officer who had ridden out of his garrison on a bicycle, and got chewed out by his sergeant for firing and giving away their position without knowing how many of the enemy were around. Fifty-eight years later, we sat in a Pennsylvania diner and he told me he has no idea how he was able to kill so coolly. He never fired a weapon after the war.

Jack Norton did not get a chance to command troops in combat during World War II. He went from being the battalion executive officer to the regimental operations officer. For a brief time before the invasion of Normandy, he was in command of Second Battalion, but when Gavin was named division commander in August 1944, he made Norton, then only twenty-six, the division operations officer. His first combat command came in 1966, when he took over the First Cavalry Division in Vietnam. He retired as a lieutenant general in 1975.

In January 1946, Norton married Cheney MacNabb. They raised three children and were married for forty-six years. Some years after Cheney's death, a friend reintroduced Jack Norton to Leslie Cameron Smith, the former Vassar coed whom he'd courted in 1941. Leslie, who had a flourishing psychiatric practice in suburban Washington, D.C., had been a widow nearly ten years when her old flame, Jack

Norton, asked her out. He proposed on their second date, and the two were finally married in 1992, when he was seventy-four and she was seventy-two.

Corinne Bennett Gorham was living at her parents' home in Wichita during the summer of 1943 when she was first notified that her husband was missing in action. Confirmation of his death came shortly afterward.

On August 20, 1943, Lieutenant General Matthew Ridgway wrote Corinne a personal letter about her husband, Arthur Gorham.

"The action which resulted in his death was typical of his inspiring leadership, for it was he [who] personally instilled the spirit of attack at a time that those around him were thinking only of defense, and in person led the attack, which succeeded. His indomitable spirit acknowledged no odds. . . . I send you personally and on behalf of the All-American Division, deep and sincere sympathy."[2]

In August 1948, the remains of Lieutenant Colonel Arthur Gorham were returned to his family for burial in Bellevue, Ohio. Arthur and Corinne's son, Bruce Bennett Gorham Clarke (the last name is his adoptive father's) graduated from West Point in 1965, twenty-seven years after the death of the father he never knew.

Corinne remarried, and she and her new husband, Ed Clarke, lived out their lives in Wichita. Corinne passed away in 2001.

Bob McGee, the demolition man who broke his leg on the Sicily jump and witnessed the shootdown of the 504th while hanging off the side of a ship, recovered in North Africa and rejoined his unit for training in Ireland and England. He jumped into Normandy on June 6, 1944. Separated from his unit, he managed to link up with a couple of other troopers, but they were so deep in enemy territory, they could barely move. He wrote in his memoir that it was "like I am trying to walk

through San Francisco without seeing an American." After a brief firefight around D + 5, McGee and a few other troopers were captured.
He survived both prisoner-of-war and work camps and made it back to
the United States in July 1945.

Alex Burns, the H Company supply sergeant who was wounded just as
he reached the top of Biazza Ridge, recalled one instance in which Ed
Krause, his battalion commander, showed good judgment. After the
fighting had ended in Sicily, Burns and his men were celebrating with
a couple of bottles of wine, and the men became loud. They apparently disturbed the sleep of a lieutenant, who turned Burns's name in
to the chain of command. Burns had to go see Krause. The sergeant
carefully buttoned his uniform and brushed off as much dirt as he
could before marching into the major's temporary office, where Krause
had installed himself behind a large desk.

"It says here you guys were celebrating last night," Krause said,
reading the complaint.

"Yes, sir, and I'm afraid we overdid it."

"Well, I'm not sure what this lieutenant would have me do with
you," Krause said. "So we might as well forget the whole thing."

"Yes, sir," Burns said happily. He snapped off a salute and turned
to go.

"Oh, Sergeant," Krause called.

Burns turned around again, not sure what to expect.

"Why don't you take this," Krause said, indicating a small wooden
barrel of wine. "Give it to your men with my compliments."

Burns saluted and left, the small barrel tucked under his arm.

Fred Morgan, the medic who ran the gauntlet of U.S. Navy shelling
and Italian tank fire to try to save an A Company GI in Sicily, served in

every major campaign with the Eighty-second Airborne Division. In a February 2002 interview, he talked about high points—saving lives— and a low point. When the 505th was loading the aircraft for the Normandy jump, an explosion and fire destroyed one of the planes on the ground. A soldier had dropped a grenade, which exploded. One of only two men who made it out of the fire and still managed to make the jump that night was Sergeant Melvin J. Fryer. On D + 3 or 4 in Normandy, Fryer was hit by shrapnel and Morgan responded to the calls for a medic, treating the wounded soldier under fire until he was also hit by shrapnel. Disabled by his own wounds, Morgan couldn't treat Fryer, who died beside him. "There isn't a day that goes by I don't think about those men," Morgan said in 2002.

Anthony Antoniou, the nineteen-year-old Cypriot immigrant who became a bazooka man in B Company, became a U.S. citizen after the fighting along the Volturno River. On June 6, 1944, D-day in Normandy, Antoniou's plane was hit by heavy antiaircraft fire. Some fifteen of the eighteen men in his stick were wounded, some severely. Antoniou and the other unwounded men thought that they should still jump; the Air Corps could take the wounded back to England. The copilot ordered the men to stay and help the wounded; when they indicated they were going to jump, the copilot pulled his pistol and said he'd shoot them before they could get out the door. Antoniou and his comrades stayed, and at dawn on D-day he was at an airfield in England, unloading the wounded and looking for a flight back over the channel to Normandy. A trooper told Antoniou to check his chute: the shrapnel that had wounded so many of his comrades the previous night had shredded his parachute without wounding him. If he had jumped, the chute would have been useless. The insistent copilot had saved his life.

Antoniou fought in every one of the Eighty-second Airborne Division's campaigns and ended the war with five Purple Hearts for combat wounds. This dubious distinction gave him the second-highest point total in the company, which meant he got to go home earlier than almost anyone else at the end of the war.

Several times throughout the war, Harold "Pop" Eatman, the North Carolinian who had run in front of the German tank on Biazza Ridge, had close calls. Always, it was the other man who got hit. In Normandy, outside Ste.-Mère-Église, Eatman and several other troopers jumped into a partially collapsed German foxhole when they were being shelled. A young trooper from another regiment tried to get in the hole, but there was no room. Seeing how frightened the young man was, Eatman gave up his spot, and the sergeant slid to the end of the hole that was partially collapsed; there wasn't room for him to hide his whole body below the level of the ground. The young soldier who had joined them lay across Eatman's legs. Then Eatman felt something hit his boot. It was a piece of shrapnel that had passed through the arm of the young trooper he'd given shelter to. Eatman applied a tourniquet and got the man to an aid station, and the soldier survived.

In Holland, Eatman and another man were trying to see what was on the other side of a berm, and they both raised their heads at the same time. Eatman heard a shot. "The ones that are aimed at you sound like someone hitting water with the flat of a shovel," he said. He dove down, then noticed the other man was still. He turned the soldier over, and a long stream of blood began pumping from a chest wound. Eatman tried frantically to find a pressure point that would stop the bleeding. The other soldier said, "I'm finished," but Eatman assured him he would be okay. The trooper died with his head in Eatman's arms. When medics came up minutes later, they said that it would not have mattered if they'd been there; the man would have bled out anyway. In an interview nearly sixty years later, Eatman does not know why he was spared when the other men died or were wounded. "I just thank the Lord every day for all my blessings," he said.

By the time of the invasion of Normandy, June 1944, Mark Alexander was the regimental executive officer of the 505th. He was involved in heavy fighting near Ste.-Mère-Église, the regimental objective, almost immediately upon landing. Alexander spent June 6 and 7 fighting for control of the La Fiere causeway and its critical access to the invasion beaches. On July 3, he took command of Second Battalion, 508th Parachute Infantry, when its commander was wounded. Sometime after dark on July 4, he was hit by shell fragments from a German mortar round.

"I felt like someone had stuck a fence post in my back," he wrote later, "and all I could do was lay there and cuss and think of all the times they were shooting at me and missed. They finally lobbed one over the hill in the dark and got me."

Alexander was still recuperating when the Eighty-second Airborne Division was caught up in the Battle of the Bulge in December. When Gavin asked for his help, Alexander left the hospital in France and flew to England, where he begged, borrowed, and stole forty antitank guns, which he rushed through the chaos that had engulfed the rear areas to reach his comrades. He delivered the guns, but the strain soon had him spitting up blood, and he was shipped back to the States.

He agreed to be interviewed in 2001, at the age of ninety, but apologized that he could not attend the East Coast reunions of the regiment, as the shrapnel he'd carried in his lungs for nearly sixty years gave him trouble in the pressurized cabins of airliners.

* * *

Former cavalryman, lumberjack, and champion boxer Otis Sampson made the combat jumps into Salerno and Normandy, where he was wounded in fighting among the hedgerows. He managed to get released from the hospital in time to join E Company for Operation Market Garden, the daytime jump into Holland in September 1944. By this time, Sampson was a platoon sergeant and jumpmaster for his aircraft. The first plane his platoon boarded lost an engine shortly after takeoff, and the pilot turned around, landed, got the troopers aboard another aircraft, and managed to catch up with the formation. In fighting along the Waal River in Nijmegen, Holland, Sampson was severely wounded by German artillery and would have bled to death except for a paratrooper named Dennis O'Loughlin, who found a jeep and evacuated the wounded man under fire. Sampson spent months in hospitals in Belgium, England, and the United States. Writing of his experiences years later, Sampson said that he could see the German border from a hill outside Nijmegen. "Had I known my fighting days were mostly over," wrote this veteran of several campaigns, "I believe I would have taken a patrol across the line, just to say I had been in Germany. I had come so far and there it was just a short distance away."

A Company platoon sergeant Tim Dyas survived nearly two years as a prisoner in Germany. He returned to the States after the war and completed his education, eventually becoming a high school principal in New Jersey. Plagued by feelings of guilt over his decision to surrender his outnumbered and outgunned patrol on D-day, Dyas eventually sought help from the Veterans Administration and was treated for posttraumatic stress disorder.

John Dixon, one of the men captured with Dyas, eventually became chief justice of the Louisiana State Supreme Court. Dixon always cred-

ited his platoon sergeant with saving his life and the lives of the other
men. In addition, Ed Sayre, Dyas's company commander, is certain that
the ambush launched by Dyas on the German armored column helped
save A Company from being overrun on the morning of D-day.

The adventurous Berge Avadanian survived two years of combat and
returned to Massachusetts after the war. He tried his hand at teaching, but felt restless and joined the OSS, the forerunner of the CIA.
His service took him to Cambridge, Paris, Vienna, Liège, and Berlin.

Ed Krause won a Distinguished Service Cross for his actions on Biazza
Ridge, and a second DSC for bravery under fire in Normandy. Krause
attended regimental reunions after the war where, mellowed by his experiences and peace, he was always the perfect gentleman.

Franklin Spencer, the communications sergeant from Second Battalion who was forced to abandon a wounded GI on the morning of
D-day, is still haunted by the vision of that man nearly sixty years later.
In an interview, Spencer said that no movie or book could ever fully
portray the horror of combat: the smell of rotting flesh and splattered
blood are with him more than half a century later.

"There isn't any glamour to it," he said of war. "It's just something
terrible that happens to young people who had nothing to do with
causing it. No winners, all losers. Anybody who glorifies it is crazy."

AUTHOR'S NOTE

This book had its beginnings in two separate conversations I had with Jack Norton, West Point Class of 1941. The first took place in the bar of the Hotel Thayer, on the grounds of the U.S. Military Academy. I had just returned from a road march with the new cadets of USMA 2002, and they had kicked up enough dust to coat my clothing, notebook, and parched throat. I was addressing the latter when a man walked up to my table; he wore a plastic nametag that said "Jack Norton '41."

Even if we hadn't been at West Point, I could have guessed he'd been a soldier. Eighty years old that spring, he still had the erect carriage and firm handshake of a much younger man. I introduced myself, invited him to sit down, and offered to buy him a drink. I was in my journalist mode—asking questions—and he was in a storytelling mood, so we hit it off well, and soon he had transported me back to 1943, when he was a twenty-five-year-old captain with the Eighty-second Airborne Division, preparing to invade Hitler's Fortress Europe.

For the price of a couple of drinks, I got to hear what the battle looked like from the door of a troop transport plane barreling in from the Mediterranean, what it sounded like to a man dangling beneath a parachute over enemy territory, how it appeared from the olive groves

above the seaside town of Marina di Ragusa as the paratroopers joined
the fight. But what most struck me in that conversation was Norton's
comment about his commander, Jim Gavin. When I asked what kind
of leader Gavin was, Norton fixed me with a dead-on stare, leaned
close, and said, "He set us on fire."

The other conversation that piqued my interest took place over
lunch in Washington's Army-Navy Club. The dining room there is lined
with tall windows that let in lots of sunlight and a view of Farragut
Square, where office workers enjoy bag lunches when the weather is
fine. The setting is formal: the china is marked with gold-script "A-N,"
the heavy silver is polished, the linen gleams. There is a dress code, and
all the men wear suits or blazers and ties.

Norton, veteran of two wars, who jumped into Sicily, Italy, France,
and Holland, who fought the Germans' last-gasp offensive in the
Battle of the Bulge, was struggling to change a dead battery in his
hearing aid. The device lay on the white linen, its tiny cover pulled off,
as Norton fished a flat metal can from a jacket pocket. Inside, amid a
variety of colored pills, was a spare battery: small, round, silver. Norton's fingers were too large to handle the battery easily, but he went
about the task patiently, talking as he worked. Without his aid, he
spoke loudly, but the other diners were too polite to look around.

"I tell high school kids today," he said with a grin, "to try to imagine
what kind of men would answer a recruiting call like this: we want
men who are strong and physically courageous, who are willing to
jump out of a low-flying airplane, at night, wearing a hundred pounds
of gear, over farms and rivers and buildings, with people on the ground
shooting at you."

He laughed as he finished, because it never fails to elicit a surprised reaction from his young audiences, and, I suspect, because it's a
way to compliment those soldiers he so obviously still admires, without gushing.

In my initial research, I learned that the men of the 505th Regimental Combat Team were not the first American paratroopers to jump into battle. That distinction belongs to the much smaller 509th Parachute Infantry Battalion, which participated in several small actions in the North Africa campaign. I also learned that the "oh-five," as the men still call it, has a very active association. When I started contacting veterans, with Jack Norton's help, they were eager to participate. They subjected themselves to interviews by telephone, and though I tried to keep these to forty-five minutes or less out of consideration for their age, most wanted to talk longer. They sent me old letters and photographs, half-finished memoirs and self-published books; they were generous, and tolerant of my questions and repeated phone calls. The most common comment I heard was "I was no hero; I was just doing my job."

Some of them broke down as they told me about young men—both their friends and the nameless enemy dead—they'd left behind nearly sixty years ago. Others are still amazed at the things they did and saw, and have no idea why they aren't haunted. Many of these men are unused to talking about their emotions—I think that's a generational idiosyncrasy—but they tried, and some succeeded. They entrusted me with their stories, and that's what I have tried to render. I have relied on the work of historians—foremost among them Carlo D'Este in *Bitter Victory,* and Clay Blair in *Ridgway's Paratroopers*—to develop the framework. I tried to capture, from the point of view of the men who were there, what it looked like and felt like to be caught up in a great and terrible war.

Wallingford, Pennsylvania
January 2003

505TH REGIMENTAL COMBAT TEAM
Killed in Action, Died of Wounds, Missing in Action
Sicily

	Rank	*Unit*	*Home State*
Adams, Thomas D.	PFC	REGT HQ	CT
Angelo, Dominic T.	PVT	G	PA
Asklar, Joseph S.	PFC	H	PA
Baldassare, John J.	PVT		NJ
Baldwin, Lewis N.		456	
Barbour, Clarence W.	SGT	H	NY
Barnett, George E.	2LT	3HQ	CT
Barnett, Walter M.	PVT	G	IA
Behary, George	PFC	3HQ	PA
Berry, Gordon R.	PFC	F	WA
Blake, Thomas J.	PVT		AL
Blount, Ben F.		456 PFAB	
Boncyk, Aloysius	PFC	G	OH
Boothe, Joe	PVT	H	TX
Bradford, James T.	PVT	C	GA
Cabali, Theodore		456 PFAB	
Cronin, Arius R.	PVT		MI
Cymerys, Charles F.	CPL	C	CT
Daniels, James R.	CPL	3HQ	TX
Derby, Charles G.		456 PFAB	
Doster, Claude A.		456 PFAB	
Downey, Harry C.	PFC	E	MI
Drake, Clyde S.*	PVT		KS

	Rank	Unit	Home State
Fiske, Raymond E.	PVT	3HQ	MA
Fulton, Donald M.	PVT		MA
Glascock, Alfred W.	PVT	G	VA
Gordon, Oscar L.	2LT	A	NH
Gorham, Arthur F.	LTC	1HQ	OH
Gousman, George H.	PFC	C	NJ
Hale, Howard W.	PFC	I	MO
Harbin, Eldridge V.	PVT	C	KY
Harris, James R.	PVT	E	GA
Hendrix, Arthur R.	PFC	F	KY
Houser, Arthur H.	PFC	G	PA
Humpich, William J.	T/5	SVC	IL
Johnson, Laross M.	PVT		PA
Kerrigan, William J.	PVT	REGT HQ	MA
Kissall, Walter F.	PVT		
Klee, Kurt B.	1LT	2MED	IN
Knight, Vernon F.	PVT	3HQ	OR
Lakomy, Edward G.		456 PFAB	
Lambrecht, Peter M.	PVT		MN
Larsen, Kolbjorn	PFC		PA
Laye, Leland	PFC	H	NY
Long, James D.	PVT	G	MO
Ludlam, Gerald L.	SGT	G	NY
Lyons, Warren	CPL	H	
McBride, Charles S.	PVT	1HQ	OH
McGuigan, John J.	PVT	REGT HQ	NY
McKeown, David J. Jr.	PVT	REGT HQ	PA

	Rank	Unit	Home State
McLaughlin, Charles R.*	PVT	MED DET	NY
Maloney, Francis G.	PVT	G	MA
Martin, Leroy V.	CPL	3HQ	PA
Mazella, Nick	PVT		PA
Meile, Carroll W.	PVT	G	MD
Moynihan, Cornelius J. Jr.	CPL	G	NY
Myrhow, Harold L.	PFC	G	WA
O'Brien, Patrick A.	PFC	A	CA
Owens, Howard S.	CPL	C	MI
Palmer, Phillip V.	PVT		OK
Plaka, Thomas	PFC		
Reed, Roy W.	PVT	H	PA
Riffle, Warren A.		B / 307 EN	
Riley, Richard S.	SSG	1HQ	ME
Rosenbush, Richard		456 PFAB	
Ross, Lee M.		456	
Scambelluri, Michael A.	PFC	C	NY
Shalonis, Anthony		456 PFAB	
Sinkovich, Frank	PFC	H	OH
Smith, Edwin R.	PFC	3HQ	NY
Smith, Walter C.*	CPL		AR
Sprinkle, John D.	1LT	D	AZ
Thompson, Floyd D.	PVT		MI
Throckmorton, Theodore H.	PVT	1HQ	NJ
Townsend, Donnell T.	PVT	G	NJ
Trail, Melvin C.	PVT		WV
Trumbull, Thomas F.	SGT	H	NY

	Rank	Unit	Home State
Veazey, Vermie T.	PVT	SVC	AL
Vidumsky, Stephen W.	PVT	3HQ	PA
Walkup, Willard W.	2LT	3HQ	WV
Whealton, Noel M.	PFC	G	NC
Williams, Trafford H.		456 PFAB	
Wilson, Brady H.	PVT	3HQ	AL
Zakrzewski, Charles		G	
Zelinsky, Anthony J.	PVT	F	NJ

*Missing in action

ENDNOTES

This book is based, for the most part, on personal interviews conducted with veterans of the 505th Regimental Combat Team between May 2001 and December 2002. Individual stories that appear in the text are drawn from these interviews. The quotations are as the veterans remember. Whenever possible, I have corroborated basic facts across several interviews, with existing records or with the work of historians. When an anecdote didn't seem to fit, I made a judgment call as to what to include and what to leave out. My goal throughout has been to tell the stories told me by these men.

PROLOGUE
1. Blair, *Ridgway's Paratroopers*, 85.
2. Gavin, *On to Berlin*, 19.

CHAPTER ONE: IN THEORY
1. Jack Norton interview.
2. D'Este, *Patton: A Genius for War*, 393.
3. Blair, 50.
4. Norton interview.
5. George S. Brown, USMA '41, later became chief of staff of the United States Air Force, 1973; and chairman of the Joint Chiefs of Staff 1974–78.
6. Blair, 29.
7. Quoted in ibid., 30.
8. Quoted in ibid., 51.
9. Kennedy, *Freedom from Fear*, 474–75.
10. Devlin, *Paratrooper!*, 92–94.

11. One of the forms that a soldier had to sign was titled "Voluntary Duty in Parachute Units." It said, "I————hereby volunteer for duty with parachute troops. I understand fully that in performance of such duty, I will be required to jump from an airplane and land via parachute." Starlyn Jorgensen, 15.

12. James Jones, who was an enlisted man before the war, skewered these traditions—and the entire officer corps—in his immensely popular 1951 novel *From Here to Eternity*.

13. Blair, 31, 51.

CHAPTER TWO: FROM EVERY CORNER OF THE LAND

1. If a family lost a son, they received a flag with a gold star. These "Gold Star Mothers" rode in Veterans Day parades and Fourth of July celebrations around the country for decades to come. All the Avadanian boys made it home from the war.

2. Kennedy, *Freedom from Fear,* 558–59.

3. Ibid., 575.

4. Quoted in ibid., 573.

5. Quoted in ibid.

CHAPTER THREE: THE OH-FIVE

1. Berge Avadanian, who would become the intelligence NCO for the Second Battalion of the 505th, had to hitch a ride from Fort Leonard Wood, Missouri, in order to report to airborne school.

2. In a 2001 interview, I asked Ed Sayre if he had volunteered for duty with Gavin. Sayre recalled, "I didn't pick him. He picked me."

3. Private Eddie Slovik, of Detroit, Michigan, was the only American soldier executed for desertion in World War II. Slovik, who had a criminal record before the war, was drafted in early 1944 and eventually assigned as an infantryman in the Twenty-eighth Infantry Division. He first deserted the convoy taking him to his unit in September 1944, resurfacing in October with a Canadian unit. Sent back to his division, Slovik again deserted, but eventually surrendered to an officer of the Twenty-eighth Division. He turned over a written confession, which said that he would desert again if he had "to go out their [*sic*]." Although warned that the confession would be damaging, Slovik insisted on a court-martial, perhaps thinking that he would merely be imprisoned for the duration of the war. On November 11, 1944, the court found him guilty and sentenced him to death. At this point in the war, desertion had become a problem in the Army, and commanders, including Eisenhower, knew that they had to send a strong signal to the troops. In December 1944, the Allies were rocked by the surprise German attack that became known as the Battle of the Bulge. The unsteady climate, coupled with the fact that the clemency board had access to Slovik's civilian criminal record, led to his appeals being turned down. He was executed by firing squad on January 31, 1945. thehistorynet.com/worldwariiarticles Uzal W. Ent.

4. In the early 1960s, Ed Sayre commanded a brigade in the Eighty-second Airborne Division, then stationed at Fort Bragg. The military police handed out traffic tickets to soldiers whose cars didn't display the right stickers. Sayre had his duty NCOs check the soldiers' cars at night, and remove the tires of cars that didn't have the proper documents. The men could retrieve their tires from the colonel's office. Usually it took only one visit to the colonel for the men to get the message, and it all happened with no black mark on a soldier's record.

5. Gavin, *On to Berlin,* 5.

6. Ibid., 4.

CHAPTER FOUR: THE ALL-AMERICANS

1. Quoted in Kennedy, *Freedom from Fear,* 586–87. General Albert Wedemeyer complained, "One might say we came, we listened, we were conquered."

2. "[T]he most effective way to seize [Sicily] would be to invade the toe of the boot . . . isolate the island and block Axis attempts to reinforce it. However, inasmuch as Roosevelt and Churchill had made no decisions about invading the Italian mainland . . . the planners were compelled to treat Sicily as though it were an isolated island sitting in the middle of nowhere." Blair, *Ridgway's Paratroopers,* 63–64.

3. Ed Sayre interview.

4. Quoted in Gavin, *On to Berlin,* 7

5. Blair, *Ridgway's Paratroopers,* 69–70.

6. Quoted in ibid., 70

7. This story is recounted in an unpublished memoir by William L. Blank of G Company. H. M. "Bill" Bishop, without prompting, told me the same story in an interview, on February 24, 2002. Bishop provided the names of the three troopers involved. *Search for Members of the 505th Parachute Infantry Regimental Combat Team of World War II 1942–1945* (Section M, p. 11) lists the names. This search, published in book form, was initiated by members of the regimental association circa 1986. James J. Meyers of D Company began the work; Robert W. "Bob" Gillette (HHC) took over in 1992. Wheatley Christensen of G Company identified the two men in a February 27, 2002, interview (Dalton L. Morris ASN 20518074; Jack A. Morris ASN 18107802). William Blank identified the shooter, Charles T. Hall (ASN 14015218), who was his bunkmate in the barracks. Blank heard the shots and saw Hall packing his gear immediately afterward. Jack Norton, who joined the unit after this incident, recalls that Myers had a tough, headstrong first sergeant named Tony Costello. Norton indicated that it would have been very easy for a relatively junior officer like Myers to be influenced by a man like Costello, and it is reasonable to assume that the first sergeant briefed the sentry. In the final analysis, as every military officer knows, the commander is responsible for everything the unit does or fails to do.

8. Mark Alexander interview.

9. Bob Fielder, "In the Beginning," unpublished memoir.

10. Dean McCandless interview; Bruce B. G. Clarke interview.

CHAPTER FIVE: TWO STEPS BACK

1. Bob McGee, "Jumping for Breakfast," unpublished memoir.

2. Allen L. Langdon, *Ready: A World War II History of the 505th Parachute Infantry Regiment* 9.

3. William H. Tucker, *Parachute Soldier,* 12.

4. Stephen E. Ambrose, *Citizen Soldiers,* 277.

5. Interview with James Rodier, February 18, 2002. Not all the units of the 505th or the Eighty-second Airborne Division operated this way. Private Fred Caravelli joined the Eighty-second in Ireland in late 1943, arriving on a train with other replacements in the middle of a rainy night. As the men assembled on the cold platform to march to the bivouac, a tall man walked up and down the line, talking to each of the troopers. Matt Ridgway, the division commander, stepped up to Caravelli and thanked him for joining the Eighty-second. "What do you do?" Ridgway asked. "I'm a rifleman, sir," the astonished soldier responded. "Good. We need riflemen." When the men in his new squad learned that Caravelli had missed out on a furlough promised after jump school, they collected nearly one hundred dollars and sent him on a weekend pass to Belfast.

6. In a December 2001 interview, I asked Thompson if perhaps his wound, which made it difficult for him to pull on the risers of his parachute, should have disqualified him from jumping. He was adamant and clear in his answer. "There was no way I was going to miss that jump," he told me. "A war is not a time for hiding out under the bushes. You're either going to soldier or you're not. If you're a soldier, you do what's expected of you."

CHAPTER SIX: THE HOUR UPON THEM

1. Berge Avadanian interview.

2. Sampson interview.

3. The Gorham letter was provided by Colonel Bruce B. Gorham Clarke (Retired). Colonel Clarke was only a few months old when his father, Arthur Gorham, was killed in Sicily.

4. Gavin, *On to Berlin,* 8.

5. Blair, *Ridgway's Paratroopers,* 85.

6. Most veterans refer to the road junction as "the Y," as if it took its name from the shape of the intersection. The "505th PIR Living History" website (*http://home.europa.com/~bessel/505thPIR/505th.html*) lists the intersection near Gela as "OBJECTIVE Y" and the road south of Niscemi as "OBJECTIVE X." This is more consistent with military planning convention. For the purposes of this book, I have deferred to the practice common among the veterans.

7. Gavin, 19.

8. Blair, 78.

9. Quoted in ibid., 79.

10. Mark Alexander interview.

11. Oldfield interview.

12. Gavin's letters provided by his daughter, Barbara Gavin Fauntleroy. Gavin's typos are included here, unchanged.

13. Letter from Corporal A. F. Cannady, undated. Supplied by Dr. James Ricci.

14. Blair, 80.

15. Personal copy of Gavin's D-day message provided by Richard Knopf, 505th Regimental Headquarters. In *On to Berlin,* Gavin did not reproduce the sentences about the countersign, the bayonet, or the American parachutist striking fear into the enemy.

CHAPTER SEVEN: DOVE PALERMO? DOVE SIRACUSA?

1. Blair uses 3,405 in *Ridgway's Paratroopers.* Carlo D'Este uses 3,045 in *Bitter Victory.*

2. Gavin, *On to Berlin,* 25–26.

3. Blair, 87–88.

4. Bob Gillette interview.

5. Ronal Lewin, in *Ultra Goes to War,* wrote that "Patton's staff had strict instructions not to inform Gavin's command [of the presence of German armor] because of the likelihood of their being captured. D-Day for Husky vividly illustrates, in fact, Ultra's inescapable limitation. It was impossible to risk disclosing its intelligence to those in actual contact with the enemy, or liable to capture for other reasons, even though the knowledge might improve their chance of success or survival" (280–1). The staff of the First Division, which went ashore at Gela, was informed of the presence of the German armor.

6. Gavin, 34.

7. D'Este, *Patton: A Genius for War,* 252.

8. Blair, 92; Gavin, 36.

CHAPTER EIGHT: SMALL BATTLES

1. Gavin, *On to Berlin,* 27.

CHAPTER TEN: THE ROAD TO GELA

1. Interview, April 2002. Leslie was a cooperative interview, but was clearly horrified by the memory of killing this Italian soldier. In his telling of the story, he jumped from the point at which he "went after the other fellow" to the point where he was "pushing him off me," then, clarifying, "pushing the body off of me." I asked Leslie's permission to describe what he did as killing the enemy soldier with his knife, and he agreed, though he said, "I don't like to talk about that."

In his book *On Killing,* the psychologist and U.S. Army officer Lieutenant Colonel Dave Grossman talks about the horror of such close-in fighting, particularly if it is face-to-face, where the killer can feel "the bucking and shuddering of the victim's body and the warm sticky blood gushing out," and hear "the final breath hissing out." Although LeRoy Leslie had been trained as a soldier, he had no experience of killing another human being before Sicily. Within minutes of his landing in hostile territory, he was forced to kill a man by the most brutal means. This is the stuff of nightmares that haunts veterans for sixty years.

2. Mark Alexander, Jack Norton, and Tommy Gore gave similar accounts of Paul Woolslayer's meltdown. Norton was the most philosophical, recalling Gavin's comment that every man has a breaking point.

3. Interview with Luis DeLosSantos, January 29, 2002. I was not able to find any soldiers from D Company or Second Battalion headquarters who could positively confirm Santos's story. However, the other men do remember him in the company, and several men remember large numbers of prisoners moving through the battalion perimeter on that very busy, very confusing morning. Santos's description of his action is plausible, and there is nothing to contradict him. Luis DeLosSantos made every combat jump with the 505th, and fought in the Battle of the Bulge. He was given an honorable discharge and became a U.S. citizen after the war.

CHAPTER ELEVEN: LANDINGS

1. Blair, *Ridgway's Paratroopers,* 91.

2. William B. Breuer, in *Drop Zone Sicily,* says that Scambelluri identified one of his captors in a group of prisoners. Breuer further implies that enraged GIs took the prisoner and shot him. Breuer cites no evidence and does not footnote his sources. In a February 2002 interview, Gerald Johnson, Scambelluri's platoon leader, said that he and his men thought Scambelluri was going to survive, and that he heard nothing about reprisals and saw none.

3. Mark Alexander interview and letter.

4. LeRoy Leslie was unclear as to whether or not Hendrix had removed the pin or it had worked itself loose in his pocket. Walter Niemeyer, another F Company trooper who was nearby, claimed that Berry had deliberately removed the pin and trusted the tape to do the job.

5. Interview with Mark Alexander, September 25, 2001. In *Drop Zone Sicily,* Breuer identifies this officer as Frank Miller. Alexander researched this point with other survivors to verify this correction to the historical record.

6. In January 1945, a wounded Mark Alexander was sent back to the States, with pieces of shrapnel lodged in his lungs. He was fit for light duty, and was assigned as director of training for the airborne school at Fort Benning. He was surprised to see Paul Woolslayer there, wearing a major's oak leaves. Alexander immediately went to the school commander to investigate, and learned that his

"unsatisfactory" efficiency report had somehow become an "outstanding" report. Based on Alexander's testimony, Woolslayer was relieved again.

7. Starlyn Jorgensen, Unpublished memoir of the 456th Parachute Field Artillery, 75.

CHAPTER TWELVE: MISSION FIRST

1. Dyas and Sayre agreed, in separate interviews, that the timing and location of their respective actions make it likely that this was true.

2. Several of Dyas's men attempted to escape as they were being moved by rail through Italy. They were recaptured.

3. Quoted in O'Donnell, *Beyond Valor*, 50.

CHAPTER THIRTEEN: SEVENTY-TWO HOURS

1. Gavin, *On to Berlin*, 27.

CHAPTER FOURTEEN: A NEW MISSION

1. Langdon, *"Ready,"* 24.

2. Gavin, *On to Berlin*, 28.

3. Gavin's antipathy is evident in his account. What's more, he does not mention whether Krause said he had been ordered to halt by Batcheller. It is hard to imagine that Krause would let Gavin imply that he had been doing nothing, without mentioning that he was following Batcheller's order. Gavin's account makes it sound as if all the Third Battalion had accomplished was to find a place to sleep, but Krause had been headed toward Gela when he ran into Batcheller. The regimental historian, Al Langdon, points out that the troopers needed a rest: they'd been on their feet for thirty-five to forty hours, and in that time had made a combat jump and fought numerous small battles with the enemy.

4. Gavin's account does not name the troopers. Star Jorgensen, in her history of the 456th Field Artillery, says the driver was Corporal Lewis Baldwin of C Battery.

5. Langdon, 27.

6. Ellis and Sampson both mention this man, though Sampson's story is secondhand.

7. According to Gavin in *On to Berlin*, Krause went back to the Forty-fifth Division headquarters to tell them what was going on at Biazza Ridge. Regimental historian Allen Langdon's account has Krause going back to retrieve men and equipment from the east of Biazza Ridge. Langdon's version is believable, but Gavin's chief complaint, that Krause should have moved into battle with the main body of his troops, is valid either way.

8. The German eastern task force started out with a company of Tiger tanks (at least seventeen as of July 10) and seven hundred infantrymen of the First Panzer Grenadier Regiment, as well as an armored artillery battalion. D'Este, 293.

9. Bishop letter January 2002. Foley was killed in January 1945. The reference book *Search* has him listed as D (died), not KIA (killed in action).

CHAPTER FIFTEEN: DESPERATE HOURS

1. Blake is listed as Thomas Blake in *Search*. The 505th monument near Ponte Dirillo in Sicily lists a "Bill Blake," and Huston, a close friend, called him "Bill."

2. D'Este writes that this unit, neither parachute nor panzer, was made up of former Luftwaffe personnel and was reconstituted after most of the division was lost in North Africa. "The division was deficient in all aspects of training and had no combat experience [as a unit]. Training effectively began only when the division began arriving in Sicily in mid-June" (207).

3. Gavin, *On to Berlin*, 31.

4. Quoted in letter from Vandervoort to Carlo D'Este, cited in *Bitter Victory*, 294. There is an apocryphal story about Gavin and Ridgway conducting a reconnaissance under fire in Normandy. When an aide suggested Ridgway withdraw, he snorted, "It would do the men good to see a dead general now and again."

5. Gavin, 33.

6. John Foster interview.

7. Blair, *Ridgway's Paratroopers*, 101–2.

8. Gavin's book says fifty or so. Langdon's *"Ready"* indicates that Wood's diary says he buried thirty-six men.

9. In 1994, around the fiftieth anniversary of the invasion of Normandy, Fred Morgan received a letter from Charles J. Lieberth of the 505th RCT. Lieberth included a newspaper clipping of an article in which he told of being wounded on D-day. Lieberth told the reporter that Morgan found him (Lieberth) alongside a road and was treating the wounded trooper when they heard tanks approaching. As Lieberth told the story, "I said, 'Morgan, get the hell out of here. I'm done for.' I was bleeding like hell. I said, 'There's no use letting the bastards get both of us.'" Morgan stayed by Lieberth's side, treating the wounded man. The tank pulled to within a few yards, and the commander looked out at the medic and the wounded GI. Then the tank moved on. Lieberth survived, amazed to find a scrap of humanity on the battlefield. Quoted in *Pittsburgh Post Gazette*, June 5, 1994.

CHAPTER SIXTEEN: "IT WAS A GOOD FIGHT"

1. In a February 2002 interview, Kenworthy recalled Lyons and a soldier he called "Lau" being killed in this ambush. There is no "Lau" listed in *Search*. There is a Leland Laye listed in both places, unit unknown. The other H Company soldiers killed in Sicily, according to Les Cruise, H Company's historian, were Joseph Asklar, Clarence Barbour, Roy Reed, Frank Sinkovich, Thomas Trumbull, and Warren Lyons. *Search* lists Asklar as KIA in Normandy. Langdon lists Trumbull as KIA in Holland.

2. Gavin, *On to Berlin*, 43.

3. Gavin letter provided by Barbara Gavin Fauntleroy.
4. Blair, *Ridgway's Paratroopers,* 113.
5. Langdon, *"Ready,"* 28.
6. Blair, 106.
7. Ibid., 107.

EPILOGUE

1. Related by General P. X. Kelley (Retired), former Commandant, USMC.
2. Letter provided by Bruce B. G. Clarke.

WORKS CITED

Ambrose, Stephen E. *Citizen Soldiers: The U.S. Army from the Normandy Beaches to the Bulge to the Surrender of Germany, June 7, 1944–May 7, 1945.* New York: Simon and Schuster, 1997.

———. *The Supreme Commander: The War Years of Dwight D. Eisenhower.* Garden City, N.Y.: Doubleday, 1970.

———. *D-Day June 6, 1944: The Climatic Battle of World War II.* New York: Touchstone, 1994.

———. *The Victors: Eisenhower and His Boys: The Men of World War II.* New York: Simon and Schuster, 1998.

———. *Band of Brothers: E Company, 506th Regiment, 101st Airborne from Normandy to Hitler's Eagle's Nest.* New York: Touchstone, 2001.

Barger, Allan C. *War and People: A Veteran's Own Story.* Port Orchard, Wash.: 2001.

Blair, Clay. *Ridgway's Paratroopers: The American Airborne in World War II.* Garden City, N.Y.: Dial Press, 1985.

Breuer, William B. *Drop Zone Sicily: Allied Airborne Strike July 1943.* Novato, Calif.: Presidio Press, 1983.

Burriss, T. Moffatt. *Strike and Hold: A Memoir of the 82d Airborne in World War II.* Dulles, Va.: Brassey's Inc., 2000.

Davidson, Edward, and Dale Manning. *Chronology of World War Two.* London: Cassell & Co., 1999.

Davis, Larry. *C-47 Skytrain in Action.* Carrolton, Tex.: Squadron/Signal Publications Inc., 1995.

D'Este, Carlo. *Patton: A Genius for War.* New York: HarperCollins, 1995.

———. *Bitter Victory: The Battle for Sicily 1943.* New York: William Collins Sons & Co. Ltd., 1988.

Devlin, Gerard M. *Paratrooper!* New York: St. Martins, 1979.

Fussell, Paul. *Wartime: Understanding and Behavior in the Second World War.* New York: Oxford University Press, 1989.

Gavin, James M. *On to Berlin.* New York: Viking Press, 1978.

Grigg, John. *1943 The Victory That Never Was.* New York: Hill and Wang, 1980.

Grossman, Dave. *On Killing.* Boston: Little, Brown and Company, 1995.

Jacobus, George R., ed. *Echoes of the Warriors: Personal Experiences of the Enlisted Men and Officers of E Company of the 505th Parachute Infantry Regiment, 82nd Airborne in World War II.* St. Simon's Island, Ga. Self-published memoir, 1996.

Jorgensen, Starlyn. Unpublished memoir of the 456 Parachute Field Artillery.

Kennedy, David M. *Freedom from Fear: The American People in Depression and War, 1929–1945.* New York: Oxford University Press, 1999.

Kimpton, Sam. Website "Casualty List for Sicily." Home.europa.com/~bessel/505thPIR/505th.htn

Langdon, Allen L. *"Ready": A World War II History of the 505th Parachute Infantry Regiment.* Indianapolis: Eighty-second Airborne Division Educational Fund Inc., 1986.

Lewin, Ronald. *Ultra Goes to War.* London: Hutchinson & Co., 1978.

Mauldin, Bill. *Up Front.* Cleveland: World Publishing Company, 1945.

McCullough, David G., ed. *The American Heritage Picture History of World War II.* New York: American Heritage Publishing Company Inc., 1966.

McManus, John C. *The Deadly Brotherhood: The American Combat Soldier in World War II.* Novato, Calif.: Presidio Press, 2001.

Murphy, Robert M. *No Better Place to Die.* Croton Falls, N.Y.: Critical Hit, 1999.

O'Donnell, Patrick K. *Beyond Valor: World War II's Ranger and Airborne Veterans Reveal the Heart of Combat.* New York: Free Press, 2001.

Rottman, Gordon, and Ron Volstad. *U.S. Army Airborne 1940–90: Elite Series.* Oxford: Osprey, 1990.

Ryan, Cornelius. *A Bridge Too Far.* New York: Simon and Schuster, 1974.

Sayre, Edwin N. *The Operations of Company "A" 505th Parachute Infantry (82nd Airborne Division) Airborne Landings in Sicily 9–24 July 1943 (Sicily Campaign): Personal Experience of a Company Commander.* Advanced Infantry Officers Class No. I, November 10, 1947.

Schock, Al. *Brothers in War.* Hills, Minn.: Crescent Publishing Inc., 1988.

Smith, Albert H. Jr. *The Sicily Campaign: Recollections of an Infantry Company Commander.* Blue Bell, Pa.: Society of the First Infantry Division, 2001.

Smith, Carl, and Mike Chappell. *U.S. Paratrooper 1941–45: Warrior.* Oxford: Osprey, 2000.

Thomas, Nigel, and Stephen Andrew. *The German Army 1938–45 Western Front 1943–45: Men-At-Arms.* Vol. 5. Oxford: Osprey Publishing, 2000.

Tucker, William H. *Parachute Soldiers.* Harwichport, Mass.: International Airborne Books, 1995.

Whitlock, Flint. *The Rock of Anzio: From Sicily to Dachau: A History of the U.S. 45th Infantry Division.* Boulder, Colo.: Westview Press, 1998.

Winchester, Jim. *The World War II Tank Guide.* Edison, N.J.: Chartwell Books, 2000.

Windrow, Martin, and Richard Hook. *The Panzer Divisions: Men-At-Arms.* Oxford: Osprey, 1982.

Winterbotham, F. W. *The Ultra Secret.* New York: Harper and Row, Publishers, 1974.

Yenne, Bill. *"Black '41" The West Point Class of 1941 and the American Triumph in WWII.* New York: John Wiley & Sons, 1941.

ACKNOWLEDGMENTS

My thanks to: Michael Gerhardt and Renate Harshaw, for finding the cover photo, and for their limitless support, encouragement, and friendship over the years. Jon Graber, Historian, U.S. Army Airborne school, who cheerfully answered my questions about the early days of the airborne; to Barbara Gavin Fauntleroy, who shared memories of her father—as well as letters and photos—and her impressions of the 505th veterans, with whom she has kept a close relationship. To Jan Bos of Nijmegen, Holland, whose dedication to these American veterans is inspiring. To John Love, Bryan Sykora, and the staff at New Vision Communications, who helped me bring this story to other audiences. To John Calabro, who offered no end of encouragement and was always ready to help. To John Anderson, Map Librarian and Director, Louisiana State University, and Lieutenant Colonel Bob Morris, USMA Department of Geography. Both of these men went out of their way to equip me with the maps that helped me make sense of a chaotic battlefield. To Colonel Bruce B. G. Clarke (retired), who shared his parents' letters and let me glimpse the affection he feels for the father he never met. To the folks at MNovak Design, New York, who helped me with "the look." To Tom Sole, American Battle

Monuments Commission, who helped me pay homage to those who made the ultimate sacrifice. To Dr. James Ricci, who helped me connect with his father. To Star Jorgensen, whose work honors her father and the men of the 456th Parachute Field Artillery Battalion. To Colin Ruggero and Robin Michener, who helped me nail down the details.

My intrepid editor, Henry Ferris; and to my agent, Matt Bialer, of Trident Media. Both these men offered no end of encouragement.

To Dealyn Ruggero, traveling partner, chief photographer, and map reader on our visit to the battlefields on Sicily.

To Marcia, coach, counselor, editor, and soulmate.

Finally, my greatest thanks to the veterans of the 505th Regimental Combat Team Association, who responded so generously to my many requests.

Jack Norton, Mark Alexander, Otis Sampson, Bob Piper, Robert Franco, Ed Sayre, Dean McCandless, John P. Cages, Ted Adamski, Allan C. Barger, Fred Caravelli, Ott Carpenter, George E. Clark, Tim Dyas, Harold Eatman, Robert A. Fielder, Willard Follmer, John J. Gallo, Robert W. Gillette, Richard S. Knopf, Harry M. Masters, Donald McKeage, William J. Meddaugh, Ed Misenick, Robert M. Murphy, Barney Oldfield, Luis DeLosSantos, Joseph Tallet, Frank W. Thompson, Bill Tucker, Charlie Turner, Walter Winton, Howard Comstock, Robert E. Coover, Ron Dent, William T. Dunfee, Samuel F. Ellis, Gene D. Fallon, John P. Foster, Howard C. Goodson, George R. Jacobus, Nick Kastrantas, Ray M. Kenworthy, Roy O. King, Stanley P. Kulikowski, John K. Lattimer, LeRoy F. Leslie, Joseph W. Lyons, Tom McClean, James P. McKenstry, Frank Miale, Fred B. Morgan, Jr., Walter H. Niemeyer, Cecil E. Prine, Jim Ricci, James Rodier, James C. Ross, Irwin W. Seelye, Henry Sha, Harold Thain, David E. Thomas, Arthur W. Tower, Theodore B. Visneski, Cloid Wigle, Vincent E. Wolf, Chuck Copping, Leslie P. Cruise Jr., William S. Farmer, Dean Garber, Douglas Howlett, Howard C. Hoye, George F. Huston,

Jerome Huth, Joseph T. Jockel, Robert R. McGee, George Nelson, Ralph W. Yeager, H. R. Zeitner, Berge Avadanian, Douglas M. Bailey, John R. Biechler, Harry Buffone, Eldon M. Clark, Ed Thomas, Anthony J. Antoniou, Edward W. Arndt, Joseph J. Basel, Alex Burns, Tommy Gore, Franklin Spencer, Charles Hinchen, and Larry Dudley.

INDEX

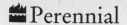 Perennial

Books by Ed Ruggero:

COMBAT JUMP
The Young Men Who Led the Assault into Fortress Europe, July 1943
ISBN 0-06-008876-1 (paperback)

The exciting story of American "citizen soldiers" who risked their lives in the first airborne invasion during World War II. In 1943 the war in Europe had reached a turning point and General Eisenhower decided a new mode of attack was needed: U.S. paratroopers. Their mission was to seize the approaches to the invasion beaches and to hold off German attacks. *Combat Jump* tells the little-known story of these paratroopers and how they changed the American way of war. It takes readers on their journey from civilians to soldiers, through training in the United States and later in North Africa, and then shows their daring jump into the darkness over enemy-held Sicily.

DUTY FIRST
A Year in the Life of West Point and the Making of American Leaders
ISBN 0-06-093133-7 (paperback)

Ruggero details the daily struggles of a dozen cadets and instructors at America's premier school for leadership—the United States Military Academy at West Point. By following about a dozen cadets and instructors over the course of an academic year, Ruggero details their tumultuous lives: the initial grueling training, the strict student hierarchy and intense classroom work, and the interaction between the lowly first-year plebes and the upper-class cadets who train them. *Duty First* also shows the roles played by the majors, captains, and sergeants, and examines the changes in West Point's approach to leadership training that have sparked controversy among its alumni.